AF574372

Icons of Modern Culture

Series Editor: David Ellis

Joan of Arc

1. *Mlle Rivière takes the lead role in* Jeanne d'Arc, *eighteenth-century print.*

Joan of Arc: Icon of Modern Culture

John Flower

HELM INFORMATION

ISBN-10: 1-903206-17-0
ISBN-13: 978-1-903206-17-1

A CIP catalogue record for this book is available from the British Library.

Published in Great Britain in 2008 by
Helm Information,
Crowham Manor, Westfield,
Hastings, East Sussex TN35
4SR U.K. www.helm-
information.co.uk

Jacket illustration: Drawn and coloured by Andrée Jaclet, it is one of a series of engravings on the life of Joan of Arc published in a limited edition by the Musée d'Epinal in 1956.

Printed on acid-free paper and bound by
Antony Rowe Ltd, Chippenham, Wiltshire

Contents

List of Illustrations

Acknowledgements

TO UNDERTAKE A STUDY of this nature of an iconic figure of the stature of Joan of Arc is like attempting to understand the expanding universe. Works of art and artefacts of all descriptions continue to be inspired by her; books about her appear with regularity on the shelves of bookstores and libraries. Any venture into this mass of material requires not simply patience but good fortune as well, and I would like to record my gratitude to a number of people whose guidance and assistance have been invaluable. In particular my thanks goes to those responsible for the two unparalleled collections of material relating to Joan in the world and who allowed me to photograph at will – to Olivier Bouzy and his colleagues at the Centre Jeanne d'Arc in Orléans and to Mary-Beth Dunhouse and Megan Fleming in the Municipal Library in Boston. I have received invaluable support as well from the Inter-Library Loans section, the Special Collections Department and the Centre for the Study of Cartoons in the Templeman Library at the University of Kent, and from the staff of the British Library in London and of the Bibliothèque nationale in Paris. In particular special thanks are more than due to Charles Young and to John Harris without whose computer skills my task would have been infinitely more difficult. I have received help and advice from my colleagues at Kent, Ana de Medeiros, Osman Durrani and David Ellis, from Ronald Knapp of the University of Los Angeles, from Sandra Boyer and Anne Ortiz at Florida State University, from Liz and Stephen Flower, Susie Burnet of the Edinburgh Festival (2004), the Royal Opera House and the British Film Institute. I would like to express my warm thanks as well to the members of the family of Andrée Jaclet (Madame André Jacquemin) for their kind permission to reproduce the cover illustration. Drawn and coloured by Andrée Jaclot it is one of a series of engravings published in a limited edition by the Musée d'Epinal in 1956.

I am grateful as well to the British Academy for grants that have financed research trips to France and the United States, and to Amanda Helm, the publisher of the 'Icons' series, and our general editor David Ellis for their patience and encouragement. Ashgate Publishing Limited kindly allowed us to incorporate in the Appendix the essay by Claude Grimal. And last but by no means least my thanks to Julia Tanney who, as it were, has had to share me with Joan for the last three years and who will be glad to see her go. Unless otherwise indicated, all translations are my own.

All possible care has been taken to trace ownership of copyright material and to make full acknowledgement. Listed below are details received at the time of going to press. In some cases it has not been possible to locate, or even identify, the owner of copyright and Helm Information would be pleased to hear from any copyright holder not acknowledged so that appropriate arrangements can be made.

We would like to thank the following for permission to reproduce this material:

Harper Collins publishers (New York, 1988) for the illustration on p. 33 'Joan abjures her recantation' by Diane Stanley;

Express Newspapers for 2 cartoons by Michael Cummings on p. 78;

Mirrorpix for the cartoon by Vicky on p. 78;

La Nouvelle République for the cartoon on p. 80;

Telegraph Media Group for the cartoon by Nicholas Garland on p. 86;

Steve Bell for the cartoon on p. 87; and

The British Film Institute for all the reproductions of film stills in Chapter 7;

Turtle Point Press for Willard Trask's English translation of quotations in Chapter 1, from *Joan of Arc in Her Own Words*, Books & Co/Turtle Point Press, New York, copyright © 1996;

We are grateful to Professors Angus J. Kennedy and Kenneth Varty for permission to quote from their edition, *Ditié de Jehanne d'Arc: Christine de Pisan*, Oxford: Society for the Study of Medieval Languages and Literatures, (Medium Aevum Monographs, n.s. IX), 1977, reprinted 2003;

The Society of Authors, on behalf of the Bernard Shaw Estate, for extracts from the preface and play of *Saint Joan*;

A & C Black publisher for the extract from Bertholt Brecht's *Die Heilige Johanna*;

Ashgate Publishing Ltd for 'The American Maid' by Claude Grimal, from Guy-Blanquet, Dominique (ed.), *Joan of Arc: A Saint for All Reasons*, Ashgate 2003.

Series Editor's Preface

Every culture has its icons, figures who populate the collective consciousness and provide it with essential points of reference. Any two members of the culture in question might well have different ideas as to what particular figures represent but both will recognise them as items in a common currency. It is in part through the different and sometimes competing meanings we give to the prevailing icons that we organise our knowledge and evince our views of the world.

In some instances the birth of an icon is an historical event, one which took place around 1412 in the case of Joan of Arc, for example, but more certainly in 1855 as far as Ned Kelly is concerned. Falstaff's first appearance in the world is also a matter of historical record but in a very different sense while that of Faust or Robin Hood is far less determinate. As these examples illustrate our icons are a varied band. They come in all shapes and sizes, quite what shape or size depending partly of course on the social or cultural position from which they are viewed, as well as the tastes and temperament of the viewer. Their essential heterogeneity and their vulnerability to private, idiosyncratic appropriation make them difficult to talk about in general, but if they have one characteristic in common it is that they have left their real, literary or mythical origins well behind. They have transcended those origins in order to represent for us qualities we admire or detest, facets of human failure or achievement which it would be uncomfortable to discuss in the abstract. It is through these figures that we often prefer to do our thinking. Close study of history is for the majority of a population esoteric, and however much 'celebrities' may temporarily engage public attention everyone is aware that they are fleeting phenomena, that they come and go. Icons on the other hand are deeply embedded. They provide a link with the generations which went before and characterise what we are quite as much as our clothes, our food or our anthems.

Each volume in this series describes and above all illustrates the process whereby a certain figure became iconic. It aims to show the different ways that figure has functioned for different interest groups and what role it plays in our culture now. Much of the illustration is literary but attention is also paid to music, painting, photography and film (how people visualise their icons can be as significant as how they write or read about them). A few recent essays of an analytic nature may also be included and the authors of individual volumes will offer their comments on some of the controversial aspects of their subject, but the chief intention is to provide a descriptive context for the *display* of material. In that way readers can watch the sometimes chequered history of an icon develop and see for themselves how the figure concerned came to play such an important role in our common awareness.

DAVID ELLIS

Foreword

30th May 1431. Early morning. Hundreds of people including women and children and soldiers are packed into the market square of Rouen, in Normandy. Towards the north end is a high stake surrounded by piles of wood. The crowd is excited. The atmosphere is tense but also one of carnival. There is to be a public execution.

A tiny, emaciated, young woman – eighteen or nineteen years of age – will be burned to death, a common enough method of execution at the time but no less grotesque for that. Dignitaries of the French church and representatives of the English crown sit on raised platforms. The girl arrives in a cart surrounded by eighty or more English soldiers. On her head is a tall cap, shaped like a mitre, bearing in Latin the words 'Heretic, Relapsed, Apostate, Idolatress' and decorated with pictures of devils – Belial, Behemoth and Satan. She is wearing a loose-fitting white dress and is in chains.

After various addresses and the sentence of excommunication have been read she is attached to the stake and the fire lit. She asks for a cross and calls on Jesus. Smoke wafts across the roofs, the stench of burning flesh fills the air.

An English lord is heard to cry: 'We have burned a saint.'

2. Joan of Arc at the Consecration of Charles VII *by J. D Ingres, 1804, engraved by Gény-Gros, Paris.*

Chapter One

Her Story, Their Story, Whose Version?

'A fickle, wavering nation.'
Shakespeare, *Henry VI*

By the early years of the fifteenth century, the country we now know as France was in the middle of the so-called Hundred Years War with England, was wracked by internal disputes and feuds, and had suffered a severe loss of population (in some places total) as a result of the Black Death in 1348. Famine, extreme poverty and continuing outbreaks of the disease were the norm. The war, which in fact lasted for 116 years in all, was not a continuous conflict but an intermittent affair. It began in 1337 when Edward III of England, whose mother was the sister of Charles IV of France, laid claim to the throne of France when Charles died without a direct heir. In 1346 Edward invaded France and on 26th August won a decisive victory over the numerically superior French army at Crécy; a year later the English also took possession of the strategic port of Calais after a year-long siege. The next decade was marked by a series of relatively minor skirmishes but in 1356, Edward's son, the Black Prince, emulating his father's previous success, defeated the French in yet another major battle at Poitiers. For the next fifty years or so France teetered on the edge of total collapse. The English gradually increased their possessions across the north of France from Normandy to Champagne and made another major move in 1415 when Henry V, who had inherited the English crown two years earlier, invaded France again and claimed a significant victory at Agincourt on 25th October. Henry married Catherine, daughter of Charles VI, and by the Treaty of Troyes in 1420 ensured that their heir would inherit the French crown and become king of both countries. Henry and Charles both died two years later; Henry VI was one year old, and the Dauphin, the future Charles VII, nineteen.

English ambitions to extend their territorial advantage further south were made all the easier by the bitter rivalries and deep unrest in France. Fewer

3. Map of France c. 1430.

than ten years before, in 1407, John the Fearless, the Duke of Burgundy had had Louis, Duke of Orléans and his rival for the French crown assassinated. Twelve years later John in turn was violently killed at Montereau, probably on the orders of the Dauphin, and Philip the Good became Duke of Burgundy. Already on a number of occasions, the English had come to the assistance of the Burgundians who now saw their best future to lie in a treaty with the English; this was the one duly signed at Troyes. Those who had supported the royal line – the Armagnacs, named after their leader Bernard d'Armagnac – remained loyal to Charles. But Charles VI was a weak king who suffered from periods of depression and madness and while, after his death in 1422, his son was named Dauphin and heir to the throne of France in defiance of the treaty of Troyes, France had no clear leadership and slipped into a state of near civil war. Moreover, when they were not fighting one another, Armagnac and Burgundian soldiers turned into marauding groups known as *écorcheurs* or 'skinners', who roamed the country devastating villages, ransacking churches and terrorising peasants as they looted. For many (and at all levels of society), mere survival was fundamental. Historians are largely in agreement that the age of high chivalry, of a society in which social stability, in theory if not always in practice, had been based on respect and mutual responsibilities and loyalty had gone. In its place was one in which, to quote the historian Jules Michelet, 'fathers were no longer fathers, nor brothers brothers.' Treachery was a password, betrayal the norm.

A Maid from Domremy[1]

4. Joan's place of birth from Maria Edmée, Histoire de notre petite sœur Jeanne d'Arc, *Paris, 1874.*

This, then, was the society into which Joan was born in January 1412 in Domremy, a small village in Lorraine on the border of Champagne. Exactly what her life was like is impossible to know. Her parents, Jacques d'Arc and Isabelle Romée,[2] were probably peasant tenant farmers, with Jacques having some kind of representative responsibility for the inhabitants of the village to their overlord, Robert de Baudricourt in the nearby town of Vaucouleurs. Their house was modest and their standard of living comfortable.

Joan had three brothers, Jacquemin, Jean and Pierre, and according to some accounts a sister, Catherine. Some have claimed that Catherine died when she was a child, others when she was giving birth, but there is no mention of Joan's having a nephew or niece. Tradition has it that Joan – or Johanette as she was known among her own people – had a quiet homely life, closer perhaps to her mother than to her father. She also seems to have had a reputation for piety. At her trial in Rouen in 1431 she would claim:

> As long as I lived at home I worked at common tasks about the house, going but seldom afield with our sheep and other cattle. I learned to sew and spin. [...] From my mother I learned 'Our Father', 'Hail Mary', and 'I believe'. And my teaching in my faith I had from her and no one else.[3]

Pictures frequently depict her carrying a distaff.

5. Joan spinning beside her father, from the Vigiles *of Charles VII, 1484.*

As a child and adolescent she shared in the village rituals and pastimes. One in particular involved a tree – the Fairies' tree (L'Arbre des Fées) – with a nearby spring with water that was said to have healing properties:

> Not far from Domremy there is a tree called the Ladies' Tree, and others call it the Fairies' Tree, and near it there is a fountain. And I have heard said that those who are sick with fever drink at the fountain or fetch water from it, to be made well. Indeed I have seen them do so, but I do not know whether it makes them well or not. I have heard, too, that the sick, when they can get up, go walking under the tree. It is a great tree, a beech, and from it our fair May-branches come; and it was in the lands of Monseigneur Pierre de Bourlemont. Sometimes I went walking there with the other girls and I have made garlands under the tree for the statue of the Blessed Virgin of Domremy.
>
> I have often heard it said by old people (they were not of my own elders) that the fairies met there. My godmother even told me that she had seen fairies there, but I do not know whether it was true or not. I never saw any fairies under the tree to my knowledge. I have seen girls hang wreaths on the branches; I have sometimes hung my own with the others, and sometimes we left them behind.
>
> I do not know whether, after I reached the age of discretion, I ever danced at the foot of the tree; I may have danced there sometimes with the children; but I sang there more than I danced.

At her trial her questioners would try to suggest that such activities implied witchcraft and a possible association with the Devil, an accusation that the Australian novelist Thomas Keneally interestingly develops in his novel *Blood Red Sister Rose* (1973). The wood in which the tree stood, the *bois chesnu* (oak wood) was also associated with a popular story according to which the wizard Merlin prophesied that from it a maid would come who could work miracles and save France. Again at her trial, Joan maintained that she 'put no faith in that', but for her followers there none the less remained a mysterious connection. And just as with her friends Hauviette and Mengotte, Joan may have been party to the traditional rural pastimes of her village, she was also more than aware of the political state of France. On more than one occasion her family was obliged to flee from the bands of *écorcheurs* and local youths skirmished violently with those from the neighbouring village of Maxey that was loyal to the Burgundians.

Joan's life was to change radically in 1425, however, when, at the age of thirteen, she heard her voices for the first time. In answer to the questions put to her later she described the experience in the following way:

> When I was thirteen, I had a voice from God to help me to govern myself. The first time, I was terrified. The voice came to me about noon: it was summer, and I was in my father's garden. I had not fasted the day before. I heard the voice on my right hand, towards the church. There was a great light all about. [...]
>
> I saw it many times before I knew it was Saint Michael. Afterwards he taught me and showed me such things that I knew it was he.
>
> He was not alone, but duly attended by heavenly angels. I saw them with the eyes of my body as well as I see you. And when they left me, I wept, and wished that they might have taken me with them. And I kissed the ground where I had stood, to do them reverence.
>
> Above all Saint Michael told me that I must be a good child, and that God

6. Joan hearing her Voices *by Henri Martin, 1884.*

would help me. He taught me to behave rightly and to go often to church. He said that I would have to go into France.

He told me that Saint Catherine and Saint Margaret would come to me, and that I must follow their counsel; that they were appointed to guide and counsel me in what I had to do, and that I must believe what they would tell me, for it was the Lord's command.

He told me the pitiful state of the Kingdom of France and he told me that I must go to succour the King of France.

Saint Catherine and Saint Margaret had rich crowns on their heads. They spoke well and fairly, and their voices are beautiful – sweet and soft.

The name by which they often named me was *Jehanne the Maid, child of France.*

At the same time, so it seems, she swore to remain a virgin 'for as long as it should please God'. Thereafter, two or three times a week over the next three years, she would be told to go to France to defeat the English and lead Charles to his coronation at Rheims. The saints also told her that de Baudricourt would provide her with a company of men and that she would raise the siege of Orléans. As Warner has noted,[4] while Joan's accusers made an important issue of the voices (as they did of the local traditions in Domremy) in order to suggest that they came from the Devil, her friends and supporters at the trials for her rehabilitation in 1456 made no special claims for them at all. The majority of those who have written biographical or imaginative works about Joan, however, follow the traditional version of her experience – her voices were of divine inspiration. In quite a few cases this may amount to little short of hagiography, but we should remember that there was nothing to be considered unusual about visions or hallucinations in the Middle Ages. Some commentators have also remarked that the statues of the three saints were in the village church and that Joan became obsessed by them. Others again, notably in recent years the film director Luc Besson in *The Messenger*, have attributed Joan's behaviour to a psychic disorder verging on madness.

Besson has a powerful scene early in the film in which Joan, hidden in a cupboard, witnesses the violent murder and rape of her sister by English soldiers, and he goes on to imply strongly that this was an experience that disturbed her profoundly and stimulated, even at an early age, thoughts of revenge.

To Chinon and Orléans

Whatever the reasons, by the time she was seventeen in early 1429, Joan was convinced of her duty and that she must set out for Vaucouleurs to seek de Baudricourt's assistance. Knowing that her parents and especially her father (described by De Quincy as 'odious' and 'horny hoofed') would be totally opposed to the idea, she persuaded her cousin Durand Laxart to invent a story that she should go with him to help care for his sick wife. It is said that Jacques d'Arc had already imagined that his daughter would run off with soldiers and that he would prefer her dead, and had instructed his sons that if they did not drown her he would do so himself. But Joan must have had a stubborn and wilful, independent streak to her. We know, for example, that she had successfully defended herself in court against a young man from the cathedral city of Toul who claimed that she had promised to marry him. The popular and traditional image of her, therefore, as a quiet, devout girl driven to act solely on account of her voices may not be entirely reliable. In 1956 the French playwright Jacques Audiberti captures some of this when he has Joan played by one actress as a silent peasant girl and by another as an energetic, confident young woman ready to embark on her mission.

Joan's first attempt to reach Baudricourt in order to try to persuade him to equip her for the journey to find the Dauphin at Chinon ended, not surprisingly, with a rebuff and advice that she should return to her village and receive a good hiding from her father.[5] But her persistence gradually won his confidence. He gave her a sword and a horse and she acquired a small retinue of six men: Jean de Metz, Bertrand de Poulengy; their servants Julien and Jean de Honnecourt; Colet de Vienne and an archer named Richard.

Again questions can be asked. While it is likely that Joan's family owned at least one horse, there is no record of her ability to ride and a journey of about two weeks over a distance of 250 miles argued for considerable strength and stamina.[6] It was also potentially dangerous as the first part of the journey crossed country frequented by roaming groups of Anglo-Burgundian soldiers,

7. Joan of Arc receiving her sword from Captain de Baudricourt.
Engraved after the painting by Gaston Merlingue, 1894.

8. *Engraving after J. S. Scherrer's* Departure from Vaucouleurs, 1886–7.

though she would later insist that she met with 'no hindrance'. No doubt for ease of riding, but also for protection, Joan chose to adopt men's clothing from this moment on: a decision that would later cost her dearly. Of this journey we know little apart from one significant event – Joan's realisation that a sword was buried behind the altar in the shrine of Saint Catherine at Fierbois where she made her final stop before Chinon and where she heard three masses. Probably on arrival at Chinon she sent for the sword, indicating where it would be found. When it was unearthed it is claimed that the rust miraculously fell away revealing five crosses on its blade and the words 'Jesus' and 'Maria' on its edge. It was later rumoured that Joan broke the sword over the backs of prostitutes she chased from her soldiers' camp.

Much has been written about her arrival at the court in Chinon and her meeting with Charles. In order to test her, the Dauphin allowed himself to be replaced on the throne by one of the knights and hid among the courtiers, but Joan's voices, so she would say, led her straight to him. Why Charles

9. Joan sees off the loose women. *André des Garçons, 1871.*

should have been convinced by her remains a mystery. Some have claimed it was because she assured him that he was the legitimate heir to the throne of France, though why he should have believed an unknown peasant girl is hard to fathom. Others have said that a vision of the crown miraculously appeared to persuade him of her mission. Much would be made of this at her trial, and Joan, either because she was confused or because she was exhausted or both, refused (or was unable) to answer. Whatever the explanation, she was successful but still had to be further examined. But if Joan succeeded in convincing Charles, she also posed a direct threat to the influence that his principal advisers, Georges La Trémouille and Regnault, Archbishop of Rheims, had over him. Joan was made to submit to an examination that lasted for three weeks by 'learned men', a tribunal of the Paris Parlement exiled in Poitiers.

10. Joan going to meet Charles VII, from the Vigiles *of Charles VII, 1484.*

She was also examined by a group of women led by Charles' mother-in-law, Yolande, Queen of Sicily, to verify her claim to be a virgin. As foreign or as crude as this may seem to us today, such a test was vital since, according to the beliefs of the time, if indeed Joan was declared intact, it proved she had had no dealings with the Devil. Joan was triumphant on both counts. Despite his debts and relative poverty, and probably against the advice of La Trémouille, Charles gave his support. Joan was provided with a banner that she had embroidered with Jesus and Maria and the emblem of the 'fleur de lys',[7] a horse and a full set of armour specially made for her in Tours in April.

This is how Joan described these events to her questioners:

> I asked my Lord's messengers what I should do. And they answered me, saying, 'Take up the banner of your Lord.' And thereupon I had a banner made.
>
> The field of it was sown with lilies, and therein was our Lord holding the world, with two angels, one on either hand. It was white, and on it here were written the names *Jhesus Maria*, and it was fringed with silk.
>
> I had the sword I had brought from Vaucouleurs.
>
> I sent to make search for another sword in the church of Saint Catherine at Fierbois, behind the altar. It was found there presently, all rusted, and on it there were five crosses. And the priests there rubbed it, and the rust fell away of itself.
>
> I loved that sword, because it was found in the church of Saint Catherine, whom I loved.
>
> But I loved my banner forty times better than my sword. And when I went against the enemy, I carried my banner myself, lest I kill any. I have never killed a man.

11. Joan examined by the learned men in Poitiers.
Watercolour by F. Dumont published in Harper's Magazine, *1895.*

Her retinue of men was enlarged as well by the Duc d'Alençon who had already signalled his support for her, a squire Jean d'Aulon and a page, Louis de Coutes. (De Coutes would be renamed de Conte and provide the 'personal recollections' on which Mark Twain would base his novel published in 1895 in New York.) Joan was also given a contingent of soldiers though her claim under examination that there were twelve thousand of them is a wild exaggeration; two or three hundred is likely to be nearer the truth.

To Orléans

Joan and her entourage left Tours on 24th April for Orléans by way of Blois. Since October of the previous year, Orléans had been under siege by the English who had built a ring of forts around the town but had left open access from the north-east. On the way from Blois, Joan learned that the soldiers with her had been instructed to approach Orléans from the south of the Loire and she angrily confronted Dunois, the illegitimate half-brother of the Duke of Orléans and in charge of the defence of the town, claiming that her voices

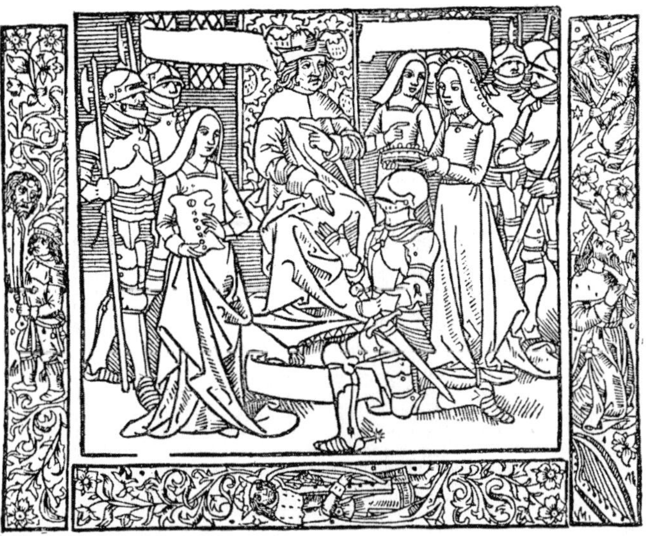

12. Joan receiving her armour from Charles VII, from the Vigiles *of Charles VII, 1484.*

had told her to arrive from the other side. Joan had no real authority of course. At this stage she was at best no more than a kind of mascot for the soldiers, a figurehead to rally their flagging morale. However, there then occurred another inexplicable event that would later be counted as one of Joan's miracles. When they reached the Loire the wind was blowing strongly against them, preventing them from crossing it with all their possessions to the northern side and the town. Rebuking Dunois, Joan claimed that God would help them, whereupon the wind changed direction. As Bernard Shaw would have Dunois acknowledge in his play, 'God has spoken' and at once (if only symbolically) he handed over command of his forces to Joan.

The news of Joan's intentions must somehow already have reached Orléans and she entered the town as the promised saviour to much adoration from the local people.

It would not be until the rehabilitation that much would be made about Joan's skills as a military leader. That her presence was inspirational is undeniable, but she clearly had no military experience and it seems unlikely that Dunois and his fellow officers would have thought fit to take her into their confidence when planning their moves at this stage. The idea that the French with inferior forces overcame well-organised and confident English troops has to be resisted as well. By now the English were disillusioned and in need of urgent supplies, and in an age when superstition was powerful, the rapidly spreading rumour among them that Joan somehow benefited from supernatural (diabolic?) help was an important factor. They had also lost one of their most prominent leaders, the Earl of Salisbury, killed by a stray canon shot soon after the siege had begun; reinforcements were on their way under the direction of Sir John Falstaff but would not arrive; their Burgundian allies had begun to desert them. According to her squire Jean d'Aulon, Joan woke during the night of 3rd May claiming that her voices had told her to attack.

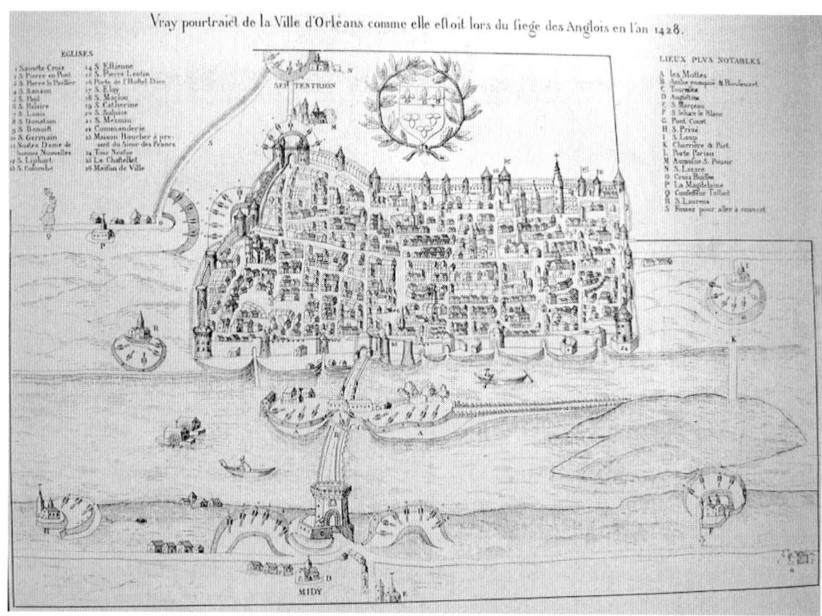

13. Map of Orléans in 1428, at the time of the siege by the English.

Without waiting for him she took a horse and joined the French under the control of Raoul de Gaucourt, the town's bailiff and insisted, much against his will, that they should move. Their assault was successful and the fort of St Loup fell. The following day was Ascension and on Joan's insistence, so it appears, there was to be no fighting. The fact that the English agreed to this can presumably only be explained by some code of chivalry and two days later they attempted to counter attack from the south. Fighting was fierce but eventually they were pushed back over the river to the fort of Les Tourelles. Did Joan sense that they were weakening? By now her popularity must have been high and any attempt by de Gaucourt, Dunois or other senior officers to call for caution and planning was unlikely to meet with her approval and, moreover, risked alienating the French soldiers. Even so, fearful of the likely bloodshed, Joan issued the commanders of the English army (the Duke of Bedford, Earl of Suffolk and Lord Talbot) with an ultimatum in the form of a letter – either they left unharmed or they would be mercilessly attacked and pursued:

14. Joan's entry into Orléans *by J. S. Scherrer, 1887.*

> Surrender to the Maid sent hither by God, the King of Heaven, the keys of all the good towns you have taken and laid waste in France. She comes in God's name to establish the Blood Royal, ready to make peace if you agree to abandon France and repay what you have taken. [...] If you do not, expect to hear tidings from the Maid who will shortly come upon you with great hurt. [...] Wherever I meet your followers in France I will drive them out; if they will not obey, I will put them all to death.

Whether the letter was received or not is uncertain, but in any event the English showed no inclination to accept the offer and hurled insults and abuse at Joan, calling her a witch and a whore. On 7th May the French attacked and the battle for Les Tourelles began, effectively marking the end of the siege.

However vividly even modern films can give an impression of conflicts such as these, it is impossible to convey fully the din, the mutilated bodies of men and horses, and the stench. The Loire at this point was quite wide, but the nature of the actual assault relatively small and the panoramic shots of swathes of French troops hurtling forward such as we have in Marco de Gastyne's 1928 film, for example, may be impressive, but are hardly accurate. The fort itself was manned by about 700 soldiers under the command of William Glasdale. Fighting was fierce and the French so hard pressed that Dunois, seeing success unlikely, gave orders for a withdrawal. As she had predicted, Joan had been wounded by an arrow in the throat or breast, descriptions vary. (Her prediction would be counted as another miracle.)

On hearing Dunois' decision, she rejoined the battle and led the final and successful assault. This was certainly made easier by the fact that the faggots piled against the fort's walls caught and set fire to it, but the sight of Joan having apparently miraculously recovered, caused many of the English to give up. This was further proof that she was a witch! In order, then, to escape from the flames, Glasdale and other knights leaped from the fort into the Loire where, under the weight of their armour, they drowned. Victory for the French was assured and those English soldiers who survived were, on Joan's

15. Poster for the quincentennial celebrations of the raising of the siege of Les Tourelles.

instructions, allowed to withdraw unmolested the next day. The 8th May, therefore, saw the liberation of Orléans and would be celebrated through the centuries thereafter.

16. *Joan wounded at Orléans, from a lithograph by Chasselat, 1819.*

While the traditional story has Joan being welcomed back into the town with even greater adoration, details are missing, however. There is, for example, no further mention of her wound. Treated at the time with a potion of herbs and oil, the risk of infection and gangrene must have been considerable. How many losses did the two sides incur? Were the hundreds (?) of bodies that must have fallen into the Loire left to rot and pollute the water? Given the intensive nature of the fighting, much of which was hand to hand, it is inconceivable that Joan should not have been more seriously wounded, especially as she would have been a major target and conspicuous with her banner. It is possible certainly that Joan did not actually fight and that she was surrounded and protected by a group of faithful followers, but in the circumstances, her later claim not to have killed anyone, even accidentally, seems equally implausible. And what effect did the victory have on Joan herself? A mass in the cathedral was held at which she gave thanks to God, but how must she have reacted? There can be no doubt that she was brave, had an aura of invincibility about her and was seen, at least by the French, to be directly inspired by God. But how did she react to those close to her? What

17. The Deliverance of Orléans, *engraved in the nineteenth century by Wittman from a painting by E. Aman-Jean.*

was her relationship with Dunois or La Hire or other knights? What did they think of her? It seems that as a result of the victory at Orléans she was given greater authority, but it is difficult (if not impossible) to judge to what extent hardened soldiers would listen to her seriously. Such questions will remain unanswered; the tributes paid to her by Dunois and others at the rehabilitation can only be taken in that particular context. But her promise to Charles to raise the siege of Orléans had been realised and she had every reason to insist that the rest of her prophecy would be as well.

From Orléans to Rheims

From Orléans, Jeanne and Dunois went first to Loches and thereafter to Tours to meet with Charles. Perhaps still not wholly convinced himself and with some counsellors advising negotiations with the Burgundians and others again in favour of pursuing them in their territories in the Île de France and Normandy, Charles had to be persuaded. Joan insisted that her voices continued to encourage her to lead him to Rheims and coronation, but whether it was this advice or simply his own understandable desire to be recognised as the legitimate king of France remains uncertain. In 1456 Dunois would make the point that, once crowned, the power of Charles' enemies would steadily decline until 'they would be powerless to harm either him or his kingdom.' Whatever the reason, Charles accepted Joan's plan but only on condition that the towns on the way to Rheims under the control of the English and Burgundians should either be persuaded to change their allegiance or be taken by force. It would seem that Joan was given a more

Armorial bearings given to Joan on 2nd June 1429 by Charles VII

central role in the planning of the campaign and a month later the army began its drive towards Rheims. Within a week (11th–18th June) the strategic towns of Jargeau, Meung-sur-Loire and Beaugency all fell to the French and at Patay the English suffered particularly heavy losses. The way forward was now assured and Charles joined the army. Auxerre capitulated (30th June) followed by Châlons-sur-Marne (14th July) and, with only token resistance, Troyes (5th–12th July). Rheims was entered on 16th July without opposition from either the Burgundians or the English and the coronation prepared.

Given the state of affairs and the speed with which everything had to be organised, this must have been a far less grand and colourful ceremony than later paintings would have us believe. Most of the dignitaries, including the Duke of Burgundy, who would normally have been present to swear their allegiance to the newly crowned king, were absent. Also absent were Charles's wife Marie of Anjou, and her mother Yolande. And there were hitches. The vial (the Sainte Ampoule) in the nearby abbey church of St Rémi, supposedly containing holy oil that had been used for the baptism of Clovis, France's first Christian king, was found to be empty and had to be refilled. And since the cathedral treasures had been removed for safekeeping, the true crown was not available and a substitute had to be used. Nevertheless, Charles was duly

18. The Consecration of Charles VII as King at Rheims, from the Vigiles *of Charles VII, 1484.*

crowned and Joan accorded pride of place at the ceremony; her mission had been accomplished. Her immediate reward, at her request, was for Charles to decree that Domremy, Greux and other local villages from her region be exempt from taxes – a privilege they would enjoy until the Revolution.

Although he was now secure as king, Charles showed little interest in continuing to fight to unite France as a single nation. He was manipulated by counsellors, notably by La Trémouille still jealous of Joan and probably afraid of her, and outwitted by the Burgundians who engaged him in a series of spurious truces. By the end of September 1429 he would have disbanded the army. Joan, whose ambition to continue to fight the English had in no way lessened and whose pride had certainly taken a blow, was furious and dictated an extraordinarily assured letter to the citizens of Rheims to say so:

> It is true that the king has made a truce with the Duke of Burgundy for two weeks, in accordance with which he is to surrender the town of Paris peaceably to him at the end of two weeks (only do not be at all surprised if I do not enter there so soon); however, I am not satisfied with this manner of truce, and I do not know if I will keep it, but if I do keep it, it will be only to preserve the King's honour; however, in any case, they will not again abuse the blood royal, for I shall keep and hold the King's army together, so as to be ready at the end of the said two weeks if they do not make peace.

But historians and biographers are of one voice – Rheims was the high point of her career. In Vita Sackville-West's words, from then on 'her feet were set on the sharply sloping path which fetched up at the stake.'[8]

The Road to Martyrdom

Ignoring Charles, and with those soldiers who remained faithful to her and with whatever mercenaries she could afford to pay out of the small amount of money she received from him, Joan embarked on a series of small and largely inconsequential battles and skirmishes before attempting to launch an assault on Paris on 8th September.

As at Orléans, she displayed courage, leading men across the ditches of the city's fortifications and, again as at Orléans, she was wounded, this time in the thigh.

Forced to withdraw from the battle she would not, on this occasion, return and was ordered by Charles to call off the attack. But Joan had not only failed as a military leader. The assault on Paris took place on the birthday of the Virgin Mary. In Orléans, Joan had called for a truce on Ascension Day, but now to encourage the soldiers to continue fighting on a day every bit as significant in the Catholic calendar was a fundamental error. The anonymous author of the *Journal d'un Bourgeois de Paris (1405–1499)* would later observe:

19. Joan marching on Paris. Jehanne La Pucelle, *engraving on wood from* La Mer des hystoires, *1491.*

'No good ought to have come to them, planning such a slaughter on Our Lady's holy nativity.' At her trial Joan would claim or admit that for once she had followed the advice of a number of her knights rather than that of her voices, but perhaps her voices had in fact been silent and that it was her own self-confidence that drove her on?

After this failure Joan's reputation waned quickly. With no royal support and dwindling resources, she continued to maintain her campaign but with no success, first at La Charité-sur-Loire in November and at Lagny the following April. It was at Lagny, though, that she was called to the local church to see a baby that had shown no sign of life for three days. As Joan prayed, it yawned and briefly recovered, enough for it to be baptised and buried in holy ground – yet another of the miracles that would be evoked in the case for canonisation five centuries later.

In August of the previous year Charles had signed a truce with the Duke of Burgundy at Compiègne and the town at once recognised his authority. By the following May, however, the Burgundians were preparing to break the agreement and a force led by John of Luxembourg laid siege to the town whose strategic position for control of the north of France was as significant as that

20. Joan wounded at Paris, *from an engraving by G. Moreau, 1771.*

of Orléans for the south. Joan was summoned to help defend the town and on 24th May rode out of Compiègne to attack the Burgundians. At the same time, a contingent of English soldiers arrived from the south forcing the French to withdraw, but before Joan could cross the drawbridge back into the town, the governor, Guillaume de Flavy, had it raised leaving her outside.

Some have interpreted his action as being deliberate, even one that had been ordered by Charles, but it seems more likely that it was simply a normal procedure to make in the town's defence. Only a few weeks before, Joan would say later, her voices had told her that she would be captured before 'Saint John's Day and that it must be so, and that I must not be frightened but accept it willingly.' That moment had now come. An archer named Lyonnel pulled Joan from her horse (is this the Lionel with whom Joan falls in love in Schiller's play *Die Jungfrau von Orleans*?) and put her in the charge of John of Luxembourg. It is thought that Luxembourg later offered a ransom for her on condition that she would no longer campaign against the Burgundians. If this is so, it may be the inspiration for the Count of Warwick's attempt to bribe Joan to change sides and join the English, a theme that we find in a number of plays over the years.

As Luxembourg's prisoner, Joan appears to have been well treated, first in Beaulieu and then in the castle of Beaurevoir where she remained for the last months of 1430. The two ladies of the castle, Jeanne, Luxembourg's aunt and Jeanne de Béthune, his wife, both of whom had sympathy for Charles and the French cause, tried to persuade him to hand Joan back to the French. Mindful of his own interests first and foremost, however, Luxembourg eventually decided to sell her to the English. Knowing what this meant, Joan tried to escape by jumping from the castle's sixty-feet-high tower, against the express

21. Joan's capture at Compiègne, from the Vigiles *of Charles VII, 1484.*

instructions of her voices. Somewhat miraculously she survived and by the end of the year had been sold and taken to Rouen to be tried by an ecclesiastical court that was supposedly neutral, but if not largely in the pay of

22. Joan being taken to Rouen Castle. Wood cut from the Vigiles *of Charles VII, printed by Jehan du Pré, 1493.*

the English, at least sympathetic to their cause. Moreover, despite her rights to be held in an ecclesiastical prison, Joan was incarcerated in Rouen castle under the authority of the Count of Warwick and subjected to the brutal attention of English gaolers. Some of Joan's supporters have maintained that, until her trial began towards the end of January, she was kept in an iron cage; others that she was shackled to a heavy beam even at night. Certainly the fear that she was a witch and had devilish powers would have been real and as frightening to those in charge of her as it had been to the English soldiers in Orléans, but in reality it is unlikely that she would have had more than her feet chained.

Together with the raising of the siege of Orléans, it is the last months of Joan's life that have attracted most attention. Looked at dispassionately, her trial, which lasted for more than three months, and her execution rank among the most extraordinary ever and have prompted frequent comparisons with those of Socrates and Christ. But to look at it dispassionately is impossible.

23. Joan insulted in prison, *by Isidore Patrois 1866.*

24. Site of Rouen castle, now an estate agent's office. Photograph by the author.

This was the trial of an illiterate girl barely eighteen years of age; she had neither legal support nor representation, nor could she call witnesses and was cross-examined by a tribunal of experienced and powerful men of the church and representatives of the pro-Burgundian University of Paris. The presiding judge was the Bishop of Beauvais, Pierre Cauchon, an ambitious, calculating man in the pay of the English, who had been preparing the trial since July and whose selection and control over the members of the court seems to have been absolute. The Deputy Inquisitor of France, Jean Lemaistre, who was legally obliged to be there and notionally had equal, if not greater, status than Cauchon (largely because of weakness or of a reluctance to become involved), appears to have played only a minimal role. The purpose of a trial by an ecclesiastical court was to have Joan admit that her voices came not from God but from the Devil and that they had deceived her. This in turn would discredit those who had supported her, most importantly Charles, whose legitimacy as king could then be questioned.

From Trial to Execution

From the transcript of the trial it is clear that Joan's defence of herself in the six public sittings and nine private ones held in her cell was brave and sometimes spirited. To the question 'Do you know that you are in God's grace?', for example, she replied:

> If I am not, God put me there, and if I am, God keep me there! I should be the saddest creature in all the world if I knew I were not in God's grace. I think, if I were in sin, that the voice would not come to me. And I wish that everyone heard it as I do!

But Joan was also obstinate, refusing to answer certain questions on the grounds that they did not directly concern the trial. 'Passez outre' or 'let's go on' or 'I'm not going to reply to that' punctuated her replies.

The two dominant issues that concerned her questioners were her voices and her refusal to discard her male clothing. Throughout the sittings, Joan constantly referred to her voices as her sole and supreme counsel. When asked on 31st March whether she would accept the judgement of the Church Militant she replied:

> Concerning what you ask I will refer myself to the Church militant, provided that it does not command me to do anything impossible.
>
> I call this impossible – that I should revoke the things which I have said and done, as they are set down in this trial, concerning the visions and revelations which I have said that I had from God. Not for anything will I revoke them. And what out Lord caused and commanded me to do, and shall command, I will not

25. Joan in prison wearing women's clothes and looking remarkably well and elegant. An engraving from a painting by J.-L. Ducis, 1824.

> cease from doing for any man living. And it would be impossible for me to revoke them. And in the case the Church wished to make me do something else, contrary to the commandment which I say God has given me, not for anything would I do it.

Similarly on 2nd May to the question 'Is not our holy father the Pope your judge?', she is no less certain: 'I will not answer further to that. I have a good master – that is, our Lord – to whom only I look, and to none other.' And when threatened by torture a week later:

> Truly, if you were to have me torn limb from limb and send my soul out of my body, I would say nothing else. And if I did say anything, afterwards I should always say that you had made me say it by force.

Her reactions to questions about her dress characteristically carry the same kind of conviction:

> My clothing is a small matter, one of the least. But I did not put on men's clothing by the counsel of any man on earth. I did not put on this clothing, nor do anything else, except at the bidding of God and the angels.

The court did, of course, have Biblical 'authority' on its side. In the Book of Deuteronomy, Chapter 22 verse 5 it is written: 'The woman shall not wear that which pertaineth unto a man, neither shall a man put on a woman's garment: for all that do so are abomination unto the Lord thy God'. Joan's accusers were not slow to use this against her, but she refused to shift: 'Since I do it at our Lord's bidding and in his service, I do not think I am doing wrong. And when he shall be pleased to direct, it [men's dress] shall be quickly laid aside.'

This obstinacy meant that the court could accuse Joan of refusing to accept the authority of the Church and thereby of being a heretic, a sin for which she would be burned. Only when faced with this horrific reality does she appear to have wavered and on 24th May in the cemetery of Saint-Ouen (now the well-tended gardens of Rouen's town hall), she signed a recantation that had been prepared for her, ('I would rather sign it than burn.') but within days she rejected it, claiming that she had been chastised by her voices:

> What I said, I said for fear of the fire.
>
> My voices have told me since that I did a very wicked thing in confessing that what I had done was not well done.
>
> They told me that God, by Saint Catherine and Saint Margaret, gave me to know the great pity of the treason that I consented to by making that abjuration and revocation to save my life, and that I was damning myself to save my life.

Quite what this document contained, however, or whether another was substituted for it later, is not known, and we have to remember as well that

26. Rouen, the site where Joan signed her recantation. Photograph by the author.

Joan could not read. But her conviction was firm. Furthermore, she had now discarded the woman's dress she had agreed to wear and reassumed her male costume. Many have claimed that in fact her gaolers had been instructed, if not by Cauchon then by Warwick, to steal the dress giving her no choice and thereby ensuring that she would effectively convict herself, but there is no hard evidence for this. It should also be added that Joan had learned that she was to be condemned to life imprisonment and to a diet of bread and water at the hands of the English, and not be transferred to the ecclesiastical authorities as she had a right to expect.

Two days later the news was brought to her that she had only hours to live. Faced with the stake her terror was unconcealed – 'I would rather be beheaded seven times than suffer burning.' – and at last she flung her accusation at Cauchon: 'Bishop, I die through you!' Joan was now classed as a heretic, but, curiously, was granted a last confession by Cauchon. Was this, as some have suggested, an oblique recognition by her judges that their sentence was unjust or a move on Cauchon's part to save his own soul? Whatever the reason her confession was heard by Martin Ladvenu, a young Dominican, who had often shown sympathy for Joan during the trial and had tried to speak in support of

27. Joan abjures her recantation, from Diane Stanley, Joan of Arc, *1998.*

her. Joan was then taken from the castle to the market square where the stake and the raised platforms for the English and dignitaries of the Church had already been prepared.

What the scene must have been like is difficult to imagine, but this was a spectacle to which the men, women and children of Rouen would flock.

Joan arrived in a cart wearing a long, loose-fitting robe,[9] with her hands and feet chained and with a mitre-shaped cap on her cropped head bearing the words 'Heretic, Relapsed, Apostate, Idolatress'. Cauchon called on her again to repent and when she refused, read out the sentence of excommunication:

> We deem you, Joan, who call yourself the Maid, to be a relapsed heretic, fallen into a diversity of crimes and offences, schisms, idolatry, invocation of demons, and sundry other evils. [...] However, because the Church never folds her arms against those who have the will to come back to her, we were of the opinion that, after full deliberation and in full good faith, you had turned away from all the

28. Joan going to the stake: Rouen 1431, *by Isidore Patrois, 1867. She is not depicted wearing her cap, nor is her hair cropped but note the anticipation and anger of several local people.*

> evils you had cast off, when you promised, vowed, and swore publicly never to embrace them again, nor any heresies whatsoever, but instead, to abide in union and communion with the Catholic Church and with our Holy Father the Pope, exactly as this is embodied in the abjuration to which you set your own hand. Nevertheless, and this we cry out with deep grief, 'You are for the second time a relapsed heretic, like a dog which has the habit of going back to its vomit!' Therefore, we proclaim, 'You have reincurred the sentence of excommunication under which you first fell. You have fallen back into your former sins. We pronounce you a heretic.

Joan was allowed to speak and protest her innocence but was soon securely chained to the stake. In front of the pyre was a board on which had been painted: 'Jehanne who called herself la Pucelle, liar, pernicious, deceiver of the people, sorceress, superstitious blasphemer of God, presumptuous disbeliever in the faith of Jesus Christ, boastful, idolatrous, cruel, dissolute, invoker of devils, apostate, schismatic and heretic.'

As the fire was being lit she asked for a cross and an English soldier made her one from two twigs that she kissed and thrust into her bosom. Isambart de la Pierre, one of the priests who had been at the trial and had sympathy for Joan, also fetched a cross from a nearby church and held it in front of her until the fire became too high and she urged him to stand away. Whether Joan died of smoke asphyxiation or from the heat or the flames or whether the executioner strangled her before the fire caught properly, as was often done, we do not know. As she died, she is said to have called on her saints and on Jesus; some claimed that as she expired a white dove rose from the flames and flew eastwards to France; the executioner is supposed to have found her heart among the ashes still intact and full of blood. On the orders of Warwick her remains were thrown into the Seine.

While the trial records allow us to have at least a reasonably objective account of the proceedings of the last two or three days of Joan's life at least up to her execution, much is left for the imagination to work on – the atmosphere and setting of the court, the reactions of the public, the bearing of Joan's judges, and especially Joan's physical state as she was summoned from the depths of the castle's cells. Centuries later, painters and film directors evoke these things in different ways: in his illustrations for an immensely popular children's book in 1896 Boutet de Monvel depicts her as a neatly dressed, defiant figure in the court room; in 1928 in his film *La Passion de Jeanne d'Arc*, the Danish director Carl Dreyer has her surrounded by the leering, mocking figures of a nightmare. And the imagination has a large part

29. A sixteenth-century woodcut of Joan at the foot of the pyre betweeen Brother Martin Ladrenu and the executioner.

to play as well in any evocation of Joan's execution. Certainly at the rehabilitation hearings in 1456 some, such as Ladvenu, for example, would recall the occasion but always to promote Joan's glory and heroism, never the full horror of what happened to her. It is true that the anonymous author of the *Journal d'un Bourgeois de Paris (1405–1499)* could write that 'the fire was put out. Her dress was pulled aside and people would see her bare with all the secrets that make her a woman and remove all doubts'. In the Middle Ages the burning of heretics was common, but not until the twentieth century, perhaps with its greater tolerance of physical horror, do we have any detailed account of what such an execution was like. The French novelist Michel Tournier, for example, in *Gilles et Jeanne* (1983), evokes the same scene: 'Hanging on to the stake, wreathed in smoke, people can see a half burned corpse, a shaved head with one eye burst open hanging down on a swollen body. All the while a dreadful smell of charred flesh drifts over the town.'

And so the English and their Burgundian supporters finally had their way, but just what impact Joan had had on the political and military situation is

30. A sixteenth-century woodcut depicting scenes of torture and execution, with local citizens enjoying the spectacle.

31. The Death of Joan of Arc *by Eugène Deveria, 1831.*

difficult to estimate and historians disagree. The Duke of Bedford recognised Charles as the rightful king of France in 1435, and while they managed to retain their hold on Calais for another 123 years, the English were driven from the rest of France in 1453. Nonetheless, Joan had been excommunicated and burnt as a heretic. Charles had been convinced by her and had supported her, and it was vital that this and any accusation of his having failed to go to her assistance during her last months should be forgotten. A popular version of events has it that Joan's mother, who must have been around sixty, (later but when?) made a pilgrimage on foot to Rome to plead with the pope, Calixtus III, to re-examine the trial and sentence. While this seems most unlikely, in 1450 Calixtus did instruct the Dean of Noyon, Guillaume Bouillé, to undertake an investigation. Charles was not going to object, but matters moved slowly. Over the next six years more than a hundred witnesses were heard, some of them contradicting or denying what they had said thirty years before. Thomas de Courcelles, the Rector of the University of Paris and one of the most brilliant men of his generation, for example, denied that he had

32. *Joan at the stake. Nineteenth-century lithograph.*

ever supported the idea of having Joan tortured. Finally, in 1456, Calixtus agreed to an annulment of the earlier trial, though without being too overtly critical of the Church's earlier role. So important were the political dimensions of the rehabilitation, however, that the central issues of Joan's voices or her dress were often either passed over quickly or ignored altogether, and Joan herself became almost incidental. While expiatory crosses were erected in Orléans and Rouen, and orders for a monument to commemorate her victory at the former were given, other images were officially banned. But whatever the official position, the popular cult of Joan had already taken root; Joan was now the creation of those who would admire her or turn her already legendary status to their own advantage.

33. Joan at the stake. *Lithograph by A.-E. Fragonard, 1822.*

34. The Pyre. *Title page of* L'Histoire de France, *vol. V, by Louis-Pierre Anquetil.*

35. Site of the stake, Rouen market place. Photograph by the author.

36. Statue of Joan, Rouen market place, by Maxime Real del Sarte. Photograph by the author.

Joan as seen by others

Not without some justification, Jacques Darras has observed that Joan was 'the creation of nineteenth-century historians'.[10] While she and her exploits were certainly mentioned in chronicles and histories, and inspired a number of poems and plays during the three and a half centuries following her death, it is not until the very late eighteenth century that they truly became part of French – and indeed international – popular culture. Initially this was through imaginative writing, but gradually she became central to a number of historical studies and biographies, many of the latter being prompted by the move to have her canonised that would begin in 1869. As the subject of imaginative writing, she was presented on the whole as a tragic heroine, truly inspired by God, who had saved France. There were exceptions, notably Shakespeare's *Henry VI* (1592) in England and, more controversially, Voltaire's *Pucelle d'Orléans* (1755), still dismissed by many of Joan's admirers as a cheap, deplorable and even vulgar work, even though its biting satire embraces far more than the phenomenon of Joan herself.

With the Revolution the principle of a feudal monarchy clearly became 'politically incorrect' in France and the 'Fête de Jeanne d'Arc' on 8th May that had been celebrated in Orléans for hundreds of years was banned, but within twenty years with the resurgence of the Catholic Church and the restoration of the Bourbon monarchy, the climate changed radically. Attempting to seek common ground with the Church, Napoleon re-established Joan's feast day and authorised the erection of a monument (now situated near where the battle for Les Tourelles took place) that has Joan symbolising the Republic, seizing a flag from an English soldier. In so doing, of course, Napoleon astutely made an important statement, effectively reducing the religious importance of Joan in favour of a more overt political one. This was the first move in what would become a debate (and often a dispute) on the one hand between the Church and those for whom Joan should remain a religious icon, and on the other, those who saw the chance to exploit her as a national Republican figurehead.

37. Joan at Les Tourelles. *Lithograph c. 1818 by Engelmann after a painting by J. B. Bosio.*

In this regard, the historian Jules Michelet was a key figure. In his first writings about Joan in the fifth volume of his immense *Histoire de France* (1841) he expressed his belief in the power of her faith, but as his anticlericalism and his political thinking evolved he saw in her the incarnation of popular, democratic values. While, therefore, when he returned to Joan as a subject in 1853, he continued to recognise and repeat the standard story about her, seeing her genius to lie rather in 'a blend of simplicity, good sense and shrewdness'; her 'uniqueness' is 'not to be sought in her visions.' His opening paragraph sets the tone not only for his own essay, but also for the works of many in subsequent generations:

> Joan's eminent quality was her common sense. This sets her apart from the multitude of enthusiasts who, in ages of ignorance, have swayed the masses. In most cases, they derived their power from some dark contagious force of unreason. Her influence, on the contrary, was due to the clear light she was able to throw upon an obscure situation, through the unique virtue of her good sense and of her loving heart. The shrewd and the cautious, the men of little faith, could not unravel the knot: she cut it. She declared in the name of God that Charles VII was the rightful heir. He himself doubted his legitimacy: she reassured him. She secured for that legitimacy the sanction of Heaven by leading her king straight to Reims; and through her swift action she won over the English the decisive advantage of the coronation.[11]

As we will see, the political value to be drawn from Joan would not be limited to those on the Left nor, indeed, to Republicans. In terms not so very different from Michelet's, the right-wing nationalist deputy Maurice Barrès would write in 1920 and in the aftermath of the First World War, for example:

> This daughter of the people was a foundling of democracy, of the people breaking into speech [...] her cult was born with the invasion of the country; she is resistance against foreign invasion incarnate.

A decade later Charles Maurras, the leader of the nationalistic Action Française movement, would see in Joan's exploits a justification for the restoration of the monarchy, and with the invasion and occupation of France by the Germans she would be exploited both by the pro-Nazi government of Vichy under Philippe Pétain and by the Resistance. In 1946 Joseph Calmette could write that Joan was 'the heroine, speaking for God, who brought the light of truth and salvation to a dark and despairing situation. She held out her powerful hand to France when the country was at its lowest and helped it climb out of the abyss.' In more recent years, however, Joan has become almost entirely appropriated by the extreme Right and by Jean-Marie le Pen's party, the Front National.

But while Michelet in the first instance may have set a political and initially broadly left-wing campaign in motion, the Church was not slow to respond. In 1869 the passionate and enthusiastic bishop of Orléans, Félix Dupanloup, began the drive to have Joan canonised. Pressure, especially from conservative Catholics, continued and in 1894 Pope Leo XIII declared her 'venerable', the first step in the process. In 1909 his successor Pius X pronounced her 'blessed' and her canonisation was authorised in 1920 by Benedict XV.

When Quicherat published his transcriptions in the middle of the nineteenth century, those who had an interest in Joan for whatever reason now had documentary material to support their case. This material also prompted the beginning of an era of substantial and serious biographies; some were certainly uncomfortably close to hagiography, others reflected the intellectual climate of the time they were written. Among the earlier ones to appear, and one that would be widely debated, was Anatole France's *La Vie de Jeanne d'Arc* (1908) in which France attempts to reconcile his genuine affection for Joan with a rational explanation of her accomplishments. France's research – largely carried out by a secretary – was later shown to be unreliable, but given that he was also an imaginative writer of distinction, it is not surprising that what might have been a simple factual account not infrequently takes on the guise of a novel. France provides pen portraits of characters about whom relatively little is known and reconstructs conversations and events; the visual impact is vital. 'Clad in a poor red gown, her heart bright with mystic love, Joan climbed the hill dominating the town', is how he describes Joan's going to Vaucouleurs, for example. In contrast and as a replique to France's work, is Andrew Lang's *The Maid of France*, published in the same year and in which the Scottish author rejects those who 'look about for any explanation that may minimize the marvel'. According to Lang, Joan was the 'Flower of Chivalry' and 'the most perfect daughter of the Church'. 'In a sense not easily defined Joan was "inspired".' Where France inclines to the rational, Lang is sentimental and romantic, but for a long time his biography was the best to have been written in English.

Not long after these two works had been published, Gabriel Hanotaux in 1911 produced another wholeheartedly admiring account of Joan's career in which, like France, he attempts to reconcile the supernatural and the rational:

> Whether we admit the intervention of divine Providence or whether we acknowledge the workings of some unknown human quality that may be one day explained by history and science, the appearance of Joan of Arc has something supernatural and mysterious about it. It is far above everyday events, it is elevated by religion and maintained there by reason.

Not surprisingly other biographers accept unquestioningly the divine inspiration behind Joan's actions. Monsignor Henri Debout in his *Sainte Jeanne d'Arc* (1907) states clearly that Joan is no ordinary mortal, but one aided directly by heaven:

> Heaven fought for her swift messenger. Just as the examination she had to undergo [in Poitiers] went in her favour, so her angelic virtue caused everyone to admire her. Her piety became increasingly edifying and when faced with the Host you would see that she had access to divine secrets hidden from the gaze of other mortals.

No matter how they might embroider their account of Joan's life and no matter whether or not they project their own religious beliefs into their work, however, the large majority of Joan's biographers are trapped by what Milton Waldman in 1935 called a story that is 'now too old, too rugged, even too hallowed to be seriously modified.' (Many creative artists are faced with the same problem as well.) The few who largely manage to avoid this do so either by the way they contextualise Joan and show – as Colette Beaume in her *Jeanne d'Arc* (2004) has done – how she was variously seen and judged by her contemporaries, or by situating her within a distinctive feminist perspective. By far the best example of this latter approach remains Marina Warner's *Joan of Arc* (1981) in which Joan is assessed as the embodiment of various types – heretic, harlot, prophet, saint, for example – against a background of both pagan and Christian beliefs and traditions. Others, usually far less successfully, continue to use Joan as a pretext or an excuse for their own political preferences or reflections on the state of the French nation. One recent example is that of the former Gaullist prime-minister Edouard Balladur. In his *Jeanne d'Arc et la France. Le Mythe du sauveur* (2003), Balladur takes Joan together with Napoleon, Clemenceau and above all De Gaulle as the personification of the true spirit of France – strong, independent and proud. His book is rambling and repetitive, but Balladur argues that if Joan no longer holds a central position in the national consciousness, it is because the French have allowed themselves to become fearful of Europe and of being neutralised. At the same time and in contrast to this by the late twentieth and early twenty-first centuries Joan has been used, as we will see, as a pretext by the extreme Right in France to justify all manner of xenophobic reactions to the European Union and to the influx of immigrants.

In addition to all these works Joan has also been the subject of biographies inspired by psychobiography, astrology, crystallography or the belief in perpetual reincarnation, inspired by the writings of Rudolf Steiner.[12] Nor should we forget those who have set out to discredit the orthodox story by attempting to prove that Joan was neither the daughter of peasant farmers in Domremy nor that she was burned to death in Rouen. This view has a long history. Not surprisingly, perhaps, there were those at the time who believed that Joan must have been replaced at the stake by another young woman and in the years following the execution a 'Maid' appeared claiming to be Joan, using the name of Armoises. It may seem inexplicable to us today, but Joan's brother, Pierre, seems to have been taken in by this subterfuge as was Charles, and she was welcomed with honour in Orléans. Within years the imposture had been discovered and the Dame d'Armoises imprisoned, but to this day her descendents claim that she was the true Joan. Another theory, first suggested in 1805 by Pierre Caze and later developed in his *La Vérité sur Jeanne d'Arc, ou éclaircissements sur son origine* (1819), is that Joan was the illegitimate daughter of Louis, Duke of Orléans and Isabeau de Bavière and hence Charles' illegitimate sister, and was sent at birth to be nursed and brought up in Domremy. However, unless the accepted year of Joan's birth (1412) is proved to be incorrect, the fact that Louis was assassinated on 23rd November 1407 immediately invalidates this.[13]

Alternative theories or versions of Joan's story, some far-fetched, will no doubt continue to surface. In 2004, for example, a Ukranian orthopaedic surgeon, Sergey Gorbenko, was invited by the French government to examine the skulls of Louis XI and his wife. In the course of this, he discovered the skeleton of a woman buried in the Basilica at Cléry near Orléans and claimed that it was the one of Marguerite de Valois, the illegitimate daughter of Charles VI. Known to have military skills, she was chosen by a group of nobles as a saviour figure said to have been sent by God – thereby fulfilling the popular prophecy – to raise morale and defend France and legitimise the Dauphin's claim to the throne. Gorbenko based his theory on the grounds that the skeleton provided evidence of a life of hard physical activity and concluded that Marguerite had in fact been Joan. Such was her success she was then seen, ironically, to be a threat to the throne and put on trial. Condemned to be burned she was none the less replaced at the stake by one of five other women condemned for witchcraft, and imprisoned for life.

While Gorbenko's conclusion seems unlikely, it has so far not been absolutely ruled out. Meanwhile, a different theory – this time subsequently disproved – concerns relics said to have come from the site of Joan's execution and held in trust for the Church by the Association of Friends of Chinon. Early in 2006, the Church gave permission for these relics to be examined and dated and a team of expert scientists in Paris became very excited and confident that, while not every piece related to Joan, enough remained to suggest they were on the right track. Several months later, however, after careful tests and carbon dating, it appeared that the bulk of the relics were of an Egyptian mummy from around 500BC! The blackened state of some fragments was shown to be the result of embalming and not burning and a tiny piece of cloth thought possibly to be from Joan's garment proved to be of recent Egyptian origin. A further factor was that traces of pine pollen could not have come from around Rouen in the early fifteenth century since pine trees did not grow in Normandy at that time. . . . The explanation appears to lie in the custom of apothecaries importing Egyptian mummies to use in the making of certain medicines.

Images of Joan: for all tastes and all times

Whether we accept the orthodox, traditional version of Joan's story or not, neither it nor any of the alternative accounts can provide answers to certain fundamental questions. The first is quite simply what she was like physically. At the rehabilitation hearing Jean d'Aulon, her squire declared her to be 'beautiful and shapely'; Quicherat reports an Italian at Charles court at Chinon to have described her as 'short [with] a rustic face, black hair, and a healthy body'. The only drawing we have of her is an imaginative one by

Clément de Fauquembergue, a clerk of the Parlement of Paris, as he recorded the raising of the siege of Orléans.

38. *Clément de Fauquembergue's drawing, 1429.*

Studies have been carried out on the kind of armour she wore; some historians have deduced from records of financial accounts that she had a taste for fine clothes and rings. But all this remains essentially speculative. Even from the time when she was under most scrutiny – the period of her

39. *A fetching portrait of Joan ordered by the dignitaries of Orléans, 1431.*

40. *Joan with banner and sword, fifteenth-century.*

imprisonment up to her execution – we have nothing. Presumably, for example, she had no change of clothes and was obliged to wear the same man's habit all the time. After four months her hair would have grown considerably. What effect did the lack of natural light and what was no doubt a very basic diet have on her? For Joan's physical appearance we are at the mercy of artists whose images almost always reflect the style and taste of their own time. Only in film is there an attempt by some directors (though not all) to recreate what Joan's life and death in fifteenth-century France must have been like.

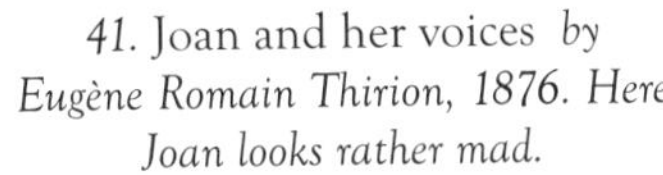

41. Joan and her voices *by Eugène Romain Thirion, 1876. Here Joan looks rather mad.*

In addition her physical condition – her virginity and amenorrhoea – also raises issues. The traditional story holds, as we have seen, that Joan promised her saints to remain a virgin and not a few of her early historians and biographers saw this directly reflected in her adding 'La Pucelle' to her name. It has been long known, however, that 'pucelle' at the time meant little more than 'young girl' (whatever Shakespeare might have made of it). Be that as it may, the claim that she was a virgin had a powerful impact and the verification of it by the 'noble ladies' was vital since it meant that she had not had dealings (and intercourse) with the Devil. But there was, of course, no scientific proof of her being intact. While she may well not have had sexual relations with any man (however improbable this may seem given the kind of life Joan was leading surrounded by soldiers), it is not impossible that her hymen would have been

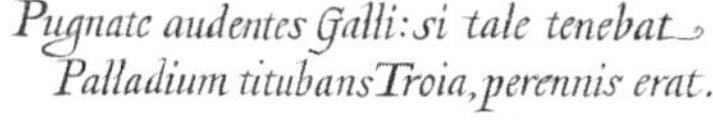

42. Engraving by L. Gaultier, 1612.

43. Joan of Arc, Flower of Chivalry, *from a seventeenth-century drawing by Vignon.*

broken by her violent physical activity, especially riding. Similar uncertainties surround the fact that, in Michelet's words, she did not suffer from 'the physical curse of women', but this strengthened the impact of her claim to be a virgin since it implied that she had not reached sexual maturity. The failure to menstruate has long been associated with anorexia, but was Joan anorexic? The little information there is about her eating habits suggest she was extremely abstemious, even after the most extreme physical efforts, and was often satisfied with bread dipped in wine, though just how conveniently symbolic such a diet is no one appears to have grasped. It is also known that anorexia is mental in origin, often suffered by women who are under great stress and, if severe, can cause them to hallucinate. While it seems likely that Joan may well have been a victim, how she found the strength for the life she led remains a mystery. It has been suggested as well that like many peasants in the Middle Ages Joan suffered from tuberculoma, a tumour in the brain, caused by the bacilli of bovine tuberculosis; this too would have resulted in her not menstruating.

When to a failure to menstruate and a claim of virginity we add Joan's insistence on wearing a man's clothes and her claims to have had visions, the substance of legend is well and truly formed. How it has been treated by

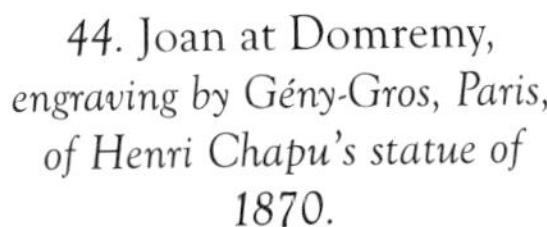

44. Joan at Domremy, *engraving by Gény-Gros, Paris, of Henri Chapu's statue of 1870.*

writers, artists, sculptors, composers, cartoonists and rock stars as well as by politicians and educationalists is what this book illustrates. Few, if any, iconic figures in European culture have attracted such attention. While most of the works inspired by and devoted to her are in French, she has been the subject of others from England, Finland, Germany, Holland, Iceland, Poland, Italy, Spain and Sweden; and beyond Europe from America, Australia, China, Japan and Russia. Many, indeed most, of these are based on the traditional story, but some focus on particular events of her life or aspects of her character, while others include episodes that have no foundation whatsoever in what we know about her.

Nor should we forget the sheer popularity and massive commercialisation of Joan's image. In France it is impossible to avoid it. A high percentage of churches have a statue or effigy of Joan somewhere; schools, colleges, streets and squares are named after her, as are religious groups, associations, clubs, cafés, hotels, restaurants, sweetshops and even an on-line dating service. Beyond France too, especially in America where the number of Roman Catholics well exceeds a billion, Joan has an immense following. As in France, schools, clubs and societies are widespread, including career advice agencies, offers of body painting, and a web site providing help with 'term papers on Joan of Arc'. In academic circles there is now a thriving discipline of 'Johannic studies', and the Saint Joan of Arc Center in Albuquerque has its own web site. In Los Angeles the Joan of Arc Commandery is part of the International Order of Chivalry and in the same city her statue stands outside a hospital in Chinatown. More prosaically, a rock group is named after her. In Belgium there is Joan of Arc beer and in Holland a giant crocus. In England – perhaps in contrition – her statue stands close to the tomb of Cardinal Beaufort in Winchester Minster and in Westminster Cathedral a mosaic designed by W. C. Symons in 1910–11 decorates the wall on the north side of the nave. Across the world Joan's image adorns broaches and pendants, porcelain bowls and plates, prayer cards, postage stamps, posters of all kinds, board and computer games, and a variety of food and goods from beans, asparagus, cheese and sardines to cosmetics, perfume and silver ware. She has inspired articles of clothing. She is used to promote insurance policies and financial investment plans. Dolls in all styles and toy soldiers have been made in her image. In

45. Statue of Joan in Winchester Minster, consecrated in 1923. Photograph by Stephen Flower.

46. Statue of Joan in Los Angeles.

many ways this has to be seen as cheap exploitation. It is also the price that has to be paid for the impact that Joan of Arc has made at all levels of society, but in no way does it diminish the fascination that she, like similar iconic figures, continues to exert. In 1994 when they were working with Jacques Rivette on his film *Jeanne la Pucelle*, his script-writers, Pascal Bonitzer and Christine Laurent, commented that the 'more we read about Joan, the deeper the mystery surrounding her; she is at the same time mysterious and transparent, simple and strange.' Few would disagree.

47. Poster promoting the national celebration of Joan of Arc, 19th May 1912.

48. Examples of products or services that have used Joan of Arc's image for promotion.

A board game using the 'epic' story of Joan of Arc's life, 1894.

Commemorative cards.

Commemorative cards.

A calendar cover from 1897.

Advertisement for an insurance company.

A US poster from 1917 commissioned by Haskell Coffin from the Treasury Department to sell war saving stamps.

As an attraction at a children's fashion show.

A cheese box.

Look Predicts a Rash of

Joan of Arc fashions

First rushes on *Joan of Arc*, starring Ingrid Bergman, revealed its fashion importance. Colors alone are so impressive that Burlington Mills will high-light Joan of Arc shades for fall. LOOK chose close-ups with costume ideas which will undoubtedly influence clothes this fall. John Frederics' sketches show how.

helmet hat

The unwieldly helmet of 15th century warfare is brought up-to-date as a casually smart hat that has a high, snugly fitting crown, juts out abruptly in front.

Fashion item in Look, *20th July 1948.*

Notes

1. Many who have written about Joan use the spelling Domrémy; there is no accent and unless it appears in the village's name in a quotation I have retained the correct form.

2. It is generally recognised that D'Arc or Darc was not Joan's name and only became established during the trial and her rehabilitation. Gradually, too, the association of her with celebrated female warriors opened the way for a play on words with 'arc' meaning a bow. In the early fifteenth century it was also customary for girls to take the name of their mother. Some have claimed that Joan's mother's maiden name of Romée was the result of her having been on a pilgrimage to Rome. This seems most unlikely. She may have made pilgrimages in France and the name may be an acknowledgement of her faith.

3. The first full transcription of the proceedings of the two trials together with a mass of supplementary material was produced by Jules Quicherat between 1841 and 1849: *Procès de condamnation et de réhabilitation de Jeanne d'Arc dite la Pucelle.* The English translation of the quotations used in this Introduction is by Willard Trask: *Joan of Arc. In Her Own Words* (New York, 1996). In order to avoid overloading the notes I have not given references to works by other writers except where they have been named or add relevant information. The Bibliography contains the titles of all major works consulted.

4. *Joan of Arc*, Berkeley and Los Angeles, 1981, 119.

5. There is disagreement about the number of visits Joan made to Robert de Baudricourt; two seem most likely.

6. There is no satisfactory explanation of how and when Joan learned to ride. One of the most colourful is given by Milton Waldman (*Joan of Arc*, New York and London, 1935, p.16). In 1428 the family was forced by *écorcheurs* to flee from Domremy and spent two weeks in a hostlery in the nearby town of Neufchâteau where Joan helped with the domestic tasks. 'In due course (the) hostelry was to evolve into a brothel for soldiers and Joan into an inmate who learned from her clients to ride and bear arms in her spare time.' More realistically Edward Lucie-Smith suggests that Joan had been a cowherd rather than a shepherdess and that she had learned to ride cattle.

7. See Warner, *op. cit.* 165–8 for a useful discussion of the symbolism of the design.

8. *Saint Joan of Arc*, New York, 1936, 225.

9. There is of course no record of what Joan wore when she was burned though the author of the *Journal de Paris* talks of her 'dress'. The long loose fitting garment is shown in early engravings and the tradition appears to have become established.

10. 'Procès d'un mythe', in *Jeanne d'Arc en garde à vue. Essais rassemblés et présentés par* Dominique Goy-Blanquet, Le Cri Edition, Brussels, 1999, 155. Translated as *Joan of Arc, a Saint for All Reasons,* Ashgate, Aldershot, 2003.

11. *Joan of Arc,* translated with an Introduction by Albert Guérard, Ann Arbor, 1959, 3.

12. See for example: Nora Wooster, *The Real Joan of Arc*, Lewes, 1992; Roger Money-Kyrle, 'A psycho-analytic study of the voices of Joan of Arc', in *The British Journal of Medical Psychology,* 13 (1933), 63–81; Philippe Vidal, *Jeanne d'Arc ... laquelle? L'énigme enfin résolu,* Nantes, 1994; Mary Stanton, *The Everlasting Ego. Lives of Joan of Arc exemplifying Reincarnation in History,* London, 1970. Perhaps the most fanciful not to say far-fetched book to have appeared to date is *Jeanne d'Arc par elle-même. Histoire de Jeanne d'Arc dictée par elle-même à Ermance Dufaux* [sic!] in the collection Vies dictées d'outre-tombe, LÉtang-la-ville, 1999.

13. This interpretation has been continued in more recent years in particular by Jean Jacoby, *Le Secret de Jeanne d'Arc,* Paris, 1932 and by Jean Grimod, *Jeanne d'Arc, a-t-elle été brûlée?*, Paris, 1952.

Chapter Two

Republican, Nationalist and Fascist Icon

As we shall see, as a subject for imaginative representation, Joan and her achievements albeit with some irregularity and not without modifications and embroidery, have preoccupied writers for well over five centuries. By contrast her potential for being exploited for the purposes of politics, education and propaganda is, as Jacques Darras reminds us, comparatively recent, having begun to be fully realised only in the early nineteenth century. Interestingly enough, one of the first overt uses to be made of her politically was not in a political essay or tract in France but in a play in Germany where, in Friedrich Schiller's *Die Jungfrau von Orleans* ('The Maid of Orleans') of 1801, she is cast as a 'resistant' figure. Schiller is addressing his fellow Germans, of course, but it was not long before Joan would appear on the political agenda in France and become in various and quite distinct guises the nation's purest heroine even if she was to be tossed from one side of the political spectrum to the other.

Given the obvious symbolic potential of Joan as the incarnation of all that was truly French and, above all, spiritual, however, it is not surprising perhaps that she would be increasingly appropriated by the conservative elements in the Catholic Church and by many of those on the Right, but the initial impetus for the role Joan was to play on the political stage came from the Left. In 1841 in his *Histoire de France* Jules Michelet portrays her quite simply as the representative of the people. In the pages he devotes to Joan and as we have already seen, he shows her to be an innocent, simple peasant girl who differs from those around her only by the extent of her religious devotion. She is a 'blend of simplicity, good sense and shrewdness. [...]. She was a very good girl, simple and sweet. She loved to go to church and to holy places. She would spin and do household chores like other girls. She went to confession frequently. She blushed when she was told that she was too devout, that she went to church too often'. For Michelet, Joan combined nationalism and republicanism, but she was also saintly and had a strength and determination unusual in a woman. Michelet's political views gradually shifted towards the Left, but even if he had no time for the kind of mysticial figure who would become central to the perception that many on the Catholic Right had of Joan, his portrayal of her contains something for everyone. After him, his pupil Jules Quicherat would reinforce this idea that Joan's appeal was universal, but gradually among those whose political sympathies lay with the Republican Left and especially non-believers the view hardened. In 1870, the answers to a series of questions asked by Pierre Larousse in his *Grand Dictionnaire du XIXème siècle* summed up what appears to have become by then the current and most generally held view of Joan:

> Did Joan of Arc have visions ? (*No*)
> Was it not a deep sense of patriotism that really motivated her ? (*Yes*)
> What did the King truly feel about her ? (*He was wary and indifferent*)
> What did the clergy always think about her ? (*They should hinder her, cause her to die and, on the pretext of rehabilitating her, make up apocryphal stories about her*).

Socialists claimed her as one of their own, not to be allowed into the clutches of the Church. And, as we shall see, would Péguy not dedicate his first work on Joan to those who had died in order to help create the 'universal socialist republic'?

At the same time the Right and conservative Catholics in particular had not been idle. By the middle of the century there was talk of Joan's being canonised and on 8th May 1869 Félix Dupanloup, the Bishop of Orléans delivered a sermon that summed up the case that he would put to the Pope later that year:

> In this lowly but intrepid village maid we cannot but discern a grand Christian character, and now that the din and dust of battle and strife have ceased, and we endeavour to find the hidden sources of these marvellous actions, we discern it in the piety which lies at the root of Christianity, the love of our Lord, of the Cross, of the Blessed Sacrament, of the Mass, devotion to the Blessed Virgin and virgin martyrs [...] (Joan was) a maiden pure and valorous, modest but ardent, simple yet grand – a soldier-maid who scatters and drives before her the ranks of the aliens and draws to her side every noble heart still burning with his country's love. Chosen by God, and wonderfully faithful to her call, this Maid gathers up in her own person the sufferings, the hopes, the strengths and the heroism of France, raises up those who were beaten down, comforts the mourning people, and finally, betrayed and deserted, she yields her life up at the stake. But scarcely has the victim been summoned to her reward, and the fire lit at her stake quenched, than light breaks anew upon the horizon of France, and the work of God, its deliverance is fulfilled. Purified by the baptism of fire and of the blood, ransomed by this holocaust, the eldest daughter of the Church is restored to her place in the plans of Providence.

Such a picture of Joan – pious, simple, courageous – is, in many respects, not so very different from Michelet's and at the time was highly appropriate. Defeat within two years at the hands of the Prussians and the consequent loss of Alsace-Lorraine would be of concern to all. But the beginning of this reappropriation by the politico-religious Right was also and ironically given impetus by changes in education introduced by the Republican Left. Already Jules Ferry's educational reforms anticipated schooling that was to be not only free but obligatory and secular. Moreover, a new radical and republican programme for the teaching of French history would be introduced, in which Joan was a central figure. The covers of children's exercise books frequently bore her image and reflected the gradually shifting political (and educational) climate.

These four illustrations from c.1840 to c.1885 clearly show how such a shift could occur. The first by Gérard Bara continues to reproduce the kind of portrait of Joan that had been common in the seventeenth century as yet untouched by controversy and debate. The next three, all anonymous, show a

49. Illustration by Gérard Bara for a child's exercise book.

50. Three further exercise book covers

distinct evolution from a traditional portrayal of her hearing St. Michael, through an anti-clerical one of her burning, to the last in which all traces of religion have gone and in which the English are blamed for her execution.

Despite some extreme views on both sides, there was none the less a general consensus for twenty years or so that Joan simply was a Christian patriot who had saved France and was to be an inspiration again for all French people. There is no better illustration of this than the gesture of the Deputy Joseph Fabre who donated the proceeds of his works and especially of the immensely popular *Jeanne d'Arc. Libératrice de la France* (1882) to the campaign to construct monuments and statues of her throughout France. He also called for a national holiday in her name. 'The date doesn't matter', he said, 'What does matter is that this solemn occasion would bring French people together in a moment of enthusiasm – men and women, monarchists and republicans, believers and free-thinkers.' Fabre was unsuccessful as he would be again in 1894 and the decision to establish a national day would not be taken in fact until Joan's canonisation, in July 1920, but the shift in opinion that would encourage such a proposal was significant. In 1894, the Prime Minister Raymond Poincaré echoed Fabre's earlier sentiments (and anticipates similar comments that would be made a century later): 'Joan belongs to no sect, no group, no school. To involve her in our political struggles would be to diminish and falsify her.' In this same year, however, the Church made an important advance; Joan was declared venerable by Pope Leo XIII, the first stage in the process of canonisation. And from this moment on the traditionalist and reactionary elements within the Church and the Right would become vociferous and the struggle for Joan's patronage increasingly intense. This struggle was fuelled by two events in particular: the Dreyfus affair and the Thalamas dispute.

The trial, condemnation and subsequent acquittal of Alfred Dreyfus, the Alsatian-Jewish officer wrongly accused of giving secret military information to the Prussians, divided France in a way never before experienced and Joan was adopted by both sides to support their positions. Those who were sympathetic to Dreyfus and considered him innocent evoked her, appropriately enough, as the symbol of the oppressed individual, tried and condemned by a corrupt court. For them, the Affair was a perfect illustration of how the state machinery embodied in the judicial system, the Army and the Church remained ever prepared to destroy an individual if he or she threated to expose its flaws or weaknesses or undermine it in any way. Those who took the opposite view considered that not only was Dreyfus a traitor and therefore rightly found guilty, but more significantly that it was impossible for such state institutions to be wrong, and they in turn called on Joan as the incarnation of the spirit of all that was truly representative of France. And not surprisingly, when Dreyfus was eventually acquitted, they interpreted this as further evidence that France – what would later be termed French sovereignty – was under attack from alien elements (notably from Jews and freemasons) that

CONTRE LES INSULTEURS DE

Jeanne d'Arc

MEETING NATIONALISTE DU 5 DÉCEMBRE 1904

Lettres et discours de MM. **François Coppée** et **Jules Lemaitre**, de l'Académie française; **Edouard Drumont**; **Auguste Longnon**, de l'Institut; **Léon Daudet**; **Antoine Baumann**, exécuteur testamentaire d'Auguste Comte; **Louis Dimier**, professeur révoqué de l'Université; **Léon de Montesquiou**, de l'*Action française;* **Copin-Albancelli**, président de la Ligue antimaçonnique.

PARIS

BUREAUX DE *L'ACTION FRANÇAISE*

42, RUE DU BAC, 42

51. Pamphlet issued for the nationalist meeting on 5th December 1894.

would have to be resisted. At a meeting of the extreme right-wing Ligue de la patrie française on 5th December 1904, for example, the following declaration by its president Edouard Drumont – author of the violently anti-semitic pamphlet *La France juive* – was read out:

> This evening it is Joan of Arc who brings men of differing views together in a patriotic and generous embrace. You know my ideas and those of my friends, and you know what name we give to the enemy who took the place of the English in our country in the fifteenth century and who tries to overwhelm us with sheer strength. For us this enemy is called Jew and freemason. Today I don't want to make too much of this, I simply want to shout aloud with you : Long live France ! Long live Joan of Arc!

Foremost in sharing these views and dominant among the right-wing groups and movements that were gaining in popularity was Charles Maurras'

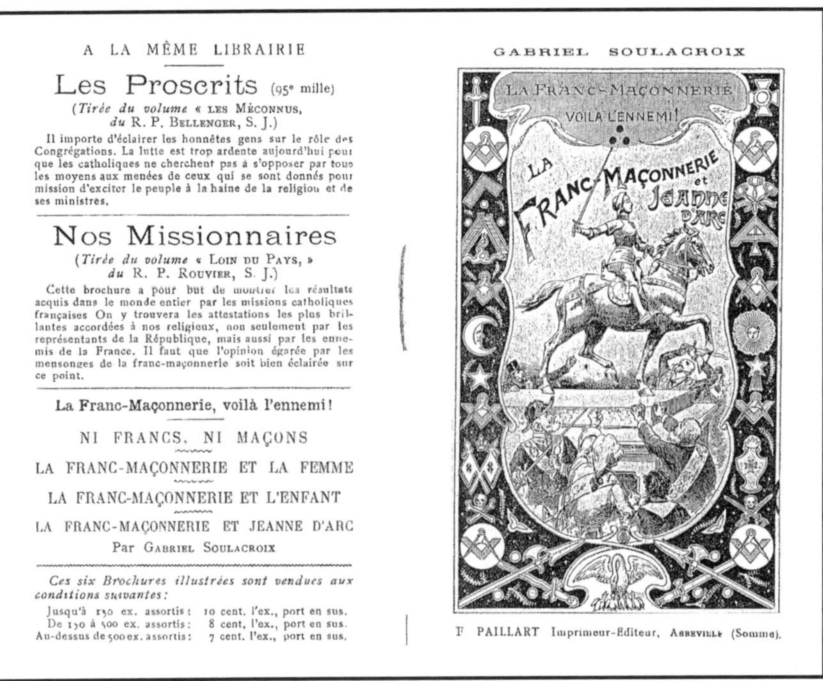

A LA MÊME LIBRAIRIE

Les Proscrits (95e mille)

(*Tirée du volume* « Les Méconnus, *du* R. P. Bellenger, S. J.)

Il importe d'éclairer les honnêtes gens sur le rôle des Congrégations. La lutte est trop ardente aujourd'hui pour que les catholiques ne cherchent pas à s'opposer par tous les moyens aux menées de ceux qui se sont donnés pour mission d'exciter le peuple à la haine de la religion et de ses ministres.

Nos Missionnaires

(*Tirée du volume* « Loin du Pays, » *du* R. P. Rouvier, S. J.)

Cette brochure a pour but de montrer les résultats acquis dans le monde entier par les missions catholiques françaises On y trouvera les attestations les plus brillantes accordées à nos religieux, non seulement par les représentants de la République, mais aussi par les ennemis de la France. Il faut que l'opinion égarée par les mensonges de la franc-maçonnerie soit bien éclairée sur ce point.

La Franc-Maçonnerie, voilà l'ennemi!

NI FRANCS, NI MAÇONS

LA FRANC-MAÇONNERIE ET LA FEMME

LA FRANC-MAÇONNERIE ET L'ENFANT

LA FRANC-MAÇONNERIE ET JEANNE D'ARC

Par Gabriel Soulacroix

Ces six Brochures illustrées sont vendues aux conditions suivantes:

Jusqu'à 150 ex. assortis:	10 cent. l'ex., port en sus.
De 150 à 500 ex. assortis:	8 cent, l'ex., port en sus.
Au-dessus de 500 ex. assortis:	7 cent. l'ex., port en sus.

GABRIEL SOULACROIX

F PAILLART Imprimeur-Éditeur, Abbeville (Somme).

52. An anti-masonic pamphlet. Joan in triumph as masons gesticulate in anger.

movement the Action française. Maurras was a royalist, deeply nationalistic and spent his life decrying the republicanism born of the 1789 Revolution. All elements alien to French life should be outlawed and eradicated, and though a non-believer himself he saw the Catholic Church as a model for the creation of the strict, disciplined, hierarchical society that alone could save France from self-destruction. As anti-clericalism gained momentum culminating in the separation of Church and State and the severing of diplomatic relations between France and the Vatican in 1905, Maurras and his ideas attracted increasing support. None the less the traditionalists and right-wing groups of whatever hue were not alone in embracing Joan. The fact that the move to have her canonised was now in fully underway and also that a fundamental debate about national identity had been raised by the Dreyfus Affair, ensured that Joan would figure prominently in all walks of life and be appropriated in various ways.

During the last decades of the nineteenth century and the early years of the twentieth, thousands of books about her of all descriptions came off the presses. Statues and monuments were erected all over France and her image appeared increasingly in advertising. In schools Joan and her exploits became a central issue though, as Olivier Bouzy has reminded us, such promotion was

Les francs-maçons fuyant devant Jeanne d'Arc.

53. Freemasons in full flight from Joan of Arc.

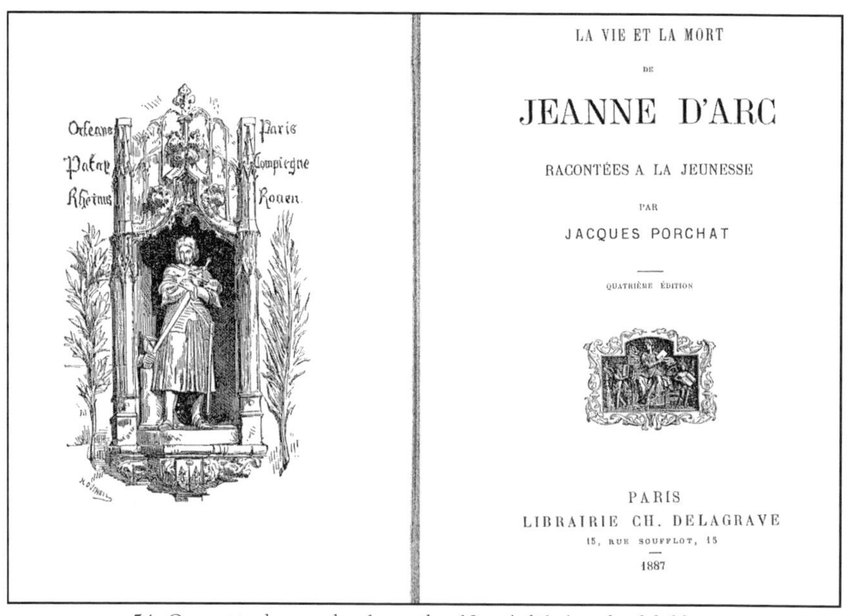

LA VIE ET LA MORT

DE

JEANNE D'ARC

RACONTÉES A LA JEUNESSE

PAR

JACQUES PORCHAT

QUATRIÈME ÉDITION

PARIS
LIBRAIRIE CH. DELAGRAVE
15, RUE SOUFFLOT, 15
1887

54. One typical example of a study of Joan's life for schoolchildren.

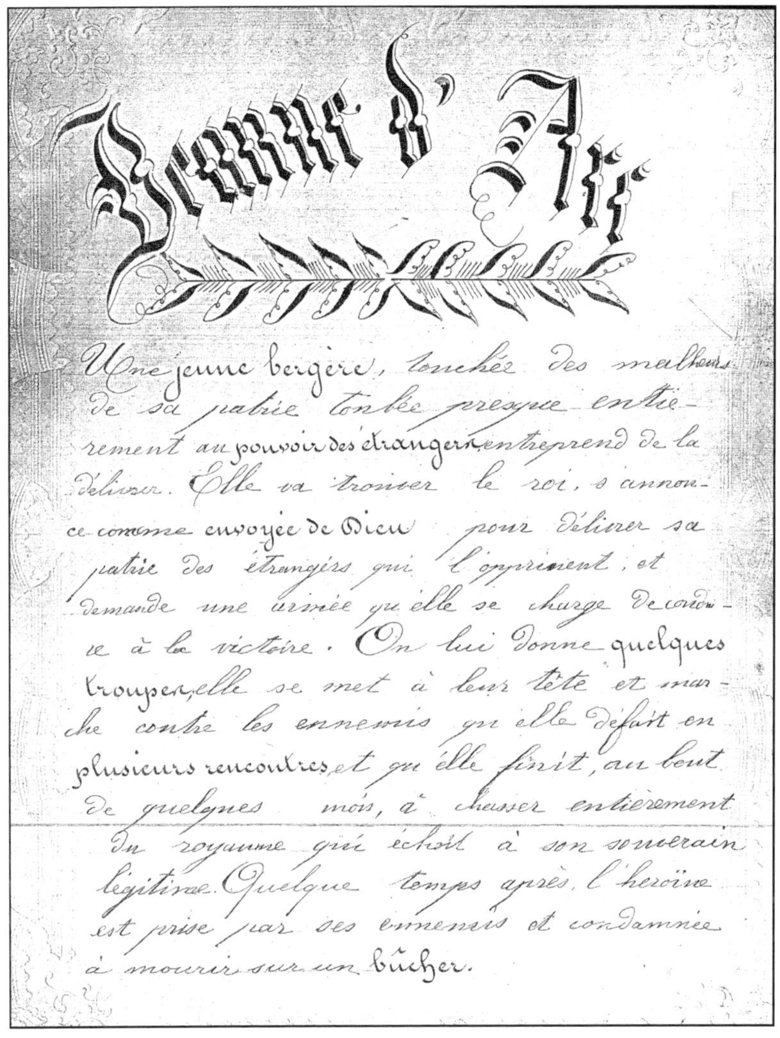

Jeanne d'Arc

Une jeune bergère, touchée des malheurs
de sa patrie tombée presque entiè-
rement au pouvoir des étrangers, entreprend de la
délivrer. Elle va trouver le roi, s'annonce comme envoyée de Dieu pour délivrer sa
patrie des étrangers qui l'oppriment, et
demande une armée qu'elle se charge de condui-
re à la victoire. On lui donne quelques
troupes, elle se met à leur tête et marche contre les ennemis qu'elle défait en
plusieurs rencontres, et qu'elle finit, au bout
de quelques mois, à chasser entièrement
du royaume qui échoit à son souverain
légitime. Quelque temps après, l'héroïne
est prise par ses ennemis et condamnée
à mourir sur un bûcher.

55. Handwriting exercise. Children were expected to complete Joan's story around key phrases. The child who completed this one clearly did not know how long Joan's campaign lasted: the 'quelques' before 'mois' is not sufficient to fill the space.

less concerned with arriving at an accurate historical account of what had happened over four centuries before than with promoting and above all consolidating the ideal of Republican nationalism for generations of pupils.[1]

And it was in the context of education that the second event in which Joan had a central role to play occured – the Thalamas dispute.

Amédée Thalamas was a history teacher at the prestigious Lycée Condorcet in Paris. His interpretation of Joan's story was at best rational and scientific, and at worst sceptical. In 1904 his teaching and the corrections he made to a pupil's essay were reported to the authorities by a right-wing deputy, Georges Bercy, after the pupil's parents had complained and an inquiry was set up. Thalamas was sanctioned and obliged to change schools, but in 1908 he was invited to give a series of open university lectures at the Sorbonne on the teaching of history. Meanwhile, in 1904 he had published a short book on Joan with a preface in which he gives an account of what had happened and defends himself.

A. THALAMAS
Professeur agrégé de l'Université
JEANNE D'ARC
L'Histoire et la Légende
60 centimes
Paul PACLOT et Cie
LIBRAIRES-ÉDITEURS
4, rue Cassette, PARIS

A. THALAMAS
Professeur agrégé de l'Université
Jeanne d'Arc
L'Histoire et la Légende
PARIS
PAUL PACLOT ET Cie, LIBRAIRES-ÉDITEURS
4, RUE CASSETTE, 4

56. Title pages of the first and a later edition of Thalamas's controversial book.

But Thalamas continued to be the target for those on the political Right and for the Action française in particular. At the Sorbonne his lectures (delivered, ironically, in the lecture hall named after Michelet) were frequently interrupted by insults from the movement's young members, the *camelots du roi*, and when it came to the last of the series he was physically assaulted. After the police had cleared the room of the disturbers (there were 54 arrests), Thalamas continued his lecture only to be interrupted again by one Lucien Lacour, a *camelot* who had managed to hide, with the words: 'that's enough! This person insulting Joan of Arc has no right to be at the Sorbonne. He should be in the Synagogue or Rue Cadet [the Masonic centre in Paris].'

57. 'Joan of Arc's voices? Pah! My voices, my 8750 voices is what history is all about!'

Thalamas hit Lacour over the head with a chair.... Two years later Thalamas would be elected as a Radical deputy for the Seine et Oise department, prompting the satirical weekly paper *Le Rire* to carry a cartoon neatly linking him with Joan and reminding its readers of his earlier escapades.

If such events as these were the most colourful the disputes that developed during and as a result of the Dreyfus affair continued to run deep. Joan became an emblem for both sides; each held held meetings and published pamphlets denouncing the other and not for the first or last time Joan in her own right was frequently overlooked.

The Church and the Right would, of course, enjoy their moment of triumph in 1920 with Joan's eventual canonisation, but with the threat and outbreak of the First World War there was a kind of truce. In December 1914, the right-wing deputy and member of the Action française, Maurice Barrès, called once more for a national day in her honour: 'the cult of Joan was born when our country was invaded; she embodies resistance against all foreigners.'

But like Fabre's, Barrès' proposal was not accepted and six years would pass before it would finally receive parliamentary approval. Despite his own political position and sympathies, Barrès' appeal was for Joan to be recognised as being above factions and parties: 'Everyone can claim Joan as theirs but she is above them all. No-one can have her to himself. Today, like five hundred years ago, the miracle of national reconciliation can be performed around her banner.' With these words Barrès echoed the feelings that had generally been expressed about national unity (the *union sacrée*) during the war. Typical are these lines from Pierre Lanery d'Arc's *Jeanne d'Arc et la Guerre de 1914*:

> She has worked to bring all parties together, the flame that has fused all hearts in one, the standard bearer around whom all have gathered in courage and confidence to face danger together. Should we not say that Joan of Arc has reawakened the national feelings she created five centuries ago? Do the same causes give rise to the same effects ? Have the circumstances not been as agonising as they were before? [...]
>
> Is it not this union which allows us to forget our disagreements, our divisions, our political rivalry and stand together in face of the German threat, raise our flag high and resolutely defend the rights of Humanity against pan-Germanism, against the madness of a megalomanic leader and the barbarity of a people out of control? Has this union not been the first obstacle for the Germans who expected to find a France divided and incapable of defending herself? Have they not run up against a nation bound indissolubly together, determined and ready to face all tests and meet all sacrifices ? Has this bonding of all parties and strengthening of resolve not been the triumphant expression of a national spirit, created, personified and renewed by the Saint of our Nation?

With the allied victory and the recovery of Alsace-Lorraine that had been annexed by Germany after 1871 this was the kind of perception of Joan held by the majority. Canonisation in the summer of 1920, the re-establishment of diplomatic relations between the Vatican and the Republic a year later, the presence of a Protestant President, Gaston Doumergue at the mass celebrating the 500th anniversary of the delivery of Orléans, as well as that of the former President Poincaré in Rouen in 1931 at a commemoration of Joan's death, all pointed to an apparently neutral state of affairs. But those on the Right were soon to reassert the claim that Joan was essentially theirs. In 1926 the Pope, Pius XI, condemned the Action française for not sufficiently upholding true Catholic beliefs. One of the consequences was the banning of the march that had become traditional (if unofficial) since the turn of the century and the laying of wreaths and flowers around the statues of Joan in the Place des Augustins and the Place des Pyramides in Paris. The year before 8th May had also been the day of national elections and celebrations had had to be postponed and, according to the Action française, the left-wing Radical government had taken this as an excuse to try to ban any subsequent major

58. A celebration of the armistice signed at Rethondes, 11th November 1918. Georges Clemenceau, nicknnamed 'The Tiger', was Minister of War.

demonstration. This was unsuccessful; the Action française refused to accept the ban and its members congregated in their customary manner. After a hommage by Charles Maurras and others, despite a massive police presence (according to the Action française eight thousand strong), hundreds of the movement's members marched from Saint Augustin to the Place de la Concorde. The result was a direct confrontation recalled in the movement's daily newspaper two years later:

Exasperated, the police called in reinforcements to stop our friends advancing. Between the Madeleine and Concorde, scenes of unheard-of butality took place. In the Place de la Concorde the considerable police force charged our friends and their march was pushed towards the Tuileries. Were they going to be caught – was it a trap? For a moment it seemed so. But they managed to escape and regrouped in the Avenue Paul Déroulède between the Louvre and the Tuileries. There was a final charge. The march moved on unflinchingly but for a moment gave ground and Pujo, who was at the head was trampled on by the police. Soon he was on his feet again and rushed towards the statue followed by thousands of supporters. Our friends covered the Place with cries of 'Long live Joan of Arc' while Pujo, hatless and covered in dust shouted in triumph : 'the traditional march for 1926 has taken place! Long live Joan of Arc! Long live France!'

ENCYCLOPÉDIE DE LA GUERRE — 1914-1916

P. LANÉRY d'ARC

Jeanne d'Arc

et la

Guerre de 1914

BERGER-LEVRAULT, LIBRAIRES-ÉDITEURS

PARIS
5-7, RUE DES BEAUX-ARTS

NANCY
RUE DES GLACIS, 18

1916

59. *Written by the compiler of* Le Livre d'or de Jeanne d'Arc *(1894), a catalogue of works devoted to Joan, this is typical of a number of patriotic history books being published at this time.*

Further skirmishes took place and, according to the Action française 221 of its members were arrested, 150 suffered casualties and 118 policemen were also wounded. While in strict political terms this event was of little importance, it clearly demonstrates the potential force of the Right. Maurras's voice was still powerful and appealed to many. In an essay on Joan (1937) he reasserts his contempt for Republicanism and his support for the discipline and order to be brought by classical civilisation, Catholicism and a hereditary monarchy. But for people to realise this, strong leadership is first necessary, and Joan is one who had provided it. As a non-believer Maurras is not concerned with her voices or visions ; for him Joan was clearsighted and determined. While she may have been inspired by a religious principle her goal was essentially patriotic. The parallel with the contemporaneous state of affairs in France was obvious, he argued. France 'is stagnating, torn by conflicting factions and led by an all-party government to the point where foreigners are invited in. As long as the country is not governed by a single person who succeeds his father and prepares the way for his son, this will continue .' But Maurras and the Action française were not alone. Even if not everyone shared his monarchist views, all right-wing groups and associations now raised Joan's flag in their demonstrations and marches. And one in

60. An anti-semitic postcard issued by the extreme Right in Orléans in 1939 in protest at Jewish 'control' of the local council.

particular, Georges Valois' quasi-fascist party, Le Faisceau, sinisterly anticipated the way Joan would be used in future. A week after a gathering in Domremy on 22nd May 1927, Valois would write: 'This was one of the most glorious days of fascism'. Throughout the next decade the same sentiments would continue to be expressed, especially in the right-wing press – in *La Liberté, Action française* and above all *Je suis partout.* Joan embodied the essence of French nationalism felt by many to be under constant threat from socialism and in particular, and at all levels, from Jews.

Joan was not entirely ignored by the Left, however. At the time of Léon Blum's socialist Popular Front government, the Communist paper *L'Humanité* could state (10th May 1936) in a retort to the Right: 'No, Joan of Arc does not belong to the royalists and the Hitler-styled fascists. The peasant from Lorraine who rose up against foreign allied forces and was abandoned by her king belongs to the people of France', and 'Jeanne avec nous' – later to be the title of a play by Claude Vermorel – was Blum's government's rallying cry. But such remarks were those of a minority, and with the invasion and occupation of France by the Germans, the image of Joan that had been coming increasingly into focus over the previous decades was firmly established.

61. The hour brings forth . . . Violently right-wing, anti-semitic and outspokenly loyal to Pétain, Patrick Weygand was appointed head of the French army and Allied commander-in-chief in May 1940. He lasted less than a month. He claimed that France should never have declared war in the first place.

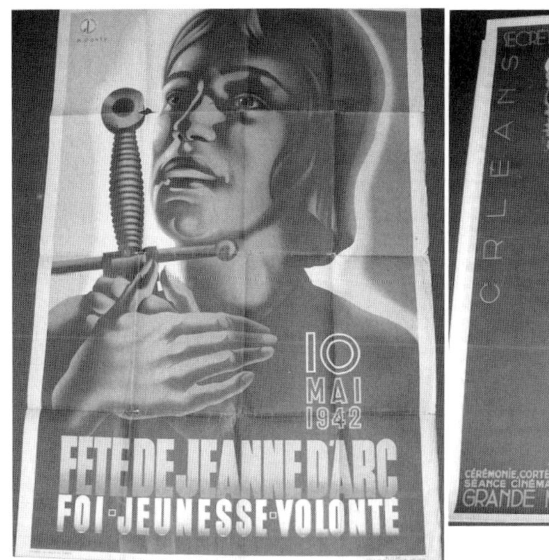

62. Posters issued by the Vichy propaganda office in 1942.

For Philippe Pétain and his collaborationist government to have depicted Joan as the warrior fighting an invading or occupying force would hardly have been appropriate. As during the First World War Joan was, initially at least, evoked as an inspirational leader, but with France's capitulation and the government's unambiguous support for Nazi policies a different image was necessary. Now she was hailed as the symbol of the new spirit of regeneration (Catholic and peasant), basic to Pétain's policy of National Revolution, and above all of anglophobia.

The Vichy propaganda office issued scores of posters, many containing pictures of Joan but others presenting Pétain in postures that clearly resemble hers, while others again associated her with the Virgin Mary and with the cult of motherhood. The collaborationist press underlined this message. On 12th May 1941 Robert Brasillach who, as we will discover, had already written a play about Joan in 1933 and who liked to identify himself with her, wrote in his antisemitic and pro-Nazi paper *Je suis partout*: 'Joan belongs to the most realistic form of French nationalism, that which runs deep and has its roots in the soil. Joan does not belong to those with money, to ideologues, and to those who pretend to defend a rotten civilisation, because she is part of eternal youth and creative vitality.' Books were published to encourage children quite openly to link Joan with Pétain. In 1942, for example, René Jeanneret concludes the preface to his *Le Miracle de Jeanne* with the following lines:

> If little boys, and even some big ones, have enjoyed reading of Joan's bravery, might not little girls, who have more of a taste for heroism than some think, not enjoy it as well? Inspired by this sublime example they will all discover, as they serve their country, that love and that faith which Marshall Pétain highlights as the two wings that bore Joan to the height of her destiny.

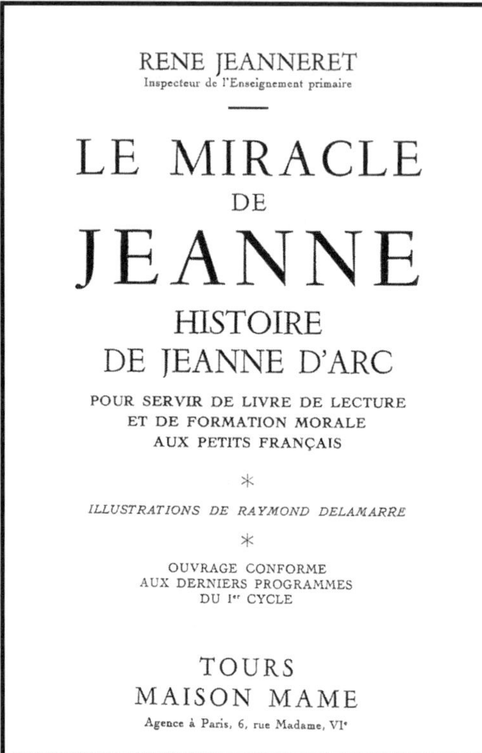

RENE JEANNERET
Inspecteur de l'Enseignement primaire

LE MIRACLE
DE
JEANNE
HISTOIRE
DE JEANNE D'ARC
POUR SERVIR DE LIVRE DE LECTURE
ET DE FORMATION MORALE
AUX PETITS FRANÇAIS

*

ILLUSTRATIONS DE RAYMOND DELAMARRE

*

OUVRAGE CONFORME
AUX DERNIERS PROGRAMMES
DU 1er CYCLE

TOURS
MAISON MAME
Agence à Paris, 6, rue Madame, VIe

63. Title page of Jeanneret's pro-Vichy book for children.

It is true, as we shall see, that Joan did feature in the literature and propaganda of the Resistance, if only to a small degree. In 1947 the Communist Edith Thomas, could say with some justification that Joan had been 'on everyone's lips and in everyone's heart, on altars and on the stage, in speeches made by reactionary officers and in the whisperings of the Resistance'. This was true. The problem was that in France not only did resistance networks not have the resources available to exploit Joan's image to any real effect, they also had to remain hidden.

But if not widely exploited by those in France who were opposed to the German presence, in London, where he had fled and exiled himself and master-minded non-Communist resistance activities, Charles de Gaulle

64. 'The killers always come back to the scenes of their crimes.' A poster from 1943 issued by the Vichy propaganda services depicting the image of Joan rising above the ruins of Rouen, bombed by the British.

adopted the cross of Lorraine as the symbol of Resistance and tellingly referred to Joan from time to time in his radio messages.[2] In 1941, while deploring the servile attitude of most of his compatriots, he acknowledged that some were willing to resist, and he reminded his listeners that 'it was from this secret hope and faith that Joan of Arc's sword caused the uprising that kicked the enemy out of France'; in June 1942 he gave her, with her courage and intransigence, as the example to follow. Indeed the American President Roosevelt reported that de Gaulle took himself to be an equal to Joan of Arc, Napoleon and Clemenceau and would receive visitors in London sitting between portaits of the first two! It says much for de Gaulle's careful self-image building that though he could have been no less aware of the political capital to be made out of Joan, at the Liberation references to her in his speeches are almost non-existent, however much he liked to consider that he was indirectly descended from her – a claim that would frequently be exploited by cartoonists in later years, both in France and abroad.

65. Cartoon by Sennep in Le Franc-Tireur, *1944. 'Let's get at the English!' Pétain's followers are depicted with the two-bladed axe that was one of his symbols. Pierre Laval urges them on from above.*

After the Liberation, France was dominated politically until the early 1980s by various shades of right-wing and predominantly Gaullist ideologies. Some attempts were made by the Left and even by the Communists, who in the late 1940s were in a position of some strength in government, to recover Joan. In May 1948 the conservative paper, *Le Figaro*, carried an amusing account of how Jeannette Vermeersch, the partner of Maurice Thorez, the French Communist party's leader, joined the annual procession and laid flowers at the foot of Fremiet's statue. 'A strange encounter' the paper's journalist observed. The following year *L'Aurore* published a cartoon in much the same spirit.

And in 1950 Jeannette Vermeersch recalled how Danielle Casanova, the head of the Communist women's organisation in the southern zone of France during the Occupation, played the part of Joan while imprisoned at Romainville, in an improvised play entitled *La France à travers les âges*:

> Danielle played Joan of Arc in the prison at Romainville. But in her life she carried on Joan's fight for our nation's independence. Joan of Arc was also arrested by the occupying forces, handed over to the French courts, to bishops who betrayed their country. The Church wasted five hundred years before

66. 'You can come down now, the joke's over.'
Cartoon in L'Aurore, *6th September 1949.*

> canonising this heroine who believed in heaven but also believed in France. Joan, the good girl from Lorraine was burned as a witch and a heretic, as a caster of spells, today Danielle's enemies talk of 'the communist, the foreign agent'. The women of our country have the same respect for Joan and Danielle (*L'Humanité*, 12th May 1950).

But the decline of the Left in France was by now gathering pace and would culminate by the early 1950s in the Cold War. The die had been cast; politically Joan was firmly embraced by the Right.

In 1957 during the Algerian War (1954–1962) General Weygand launched his 'Alliance Jeanne d'Arc', ostensibly a non-party organisation whose aim was to 'reinvigorate the sense of the French nation in the light of Christian principles' and 'to interpret papal teaching over civil and family matters to as many people as possible'.

But Joan rapidly became a champion for the *pieds-noirs* and all those who wished to keep Algeria as part of France. Her image was also used by cartoonists in France and Great Britain during the next half century to comment on various matters in which French interests were seen to be under threat such as the Treaty of Rome, the Common Market, the construction of Concorde and, more recently, Mad Cow disease, over which there were acrimonious disputes with the British. In 1965, at the time of the Presidential elections which de Gaulle only narrowly won she was regularly evoked.

'Wake up, Mr. Macmillan – history never repeats itself!'

67. De Gaulle's own cult of Joan was frequently ridiculed by cartoonists in the British press. Cummings, Daily Express, *6th March 1963 and 31st October 1964; Vicky,* Daily Mirror, *21st May 1958.*

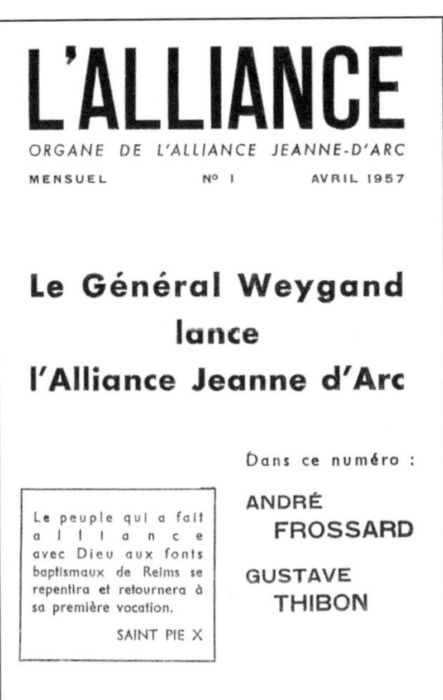

L'ALLIANCE

ORGANE DE L'ALLIANCE JEANNE-D'ARC

MENSUEL N° 1 AVRIL 1957

Le Général Weygand lance l'Alliance Jeanne d'Arc

Dans ce numéro :

ANDRÉ FROSSARD

GUSTAVE THIBON

Le peuple qui a fait alliance avec Dieu aux fonts baptismaux de Reims se repentira et retournera à sa première vocation.

SAINT PIE X

68. The first issue of a right-wing review edited by Weygand. After the Liberation, Weygand supported most (if not every) reactionary movement.

69. Maggie, please, kick the Brits out of the Common Market.'
'I'm really sorry but only French shepherdesses hear voices.'
Cartoon in Le Figaro, 30th November 1979.

When the socialist François Mitterand was finally elected as President of the Republic in 1981, *L'Humanité* published a cartoon recalling the one of Thalamas in *Rire*.

70. *'My little one, on the 10th May I heard more voices than you did.' Cartoon from* Le Canard enchaîné, *14th October 1981.*

71. *On the anniversary of Joan's death, President Giscard d'Estaing dreams of ridding himself of Margaret Thatcher: 'There are times when it would be good to set fire to memories again.'* La Nouvelle République, *11th May 1993.*

72. *'My God, we're going to eat saint!'*
Le Nouvel Observateur, *1st–10th November 1999.*

73. *Reactions to France's embargo on British beef often featured in French cartoons.*
La République du Centre, *28th October 1999.*

While Joan's image continued to be used in such various ways, she was not appropriated by any single group to the extent that she had been by the Action française, however. But in the early 1980s this was to change with the foundation by Jean-Marie le Pen of his extreme right-wing party, the Front National.

Le Pen's message and methods are clear. Over the years he has regularly claimed that the policies of his party are intended to respond to the deep but

74. 'Joan, I understand you better and better.' Before Le Pen had the impact he would have a few years later, the satirical Le Canard enchaîné *published this cartoon on 11th March 1992.*

75. National Front publicity for the rally in 2003

often unvoiced xeno-phobic feelings of all French citizens who resent and wish to resist any intrusion from outside. But behind this apparantly all-embracing, popu-list message lies a policy that is fundamentally exclusive and racist. Le Pen's party's annual rally was organised to coincide with that of Joan in Paris on 8th May, but in 1984 Le Pen moved its date back to 1st May, so that it would coincide with the International Workers' Day, the Fête du travail.

This was not done as a challenge or with the intention of staging a confrontation, however, but so that it would appear to bring the full spectrum of parties together in a show of national unity with Joan as their figurehead. Not surprisingly the change of date had no effect; nor have the nature and composition of the Front's demonstrations or Le Pen's basic message varied, in spite of any token gestures he may have made to the workers. And if the direction of the march has changed slightly over the years it always takes in the Place du Palais Royal, the Place des Pyramides, the Place des Augustins and , in recent years, the Place de l'Opéra.

Flowers are laid at the foot of Fremiet's statue, stirring music is played loudly (selections from Carl

Orff's *Carmina Burana* and Tchaikowsky's *Sixth Symphony* are favourites) and Le Pen, rapturously received by his followers, speaks. Joan is still mentioned and is often the launch pad for Le Pen's initial comments , but in general the significance he is willing to attribute to her appears to be decreasing. In 2003 she was still central to his appeal:

> Thank you and greetings to all of you who have come once again from all parts of France to celebrate Joan of Arc and the workers' day that we consider to be one of the most noble social values. We must pay you a special due as well since you have come without being told of this event by the media who have kept their announcements for their friends on the unionist Left – or what is left of it [...]. A young girl of the world and of heaven whose task was to save France from disappearing because of violence and treason, and of being taken over by an enemy, stripped of her sovereignty, her independence, her language and her identity. [...].
>
> Today we celebrate work and the workers, not laziness and parasites. We also celebrate our nation and those patriots who honour Joan. Of course, no one would dream of comparing himself or herself to Joan whose amazing epic story is unique, miraculous and inimitable, but there is no reason why she should not be an inspiration for each of us in our struggle to maintain those virtues she embodied : patriotism, courage, devotion, the spirit of sacrifice. [...]
>
> Like her we love our country and our people, not against others but before them. We know that the main enemy within us is doubt, effort and independance are replaced by discouragement and despair. We know that if mass immigration is the greatest danger we face, we blame politicians of the Right and Left and all their accomplices in an impotent and corrupt system. Let the people of France wrench themselves from the listlessness of a comfort that is disintegrating before it is too late.

76. National Front rally, 1st May 2005 outside the Opéra in Paris. Photograph by the author.

Like most political leaders Le Pen is an astute manipulator of the media and the Front's annual gathering of his movement's supporters offers him an unparalleled opportunity for propaganda. The similarity with the Action française's rallies in the late 1920s and 1930s, which attracted groups of veterans from the First World War and conservative Catholics, is striking. Over the years, in addition to the representatives of the provincial and Parisian sections of the Front there has been a variety of groups from *anciens combattants* and ultra-conservative (integrist) Catholics opposed to all modernisation in the Church, to scouts, nostalgic Pétainists and pro-Nazi skin-heads. And the police presence is equally massive. Rightfully fearful of the possibility of counter demonstrations and violence, the Parisian authorities have monitored the event carefully and have increasingly clamped down on the participation of potential trouble makers. One of the consequences is that the rally has become a more narrowly conventional political one. Hommage is still paid to Joan; flowers and wreaths are still strewn around Joan's statue, pamphlets and magazines bearing her image are much in evidence and as ever it adorns the massive backdrop for the platform where party officials sit and from which Le Pen addresses the faithful. But Joan appears to have become little more than a pretext. In 2005 she was represented on a single banner only in the demonstration and Le Pen's acknowledgement of her as an inspirational force

77. National Front rally in 2005: the sole banner depicting Joan. Photograph by the author.

simply occupied a few seconds of a ferocious attack on those in favour of the new European Constitution on which there was to be a referendum on 29th May: 'The one person who holds first place in the long line of those who have fought for our nation is Joan of Arc, Joan the patron saint of our fatherland, Joan the nation's heroine, the symbol of all who say "No" '.

78. Le Pen rally in 2005. Joan appears on the backdrop to the speakers' stand. Photograph by the author.

Over the years Republican reaction to Le Pen's exploitation of Joan in his campaigns has been curiously muted. In 1989 on 8th May at Orléans, François Mitterrand, with Le Pen obviously in his sights, commented that : 'It is not possible to accuse Joan of speaking of hate and scorn for the other person. The opposite is true.' Jean-Pierre Sueur, the city's mayor, produced the well-worn and much rehearsed view that Joan 'belongs to the people of France. No-one can appropriate her. No-one has the right to annex her, especially those adepts of xenophobia [...] Joan's message is one of freedom, justice and brotherhood and is addressed to all, not to a minority or particular faction.' Seven years later Jacques Chirac would repeat the same kind of vague non-partisan sentiments: 'the values that Joan incarnates are those of justice, love, freedom and peace. The purity of her ideal, the nobility of her struggle place her above all ambitions and calculations. She belongs to all French people'. In 1999 Elisabeth Gigou claimed that it was Republicans' responsibility not

79. 'I've gone to the anti-Le Pen demonstration as well.' La Croix, 4th May 2002.

to let Joan be taken over by those who would use her image in the wrong way.[2] And perhaps within the context of politics there is little more to be said. Joan and her story are central to France's heritage; serious historical studies and popular books continue to be published and her image is

80. Two cartoons depicting Joan clearly disapproving of having been appropriated by Le Pen: by Nicholas Garland, The Daily Telegraph, *3rd May 2002 (see opposite) and Steve Bell,* The Guardian, *2nd May 2002.*

preserved in literature and film. She remains an object of devotion for many. It appears unlikely, however, that at least in the foreseeable future she will be appropriated by a political party of any colour to the degree that she has in the past.[3]

Notes

1. 'Historiographie de Jeanne, du XVe siècle à nos jours', in *Jeanne d'Arc, mythes et réalités,* Paris: L'Atelier de l'Archer, 1999.
2. Yann Rigolet, *Jeanne d'Arc ou l'étonnante pérennité d'un mythe, à Orléans, de 1945 à nos jours*, unpublished Masters thesis, Univesity of Orléans, 2003.
3. This chapter has concentrated on the use made of Joan in a variety of political contexts in France. From the eighteenth century she has been evoked for political purposes on a number of occasions in the United States. For a discussion of this see the article by Claude Grimal in the Appendix.

Chapter Three

Warrior, Saint or Harlot?

As we noted in the first chapter, the story of Joan and her exploits has inspired world-wide thousands of pieces of all possible kinds of creative works and imaginative writing – poems, plays, novels, stories for children, ballets, operas, film scenarios, pantomimes and comic strips. . . . No single historical figure has been subjected to such creative scrutiny and exploitation. Most of the literary works originate, inevitably, in France and are often no more than simple, popular adaptations of the 'facts' of Joan's life; some pay scant attention to historical detail and even chronology, some introduce scenes and characters for which there is no factual support and some are entirely fanciful. As we saw in the last chapter they have, on occasions, also been prompted by shifts in the political and religious climate of the time. While, beyond France, factors such as these are on the whole less important or less influential, they can be significant, as Shakespeare's *Henry VI*, Southey's poem or Shaw's play in England, Brecht's plays in Germany or Panilov's film in the Soviet Union for example clearly demonstrate.

To pretend to be able to offer even a remotely comprehensive survey of this extraordinarily rich field would be absurd. In what follows therefore I try to highlight what I consider to be key and often distinctive texts, and show how many of them encourage us to go beyond the traditional Joan story to reflect on wider issues of a socio-religious and political nature.[1] This is particularly noticeable, to choose but three examples, in the seventeenth century when Anglo-French rivalry was running high, in the early nineteenth century when the idea of nationhood was beginning to develop throughout Europe and during and immediately following the period of the Occupation of France by Hitler's Nazi forces in 1940–1944.

The Making of the Myth: the Fifteenth and Sixteenth Centuries.

Such was the impact of Joan's military success and the notoriety of her trial and execution it is perhaps surprising that not more contemporaneous accounts or tributes to her have survived. Of those that have the best known is the *Ditié de Jehanne d'Arc* ('The Song of Joan of Arc') by Christine de Pisan, written in 1429. Passionately attached to her homeland Christine was herself militantly anti-English; she was also a self-conscious feminist. In her poem Joan is compared to and shown to be greater than a number of heroic biblical figures. Christine describes her not only as a warrior, but as the saviour of God's chosen people. These are themes that will be repeated endlessly in writings about Joan across the centuries, but behind Christine's fulsome praise and tribute it is difficult not to detect her own values:

> And you blessed maid, are you to be forgotten, given that God honoured you so much that you untied the rope which held France so tightly bound? Could one ever praise you enough for having bestowed peace on this land humiliated by war?
>
> Blessed be He who created you, Joan, who were born at a propitious hour! Maiden sent from God, into whom the Holy Spirit poured His great grace, in whom [i.e. the Holy Ghost] there was and is an abundance of noble gifts, never did Providence refuse you any request. Who can ever begin to repay you?
>
> And what more can be said of any other person or of the great deeds of the past? Moses, upon whom God in His bounty bestowed many a blessing and virtue, miraculously and indefatigably led God's people out of Egypt. In the same way, blessed Maid, you have led us out of evil!
>
> When we take your person into account, you are a young maiden, to whom God gives strength and power to be the champion who casts the rebels down and feeds France with the sweet, nourishing milk of peace, here indeed is something quite extraordinary!
>
> For if God performed such a great number of miracles through Joshua who conquered many a place and cast down many an enemy, he, Joshua, was a strong and powerful *man*. But, after all, a *woman* – a simple shepherdess – braver than any man ever was in Rome! As far as God is concerned, this was easily accomplished.
>
> [...]

I have heard of Esther, Judith and Deborah, who were women of great worth, through whom God delivered His people from oppression, and I have heard of many other worthy women as well, champions every one, through them He performed many miracles, but He has accomplished more through this Maid.

She was miraculously sent by divine command and conducted by the angel of the Lord to the King, in order to help him. Her achievement is no illusion for she was carefully put to the test in council (in short, a thing is proved by its effect)

and well examined, before people were prepared to believe her; before it became common knowledge that God had sent her to the King, she was brought before clerks and wise men so that they could find out if she was telling the truth. But it was found in history-records that she was destined to accomplish her mission;

for more than 500 years ago, Merlin, the Sibyl and Bede foresaw her coming, entered her in their writings as someone who would put an end to France's troubles, made prophecies about her, saying that she would carry the banner in the French wars and describing all that she would achieve.

And, in truth, the beauty of her life proves that she has been blessed with God's grace – and for that reason her actions are more readily accepted as genuine. For whatever she does, she always has her eyes fixed on God, to whom she prays and whom she invokes and serves in word and deed; nowhere does her devotion ever falter.

Oh, how clear this was at the siege of Orléans where her power was first made manifest! It is my belief that no miracle was ever more evident, for God so came to the help of His people that our enemies were unable to help each other any more than would dead dogs. It was there that they were captured and put to death.

Oh! What honour for the female sex! It is perfectly obvious that God has special regard for it when all these wretched people who destroyed the whole Kingdom – now recovered and made safe by a woman, something that 5000 *men* could not have done – and the traitors [have been] exterminated. Before the event they would scarcely have believed this possible.

A little girl of sixteen (isn't this something quite supernatural?) who does not even notice the weight of the arms she bears – indeed her whole upbringing seems to have prepared her for this, so strong and resolute is she! And her enemies go fleeing before her, not, one of them can stand up to her. She does all this in full view of everyone,

and drives her enemies out of France, recapturing castles and towns. Never did anyone see greater strength, even in hundreds and thousands of men! And she is the supreme captain of our brave and able men. Neither Hector nor Achilles had such strength! This is God's doing; it is He who leads her.

[...]

And know that she will cast down the English for good, for this is God's will: He hears the prayer of the good, whom they wanted to harm! The blood of those who are dead and have no hope of being brought back to life again cries out against them. God will tolerate this no longer – He has decided, rather, to condemn them as evil.

She will restore harmony in Christendom and the Church. She will destroy the unbelievers people talk about, and the heretics and their vile ways, for this is the substance of a prophecy that has been made. Nor will she have mercy on any place which treats faith in God with disrespect.

She will destroy the Saracens, by conquering the Holy Land. She will lead Charles there, whom God preserve! Before he dies he will make such a journey. He is the one who is to conquer it. It is there that she is to end her days and that both of them are to win glory. It is there that the whole enterprise will be brought to completion.

Therefore, in preference to all the brave men of times past, this woman must wear the crown, for her deeds show clearly enough already that God bestows more courage upon her than upon all those men about whom people speak. And she has not yet accomplished he whole mission! I believe that God bestows her here below so that peace may be brought about through her deeds.

And yet destroying the English race is not her main concern for her aspirations lie more elsewhere: it is her concern to ensure the survival of the Faith. As for the English, whether it be a matter for joy or sorrow, they are done for. In days to come scorn will be heaped on them. They have been cast down!

> And all you base rebels who have joined them, you can see now that it would have been better for you to have gone forwards rather than backwards as you did, thereby becoming the serfs of the English. Beware that more does not befall you (for you have been tolerated long enough!), and remember what the outcome will be!
>
> Oh, all you blind people, can't you detect God's hand in this? If you can't, you are truly stupid for how else could the Maid who strikes you all down dead have been sent to us? – And you don't have sufficient strength! Do you want to fight against God?[2]
>
> (Stanzas XXI–XXV; XXVII–XXXVI; XLI–XLVII)

Probably from the same year as well, and possibly slightly earlier than the *Ditié*, we have an anonymous poem *Ballade contre les Anglais* ('Ballad against the English')[3] :

> Go back, Englishmen, go back
> You no longer rule here;
> Drag away your flags
> Which the valiant French have beaten down,
> Willed on by our Lord Jesus,
> And the sweet Maid, Joan,
> Who has overcome you
> In a way you find hard to take.

Joan was also commemorated in the early part of the fifteenth century in works by Martin le Franc and Georges Chastellain. In a collection of poems in praise of women, le Franc wrote, in 1440, a kind of debate in which Joan's skills and exploits are described and once again, as in Christine de Pisan's poem, she is seen as a saviour figure:

> It was she who regained
> The French their honour and in such a way
> That she will rightfully
> Be ever remembered for it.

Chastellain's two verses are brief and to the point with Joan already referred to as a saint. (Chastellain also interestingly alludes in the last lines of his tribute to the first of the 'false Joans', Jeanne des Armoises [*sic*].)

> In France, the finest
> Flower in Christendom,
> I saw a Maid
> Rise with authority
> And raise the siege

Of Orléans with her own hands,
And then lead the king
To his coronation in Rheims

The Saint was adored
On account of her deeds
But then was overcome
And taken without trial.
She was burned to a cinder in Rouen
Much to the distress of the French
Who have since caused her to live again.

Better known, and as famous as Christine de Pisan's poem, is François Villon's *Ballade des dames du temps jadis* ('Ballad to ladies of former times') from 1460 in which he records the names and evokes the deeds of a dozen women, many of whom were courtesans or lived debauched lives. His reference to Joan is brief and his intention unclear. Is she 'The good girl from Lorraine / Whom the English burned at Rouen' an exception in this list or is Villon as mocking of her as he is of the others? Or again, is she, irrespective of her achievements, lost in time like them all?[4]

Nearly a quarter of a century later Martial d'Auvergne took up Joan's story again in his beautifully illustrated *Vigiles du roi Charles VII* (1484) ('The Vigils of King Charles VII'). He passes over many of the early episodes of her life except to comment that her family was honest and of 'small means' and makes no mention of Joan's voices. Instead he emphasises her warrior spirit and appearance. In the company of Charles, for example:

She resembled neither a scholar nor a merchant;
But was robust, strengthened by prowess.
It amazed me to see a woman so firm,
Of such great courage that the people are aroused and taken in,
And each citizen is made to fight, as if at all times
She keeps the soldiers safely under her wings.

Even more strident in tone is a popular anonymous *La Chanson de Jeanne d'Arc* ('The Song of Joan of Arc') in which she is compared again with ancient heroines and especially the Amazons:

Dressed like an Amazon,
Sword in hand
Like a warrior she is given
Her share of the spoils.
Her reputation is so great that
The best soldiers
And all the army chiefs
Follow in her footsteps.

In addition to poems and songs such as these we should also note the existence of the immensely long and ponderous *Mistère du siège d'Orléans* ('The Mystery of the Siege of Orléans') by Jacques Milet (1450)[5] which ploddingly retraces in diary-like style Joan's story from Domremy to her victory in which even God is given a small part. Over a century later, and rather more interesting, is the publication of what is probably the first playable five-act drama about Joan, Fronton du Duc's *L'Histoire tragique de la Pucelle d'Orléans* ('The Tragic History of the Maid of Orléans') which brought some fortune if not fame to its author, a 22 year old Jesuit priest.

In 1580 the King, Henry III and his wife Queen Louise decided to take the waters at Plombières in May. To amuse them, Fronton wanted to have played to them a tragedy that he had called 'Joan, Maid of Orléans' but so widespread were contagious diseases becoming at the time that the project was abandoned. However, the tragedy was performed on 7th September in the presence of Charles III of Lorraine. So pleased with it was he that he wanted to pay the author whose gospel-like poverty was such that he wore only poor, torn clothes. He immediately had him paid one hundred *écus* saying that he wanted him to buy the new clothes of which he had such a need.

Fronton's play raised an important issue – Joan ultimately refused to obey the authority of the Church, a refusal based on two principles; first her unshaken belief in the truth of her voices and secondly her acceptance of male dress. 'Must I, forgetting my sex, dress myself as a man?' she asks in her opening lines. As challenging as these views were it is difficult to imagine that the play had any effective dramatic impact. Its 12 syllable alexandrines show the influence of the contemporary neo-classical theatre. Each act concludes with a Pindaric ode recited by a chorus and all actions are reported. But too many of the play's exchanges are stilted for it ever to come alive.

The English Counter-attack: Shakespeare's *Henry VI, Part I.*

While Joan's story then was already prompting a certain amount of interest in France in both popular and in more formal writing, it had also, not surprisingly, not gone entirely unnoticed in England. The first reference appears to be by William Botoner who in 1430 recorded that on '23rd May a young woman called the Maid of God, was captured by the English at the town of Compiègne.' More substantially in *The Chronicles of England with the Fruit of the Times* (1480), William Caxton, introducing a new factor that would be exploited by later authors, wrote: 'Armed like a man and with many other captains she was captured on 22nd May in the field outside the town of Compiègne. All were brought to Rouen where she was put in prison and judged by the law to be burned. And then she said that she was with child, whereby for a while she was given respite. But in conclusion it was discovered that she was not with child and then she was burned in Rouen.' However, it would not be until Shakespeare wrote his plays about Henry VI that Joan would be treated to any serious degree by an English author.

Unlike the works of the earlier French authors *Henry VI, Part I,*[6] in all probability first performed in 1592, pays little or no attention to the accepted chronological sequence of events and Shakespeare has no compunction in having Joan appear in scenes depicting events that took place after her death. For example, she does not first meet Charles at Chinon but at Orléans where she is brought by Dunois. There is then a period of 24 years between this meeting and the recapture of Bordeaux by the French in 1453, the town in which we can assume Joan will be burned. But it is less this kind of manipulation of or even wilful disregard for historical accuracy that concerns us as Shakespeare's portrait of Joan. According to the list of characters she is simply 'Joan Puzel, a peasant'. Various commentators, including Marina Warner and Edward Burns, have debated this name. 'Puzel' could, of course be an anglicised pronunciation of 'pucelle', but 'puzel' in English at the time also meant whore. Nor, as Burns, reminds us, should we overlook the fact that 'pizzle' was an Elizabethan term for penis. As he rightly and amusingly comments: 'The woman in man's clothes wielding a sword is a pucelle with a pizzle, and therefore a puzzle'. But Shakespeare's punning on this description of Joan already points to one of the major problems to face any but the most blinkered and credulous among those who would choose to write imaginatively about her over the next four centuries.

It has often been pointed out that Shakespeare's portrait of Joan is precisely one that is coloured by the political climate in England at the time – anti-French and xenophobic. Certainly for her English opponents Joan is the 'damned sorceress', 'vile fiend and shameless courtesan', 'foul fiend of France and hag of all despite', 'ugly witch' and 'fell banning hag'. Nor in her final appearance does she emerge with any credit, despite her vigorous last words. She brutally denies her father and then claims to be pregnant:

YORK: Bring forth that sorceress condemned to burn.
SHEPHERD: Ah, Joan this kills thy father's heart outright.
Have I sought every country far and near
And – now it is my chance to find thee out –
Must I behold thy timeless cruel death?
Ah, Joan, sweet daughter Joan, I'll die with thee.
JOAN: Decrepit miser, base ignoble wretch,
I am descended of a nobler blood.
Thou art no father, nor a friend of mine.
SHEPHERD: Out, out! My lords, an please you, 'tis not so.
I did beget her, all the parish knows.

Her mother liveth yet, can testify
She was the first fruit of my bachelorship.

WARWICK: Graceless, wilt thou deny thy parentage?

YORK: This argues what her kind of life hath been –
Wicked and vile, and so her death concludes.

SHEPHERD: Fie, Joan, that thou wilt be so obstacle.
God knows, thou art a collop of my flesh,
And for thy sake have I shed many a tear.
Deny me not, I prithee, gentle Joan.

JOAN: Peasant, avaunt! [*to York*] You have suborned this man
Of purpose to obscure my noble birth.

SHEPHERD: 'Tis true, I gave a noble to the priest
The morn that I was wedded to thy mother.
Kneel down and take my blessing, good my girl.
Wilt thou not stoop? Now cursed be the time
Of thy nativity. I would the milk
Thy mother gave thee when thou suck'st her breast
Had been a little ratsbane for thy sake –
Or else, when thou didst keep my lambs a-field,
I wish some ravenous wolf had eaten thee.
Dost thou deny thy father, cursed drab?
O burn her, burn her, hanging is too good.

YORK: Take her away, for she hath lived too long,
To fill the world with vicious qualities.

JOAN: First let me tell you whom you have condemned:
Not me begotten of a shepherd swain,
But issued from the progeny of kings:
Virtuous and holy, chosen from above
By inspiration of celestial grace
To work exceeding miracles on earth.
I never had to do with wicked spirits;
But you, that are polluted with your lusts,
Stained with the guiltless blood of innocents,
Corrupt and tainted with a thousand vices,
Because you want the grace that others have,
You judge it straight a thing impossible
To compass wonders but by the help of devils.
No – misconceived, Joan of Aire hath been
A virgin from her tender infancy,
Chaste and immaculate in every thought,
Whose maiden-blood, thus rigorously effused,
Will cry for vengeance at the gates of heaven.

YORK: Ay,ay: away with her to execution.

WARWICK: And hark ye, sirs: because she is a maid,
Spare for no faggots, let there be enough.
Place barrels of pitch upon the fatal stake
That so her torture may be shortened.

JOAN: Will nothing turn your unrelenting hearts?
Then, Joan, discover thine infirmity,
That warranteth by law to be thy privilege.

> I am with child, ye bloody homicides:
> Murder not then the fruit within my womb,
> Although ye hale me to a violent death.
> YORK: Now heaven forfend, the holy maid with child?
> WARWICK: The greatest miracle that e'er ye wrought.
> Is all your strict preciseness come to this?
> YORK: She and the Dauphin have been ingling.
> I did imagine what would be her refuge.
> WARWICK: Well, go to, we'll have no bastards live;
> Especially since Charles must father it.
> JOAN: You are deceived, my child is none of his.
> It was Alençon that enjoyed my love.
> YORK: Alençon, that notorious Machiavel?
> It dies, an if it had a thousand lives.
> JOAN: O give me leave, I have deluded you.
> 'Twas neither Charles, nor yet the Duke I named,
> But Reignier, King of Naples, that prevailed.
> WARWICK: A married man, that's most intolerable.
> YORK: Why, here's a girl! I think she knows not well –
> There were so many – whom she may accuse.
> WARWICK: It's a sign she hath been liberal and free.
> YORK: And yet, forsooth, she is a virgin pure.
> Strumpet, thy words condemn thy brat and thee.
> Use no entreaty, for it is in vain.
> JOAN: Then lead me hence – with whom I leave my curse.
> May never glorious sun reflex his beams
> Upon the country where you make abode,
> But darkness and the gloomy shade of death
> Environ you, till mischief and despair
> Drive you to break your necks, or hang yourselves.
> (Act V, Scene iii, 271–277.)

For the French, not surprisingly, she is, in Dunois's words:

> A holy maid [...]
> Which by a vision sent to her from heaven
> Ordained is to raise this tedious siege
> And drive the English forth to the bounds of France.
> (Act I, Scene ii, 132,3.)

And after the first defeat of the English and the realisation that the siege will be raised, Joan is praised in language full of Classical allusions and is elevated, by Charles, to the status of a national saint:

> 'Tis Joan, not we, by whom the day is won:
> For which I will divide my crown with her,
> And all the priests and friars in my realm
> Shall in procession sing her endless praise.

A statelier pyramis to her I'll rear
Than Rhodope's or Memphis' ever was.
In memory of her, when she is dead,
Her ashes, in an urn more precious
Than the rich-jewelled coffer of Darius,
Transported shall be at high festivals
Before the kings and queens of France.
No longer on Saint Denis will we cry,
But Joan de Puzzel shall be France's saint.
(Act I, Scene v, 161,2.)

Between these two extreme perceptions of her and in addition to the conundrum of her name, Shakespeare's treatment of Joan opens up a wealth of uncertainty and ambiguity. If she is the witch the English proclaim her to be, why do the fiends she calls on for help in Act V Scene ii fail to respond? At her trial she had maintained that she did not fight, but Shakespeare depicts her in combat on at least three occasions – with Charles who tests her claims ('In single combat thou shalt buckle with me, / And if thou vanquishest thy words are true'); with Talbot, and with York who captures her. She protests her virginity and yet maintains she is pregnant. And while in her last scene her claim to be of noble blood may simply be a way of trying to avoid being burned alive, it anticipates the debates surrounding her possible royal origins that will emerge in the nineteenth century.

Within the play itself Shakespeare provides us with no neat answers. While Joan may be the most interesting and for some the most important character in the play, *Henry VI, Part I* is, after all, about the internal politics and power struggle in fifteenth-century England. But Joan remains something of an enigma, and precisely because there are no answers, she and her role acquire a resonance that goes beyond the text. Writing with hindsight Shakespeare may have wanted to suggest little more in his portrayal of Joan than that she had been a genuinely inspirational but misguided young woman, whose impact on the morale of those supporting the Dauphin's cause went far beyond the brief span of her real exploits. But with the strong hints of bisexuality, of her belonging, as Charles acknowledges, to the ranks of virgin warriors ('Thou art an Amazon / And fightest with the sword of Deborah'), and not least with suggestions that she might be compared to the Virgin Mary, Shakespeare clearly reveals how aware he was of the rich potential of a character around whom a legend had already begun to form.

Classical Consolidation: The Seventeenth and Eighteenth Centuries

Given the rivalry between France and England it is not surprising perhaps that many works written in France in the seventeenth century were in reaction to Shakespeare's play. And yet, as we shall see, there was not unequivocal admiration for Joan and what she had achieved. In 1642 the English writer Thomas Fuller anticipated some of the controversies to come when, in his *The Holy State and the Profane State,* a chronicle of his times containing a number of portraits including one of Joan, he wrote:

> Here lies Joan of Arc, the which
> Some count saint, and some count witch;
> Some count man, and something more;
> Some count maid, and some a whore.
> Her life's in question, wrong or right;
> Her death's in doubt, by laws, or might.
> Oh innocence take head of it,
> How thou too near a guilt dost sit.
> (Meantime France a wonder saw
> A woman's rule 'gainst Salique law.)
> But, Reader, be content to stay
> Thy censure, till the Judgement-day:
> Then shalt thou know, and not before,
> Whether Saint, Witch, Man, Maid, or Whore.

In France, however, the dominant tone, initially, was one of approval. The best known work devoted to Joan is Jean Chapelain's massive but unsuccessful epic *La Pucelle ou la France délivrée* ('The Maid or the Salvation of France'). Cavalier with historical detail and much given to exaggeration, Chapelain took twenty years to write the first twelve cantos, the only ones to appear in his lifetime in 1656. (A further twelve would not be published until 1882 by which time Joan would be in the forefront of religious and political debate.) In his poem's Preface, Chapelain staunchly supports the idea of female heroism: 'It would be easy', he writes, 'to provide thousands of examples from all centuries demonstrating that women are in no way inferior to men and how they often show extreme assurance in the face of danger when men react as cowards.' 'A holy warrior', Joan is a perfect illustration of this, and yet in the poem the true hero is Dunois, who is seen to fall in love with her, leaving Marie Louvet to whom he has been married for four years. When Joan arrives at the court at Chinon her perfection is clear and she is already divinely inspired:

> Her brown hair shining with an innocent glow
> Surrounds her head like a crown,
> But her gaze is like a divine fire
> Piercing and burning everything with its power.

81. Frontispiece from the first edition of La Pucelle ou la France délivrée. *Charles looks both pathetic and grateful as Joan helps him to his feet.*

Dunois is powerless to resist her, as he admits to Marie at the end of the second Canto:

> There is no mortal equal to you in merit,
> And nothing mortal that makes me leave you.
> What tears me away from you deserves an altar
> And can claim a place among the immortals.
> I love, I adore a saintly warrior,
> Who has come to me from heaven in my last hours.
> Forgive me if I prefer the divine light of her eyes
> To that of your own.
> But what is this fire that excites my soul?
> Dare I call it love?
> Is it love to love without reason
> And hope to serve with no hope of success?
> I have only respect and esteem
> For these heavenly eyes, for this noble brow.
> I wish for nothing and if I am a lover
> I am so without desire.

Chapelain's verse is ponderous and he insists throughout the poem on showing how the French cause is not only just, but divinely inspired against an England in the service of Satan. But there are moments when he indulges in a kind of melodramatic realism as in his description in Canto XI of the violent and bloody hand-to-hand struggle between Joan and Talbot at Orléans:

> A blow causes the Saint's blood to gush out;
> Seriously weakened and slower in her fight

82. *Joan at the siege of Paris from* La Pucelle ou la France délivrée. *Engraved by Abraham Boss after Vignon.*

She decides on a dangerous move
And leads the struggle to the edge of the terrace
Causing Talbot to have a terrible fall.
But with arms and legs closely linked in their struggle
They fall together to the very bottom.
The spirit of the great Talbot is so surprised
That he is shattered on the rocks below.
The saintly warrior disentangles herself
And points her shining sword at Talbot's brow.

Shortly after this success, and having rapidly recovered from her own wounds, Joan is rewarded with a vision of the heavenly hosts coming to her aid and she returns to the battle.

In addition to Chapelain's work the seventeenth century produced a number of plays, smaller poems and inscriptions destined for statues erected in Joan's honour in Orléans. Typical of the last is this small fragment of a poem by Le Père le Moyne probably written in 1647:

> Fatal for England and fatal for France,
> I destroyed the arrogant pride of the one
> And the other, freed by my efforts,
> Saw its unstable throne supported by my spear.
> No matter how black it was, the fire
> Lit against my innocence could not sully its purity.
> And the death I suffered showed me to be even braver
> In the face of those who instigated this cruelty.
> With a heart equal to those of the most famous warriors
> And crowned with laurels,
> I protected the flower of my body.
> And chaste and courageous like the bee,
> I stung, I hunted down the English leopards
> And defended the lilies that crown our kings.

Elsewhere we find endless allusions to classical mythology and epics not only for the purpose of direct comparisons with Joan (for Jean Dorat she is 'The Amazon of the Heavens'), but also, as in Chapelain's poem, to raise the general tenor of the work in question. In an anonymous play from 1611, for example, the *Tragédie de Jeanne d'Arques dite la Pucelle d'Orléans* ('The Tragedy of Joan of Arc, the so-called Maid of Orléans'), Joan herself displays a knowledge of classical mythology that is completely out of place. Most of the play is composed of long, heavy declamatory speeches, with no action, little effective dialogue or repartee. The first three acts are concluded by a Chorus offering a form of summary of past events, while in the last 'Les filles de France' lament Joan's execution, which in true neo-classical tradition is carried out off-stage. Rather more successful would be *La Pucelle d'Orléans,* attributed to Censerade and La Mesnardière in 1642. In this play Warwick (Le Comte de Varvic) falls in love with Joan and plans to arrange her escape. The play was based directly on *Jeanne d'Arc* by François Hédélin d'Aubignac of the same year. D'Aubignac's play, in strict neo-classical form, takes the day of Joan's death (a device used much later in film by the Danish director, Carl Dreyer, for example), and recounts what she has achieved through a series of flash backs. As far as I know, the introduction in these two plays of the idea of Warwick as a suitor for Joan's affection is novel and, however improbable, is not without dramatic and psychological effect. Joan rebuffs the Englishman's advances but is sufficiently immodest to acknowledge her physical attractiveness:

> Charles witnessed my brilliance at his court
> Where a hundred young knights thought only of love,
> But not even the boldest offended my virtue.

Even so her resolve is unshakeable: 'Because God wishes me to die, but to die pure [...] In saving my honour I preserve the one thing / That triumphs over time and that nothing can destroy.' By concentrating on the very end of her

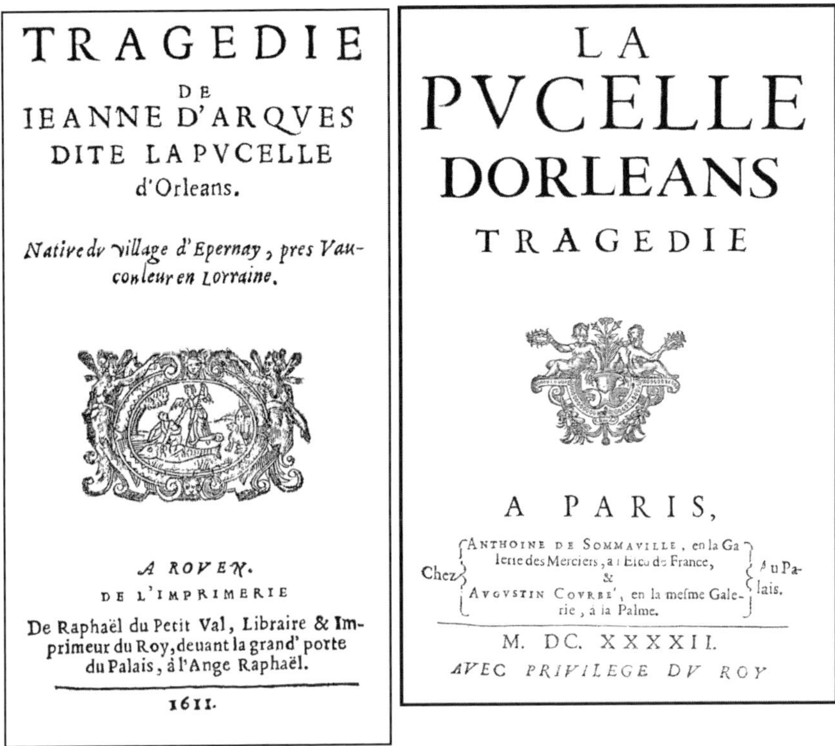

TRAGEDIE
DE
IEANNE D'ARQVES
DITE LA PVCELLE
d'Orleans.

Native dv village d'Epernay, pres Vau-
couleur en Lorraine.

A ROVEN.
DE L'IMPRIMERIE
De Raphaël du Petit Val, Libraire & Imprimeur du Roy, deuant la grand' porte
du Palais, à l'Ange Raphaël.

1611.

LA
PVCELLE
DORLEANS
TRAGEDIE

A PARIS,
Chez ANTHOINE DE SOMMAVILLE, en la Galerie des Merciers, à l'Escu de France, & AVGVSTIN COVRBE', en la mesme Galerie, à la Palme. Au Palais.

M. DC. XXXXII.
AVEC PRIVILEGE DV ROY

83. *Title pages of* Tragédie de Jeanne d'Arques dite la Pucelle d'Orléans, *1611 and* La Pucelle d'Orléans Tragédie, *1642.*

life and by introducing this personal issue, this play has an immediacy and a genuine human quality that is often absent from others which attempt to cover all Joan's exploits. Furthermore it goes beyond her death that, once again, occurs off-stage and is merely reported. At the close of her trial in Act III she foresees the ends of her judges; in Act V, Scene vii, Cauchon is indeed struck down by the 'sudden death' Joan had predicted.

With few exceptions then the seventeenth century offers us only a handful of works of note that deal with Joan, and clearly none of the major imaginative writers of the period saw in her story matter for their talents. For many years during the eighteenth century there would be little change. Although there were in all probability over a hundred works about her, most were in French and most were histories. But changes were to occur. Moreover Joan began to attract the attention of writers outside France, notably of the English poet Robert Southey whose *Joan of Arc* would appear in 1796 and of John Daly Burk who fled from Ireland to America and published his play *Female Patriotism or the Death of Joan of Arc* two years later.

Another important development was a change in the intellectual climate of France. In an age when reason was beginning to replace superstition and religious faith was increasingly challenged, there was a tendency to disregard Joan's divine inspiration and instead to attribute her determination to some kind of auto-suggestion or even claim that she had been manipulated by political forces. This did not mean that Joan was any less a national heroine and saviour but that the matter of her voices and of her being visited by the saints tended to be brushed aside. An example of this is the typically patriotic epistle addressed to Jacques Ducoudray, the mayor of Orléans in 1772 by the grammarian Martial Servant in which he celebrates

> this young warrior
> Who, saving our city walls, saved all of France,
> Repulsed the enemy with her acts of bravery
> And saw her king finally confirmed on the throne.

But while Servant acknowledges that the English have been overthrown by 'a divine hand', he remains silent about how and when this celestial help came to Joan.

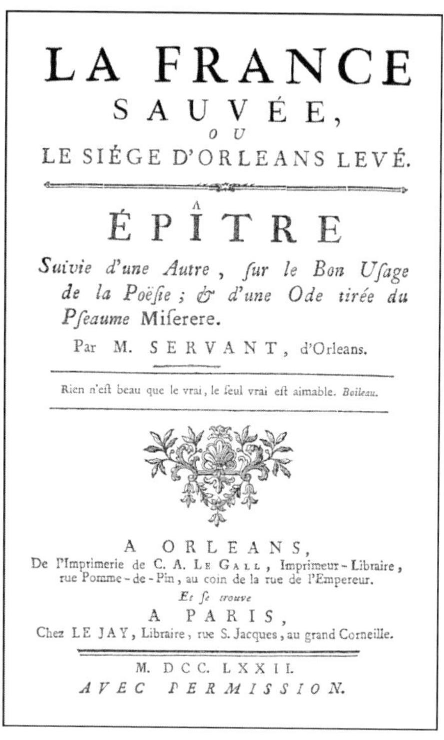

LA FRANCE
SAUVÉE,
OU
LE SIÉGE D'ORLEANS LEVÉ.

ÉPÎTRE

Suivie d'une Autre, sur le Bon Usage de la Poësie ; & d'une Ode tirée du Pseaume Miserere.

Par M. SERVANT, d'Orleans.

Rien n'est beau que le vrai, le seul vrai est aimable. *Boileau.*

A ORLEANS,
De l'Imprimerie de C. A. Le Gall, Imprimeur-Libraire, rue Pomme-de-Pin, au coin de la rue de l'Empereur.
Et se trouve
A PARIS,
Chez LE JAY, Libraire, rue S. Jacques, au grand Corneille.

M. DCC. LXXII.
AVEC PERMISSION.

84. *Title page of* La France Sauvée, ou le Siège d'Orléans levé *by Martial Servant, 1772.*

Voltaire's 'filthy poem'.

Such silence and even scepticism would be taken further, especially of course by Voltaire who, for all his genuine admiration of Joan, turned his massive poem, *La Pucelle d'Orléans,* into a satirical attack not only on all aspects of religion, on government and on learning but on human credulity as well.[7] From a remark he is reputed to have made to Cardinal Richelieu in 1730 or 1731, Voltaire appears to have been of the opinion that it was unlikely that a serious work could be written about a girl who had been 'born in an inn', and who died at the stake, and that only a light-hearted or trivial treatment would be appropriate. His deliberate lack of concern for the facts of Joan's birth are followed in his poem by an almost total disregard for chronology and for many of the circumstances of 1429. He also portrays a number of characters who bear only the slightest resemblance to their historical models – and some are pure invention. Theodore Besterman once pertinently remarked that 'the main theme [of *La Pucelle*] is a huge joke: the mystical importance attached to Joan's virginity'.[8] Voltaire himself is clear about the matter from the opening Canto. When St Denis appears to Charles and promises to produce a virgin who will save France, Richemont, commander in chief of the royal army, sarcastically responds that 'virginity is useless as a weapon'. Voltaire's title is also comic. Joan may be a virgin at the time Orléans is taken from the English, but this is only discovered and announced by Dunois when, in the last lines of the poem, he finally beds her:

> Joan fierce and tender, having sent away
> That same night, to Heav'n her Donkey grey,
> Of sacred oath accomplishing the law,
> Kept promise made to well belov'd Dunois,
> As Lourdis, midst the faithful cohort stray'd
> Bawling out still: 'Ye Britons! she's a maid!'.
>
> (Canto, XXI, 259)

In addition to this comic but provocative treatment of his subject Voltaire plays with the events of Joan's life, invents and adds others – many of them preposterous, fantastic and farcical – as he thinks fit. His poem is frequently not about Joan at all but tells instead of the escapades of those close to her or who crossed her path in some way – Dunois, La Trémouille, or the Dauphin who has already been crowned as Charles VII. Despite episodes in which he describes her relentlessly cutting down scores of English soldiers, Voltaire's picture of Joan is not that of the virgin warrior who had hitherto been idolised and would increasingly be seen as a symbol of French patriotism; but this is not to say that he did not admire her or what she had achieved. This is evident if only briefly from *La Henriade* (1728), but much later in his *Essais sur les moeurs* (1775) he describes Joan as having 'a strength and courage beyond her years' and that when she was finally captured, was 'judged to be a witch by an ignorant and barbaric ecclesiastical court and burned by the English who ought to have honoured her for her courage.' For a country girl 'who had been used only to keeping sheep, her determination and resolve were remarkable and as a military leader she never failed to keep her promises.' Her claims to the Dauphin in 1429 were made 'with the modesty befitting her sex and age.' Was it not extraordinary, Voltaire asks, that 'a poor girl without talent or experience should overturn the best laid plans drawn up by cautious and experienced statesmen, that she should throw the most redoubtable army ever known into confusion?' In *La Pucelle* therefore, rather than directing his satire or mockery at Joan or even at those who had sought previously to explain and extol her (though many are dismissed as insignificant writers 'buried deep in their schools'), Voltaire is more concerned with the political, social and religious climate of his day. As Bernard Shaw would observe in the Preface to his play, *Saint Joan,* more than a century and a half later, Voltaire set out 'not to depict Joan, but kill with ridicule everything [he] righteously hated in the institutions and fashions of his own day. He made Joan ridiculous, but not contemptible, nor (comparatively) unchaste.'

To the modern reader this is evident enough, but during the years following the poem's publication reactions were varied. *La Pucelle* became the victim of censorship and was outlawed in the public domain well into the nineteenth century and booksellers in France and abroad discovered with copies in their possession could be fined or imprisoned. It might be thought that after Voltaire's death in 1778 and the Revolution that the poem might have benefited from a more liberal reaction in intellectual circles, but few were the voices to express admiration or approval. While Flaubert would note in passing that *La Pucelle* was Voltaire's masterpiece, in many quarters both in France and abroad it continued to provoke scorn and moral and even patriotic outrage. Bernardin de Saint-Pierre considered that it was 'ridiculous', Southey that it was 'worthless', Abel-François Villemain that it was 'frivolous and licentious'. In his preface to the first French translation of Schiller's play in 1802, Louis Mercier called it immoral, taxed Voltaire with anti-nationalism and praised the German writer for teaching the French 'to venerate Joan of Arc and give her the respect she is due.' Nearly sixty years later Jules and Edmond Goncourt accused Voltaire of writing a 'filthy' (*ordurier*) poem.

But what is this poem? Described by Voltaire himself as a 'epic poem', it has twenty-one Cantos of varying length, most of them introduced by an appeal to the reader or, in true classical style, with allusions to Classical mythology, intended here to provide a tongue-in-cheek dignity. Voltaire's 'anonymous' Preface is also delightfully defensive:

> The present poem ought to be regarded in the light of a work destined to

> inculcate lessons of wisdom and common sense, under the mask of folly and voluptuousness. The author may in some instances have wounded taste, but has never injured the cause of morality.

It becomes quickly apparent, however, that the poem is full of accounts of sexual adventures involving all but Dunois; the tone is, as we also learn from the Preface, 'bold and racy'. Ironic, satirical and witty as well it moves forward – and in this resembles so many of Voltaire's stories – with the pace of a modern comic strip. All is launched by a beautifully crafted opening:

> The praise of saints my lyre shall not rehearse,
> Feeble my voice, and too profane my verse:
> Yet shall my Muse to laud our Joan incline,
> Who wrought, 'tis said, such prodigies divine;
> Whose virgin hand revived the drooping flow'r,
> And gave to Gallia's lily tenfold pow'r;
> Rescued its monarch from the impending fate,
> So dreaded from victorious England's hate;
> Made give him praise at Rheims, to God adored,
> While on his temples holy oil was pour'd:
> Although in visage Joan appear'd the maid,
> Although in stays and petticoat array'd,
> With boldest heroes she sustained her part,
> For Joan possess'd a Roland's dauntless heart:
> For me, much better should I love by night,
> A lamb-like beauty, to inspire delight;
> But soon you'll find thro' ev'ry glowing page,
> That Joan of Arc could boast the lion's rage;
> You'll tremble at those feats she dared essay,
> How dauntlessly she braved the bloody fray;
> But greatest, of these rare exploits you'll hear,
> Was, that she kept virginity – a year.
>
> (Canto I, 1,2)

Later in the same Canto, St Denis arrives in Charles's debauched court in Tours and announces that he will find a virgin to free France from the English. In the following Canto Joan duly appears and Voltaire delights in describing her as a sexually robust, earthy young woman who, with St Denis's aid, only narrowly escapes the clutches of an English monk, Grisbourdon, and a mule-driver. Comforted by the saint and told of her mission Joan is instantly equipped with armour and weapons. She is also provided not with a noble horse as her steed, but with a winged donkey (with the inevitable reference to Pegasus) whose lust for Joan will grow to the point when, in the last Canto, he will attempt to have sex with her. Voltaire's humorous and iconoclastic account of Joan's preparation continues with the descriptions of the tests carried out on her to ascertain whether she is a virgin and of the award of a 'certificate':

Thus spoke the king, in a majestic tone
Which might have fear'd, but she alone:
'Joan hear me: Joan if thou'st a maid, avow'
Joan answer'd: Oh! great sire, give orders now
That doctors sage, with spectacles on nose,
Who versed in female myst'ries can depose,
That clerks, apothecaries, matrons tried,
Be called at once the matter to decide;
Let them all scrutinize, and let them see.
By this sage answer Charles knew she must be
Inspired and bless'd with sweet virginity.
'Good,' said the king, 'since this you know so well,
Daughter of Heav'n, I prithee, instant tell
What with my fair one pass'd last night in bed?
Speak free.' 'Why nothing happen'd', Joan then said;
Surprised, the king knelt down and cried aloud –
'A miracle!' then crossed himself and bow'd
Immediately approv'd the fur-capped band,
Their bonnets on, Hippocrates in hand,
They came to view the bosom purely fair
Of warrior chaste committed to their care.
Naked they stripp'd her, and the senior sage,
Having consider'd all that could engage,
Above, below, on parchment then displayed
An attestation, that Joan was a maid.
(Canto II, 53,4)

For the remaining fourteen Cantos, Voltaire indulges himself and his reader with a series of riotous, farcical adventures involving heaven and hell, magic castles, transvestism, incest and a hymn competition between St Denis and St George. From many of these Joan is absent but she returns in Canto XX where, reflecting on what she has achieved so far, she succumbs to vanity. As a punishment St Denis causes the donkey to make sexual advances to her, but Dunois is close at hand and together they force the animal to leave. By the end of the poem the way is open for Joan and Dunois to declare their love, but the moment of their consummation is delayed – with St Denis's approval – until their victory at Orléans is complete:

In fine, this point, to set forth free from varnish,
Shewing of Joan nought could the lustre tarnish,
To prove that to the malice foul of Hell,
The Donkey's eloquence and transports fell
Her heart was proof, in virtue's armour clad.
Know, that the maid, another lover had:
'Twas Dunois, as my readers all well know,
The bastard bold, who had inspir'd the glow,
At speech of ass; surprise the mind may seize,
One may indulge a vain desire to please,

A turn so innocent and light, 'tis clear,
Could ne'er the traitor prove, to love sincere.
On page historical, the truth is told,
How Dunois the sublime, the hero bold
Felt, with a golden shaft, his heart pierc'd through,
Which Cupid smiling, from first quiver drew;
He ever in obedience kept the flame,
Weakness in his proud heart ne'er took the rein,
Nought save his monarch, and the state he saw,
In him their int'rest reigned, the ruling law.
He knew, Oh! Joan, thy blooming virgin flower,
Of victory the pledge in battle's hour.
Respected were thy charms and Denis too;
Just like the pointer-dog, well taught and true,
Who staunch the calls of hunger can defeat,
The partridge holding, which it will not eat;
But, when celestial Jack-ass, thus he found,
On flame descanting of Love's bleeding wound,
Dunois conceiv'd that he might speak in turn;
Sages sometimes forget themselves, we learn.
No doubt, a flagrant folly it had proved,
To sacrifice the state for her he lov'd;
'Twas all to lose, and Joan still feeling shame,
For having donkey heard avow his flame,
Resisted ill her hero's ardent speech,
Love strove in soul so pure, to make a breach;
All had been done; when lo! her patron bright,
His ray detaching from celestial height,
That golden beam, his glory and his steed,
Bearing his saintly form in time of need,
As when he sought, impelled by pressing call,
A virgin flow'r to rescue Orléan's wall;
This heavenly ray that pierc'd Joan's better sense,
Each sentiment profane remov'd from thence:
'Dear Bastard stop:' she cried, 'O! shun the crime,
Our Loves are reckon'd, 'tis not yet the time;
Let us nought mar of sovereign fate's decree,
My solemn faith is plighted but to thee,
Thine I protest the virgin bud should be:
Let us await until your vengeful arm,
Your virtues, which in Britons strike alarm,
Have from our soil the vile usurpers driv'n,
Then, 'neath the laurel stretch'd, we'll taste our love's heav'n.'
At this address the Bastard calmed his rage,
And hearing oracle, submitted sage;
Joan modestly receiv'd his homage spoken,
So pure, so soft, and gave him straight for token
Chaste kisses thirty, with a glow replete,
Such as when brother's lips, a sister's meet!
Each bridled in the torrent of desire,

And modestly agreed to quench the fire:
Denis behold; - the saint was satisfied,
And straight his projects hast'ned to decide.
(Canto XXI, 243,4)

In order to avoid the censorship that *La Pucelle* was inevitably going to attract, Voltaire had it published anonymously in Louvain in Belgium in 1755. (There were also several versions printed with explicit erotic and sometimes pornographic illustrations.)

A naked Dunois gazes longingly at Joan.

Chant XX.

Heureux cent fois qui trouve un pucelage

a) The donkey makes amorous advances to Joan who appears to take pleasure in them.

b) Dunois chases off the donkey.

c) Voltaire has only male doctors examine Joan's claim to be a virgin. Does Charles's mother-in-law, Yolande, look on anxiously from the doorway?

85. Four illustrations from various editions published between 1762 and 1790.

This first publication was followed by a large number of pirated editions and it was not for another seven years that the first authentic version by Voltaire appeared. As we have seen, reactions on the whole were unfavourable and would continue to be so, and even in recent years the poem can be dismissed as 'deplorable' and as a piece of 'vulgar and licentious' writing.[9] Such a view from a modern historian may surprise us even if at the time of the poem's appearance it was more understandable. But Voltaire was no stranger to criticism and attacks. His targets in *La Pucelle* were many and varied and in many respects Joan was little more than a pretext. Nonetheless his treatment of her and her exploits was a welcome change from the generally gushing and pompous verse in which she had been proclaimed during the previous three centuries.

Notes

1. In this and the next three chapters I only include references to the editions of texts I use and from which I quote where they are especially helpful.
2. Extracts are from the edition of the *Ditié* by Angus J.Kennedy and Kenneth Varty published by the Society for the Study of Medieval Languages and Literature, Oxford, 1977.
3. The earliest poems about Joan are contained in Quicherat, *op. cit.* Vol. 4. The *Ballade contre les Anglais* was discovered in the late nineteenth century by Paul Meyer. See *Romania* Vol. 21, 1892.
4. See Warner, *op. cit.* 285.
5. See the modern edition by V. L. Hamblin, Droz, Geneva, 2002.
6. All references to the play are to the edition by Edward Burns, The Arden Shakespeare, London, 2000.
7. I am indebted to Jeroom Vercruysse's critical edition of *La Pucelle d'Orléans* in *The Complete Works of Voltaire,* Vol. 7, Geneva, 1970 and in particular to Section viii, 'L'accueil'. The English quotations are from *The Maid of Orléans or La Pucelle of Voltaire*, translated into English verse with notes by W. H. Ireland, 2 volumes, Miller and Wright, London, 1822.
8. Quoted by Vercruysse, *op.cit.*,219.
9. See, for example, Regine Pernoud, *J'ai nom la Pucelle*, Gallimard, Paris, 1994, 123.

Chapter Four

Into the Public Arena

For all Voltaire's biting criticism of the established institutions, values and attitudes of eighteenth-century France in *La Pucelle*, he was not using the work to advocate a new political direction either for his country or in the abstract. This instead would come from outside France in the works of Robert Southey in England and John Daly Burk in America.

Like Voltaire, Southey had little concern for historical accuracy and readily introduced entirely fictional characters and episodes in Joan's life.[1] Like any other soldier Joan kills her enemies including Talbot's son, she is in love with Theodore, a childhood friend, yet mindful of her duty she rejects him, she is wounded specifically by Glacidas and not by a stray arrow, Charles'mistress, Agnes Sorel, plays an important part, the siege of Orléans is recounted by a young couple, Isabel and Francis, Joan personally anoints Charles and so on. But beyond the emboidery and invention, Southey's *Joan of Arc* was important for its message of anti-authoritarianism and radical romanticism. As the essayist William Hazlitt commented, it was 'a work in which the love of liberty is inhaled like the breath of Spring.' In a prefatory note written to a later edition in 1837 Southey himself states that the poem had originally been written 'in a republican spirit', at a time when 'such opinions were [...] as unpopular in England as they deserved to be well received.' Most of the open 'political prejudices of a young man' would be removed from this later edition of the poem, but the spirit so evident in the first remains essentially the same. For Southey, Joan is simply a young woman acting 'wholly from the workings of her own mind, from the deep feeling of inspiration.' His 1795 Preface makes his interpretation and intention clear:

> The history of Joan of Arc is one of those problems that render investigation fruitless. That she believed herself inspired, few will deny; that she was inspired, no one will venture to assert; and who can believe that she was herself imposed on by Charles and Dunois? That she discovered the king when he disguised himself among the courtiers to deceive her, and that as proof of her mission, she demanded a sword from a tomb in the church of St Catherine, are facts in which all historians agree. If this had been done by collusion, the maid must have known

> herself an impostor, and with that knowledge could not have performed the enterprise she undertook. Enthusiasm, and that of no common kind, was necessary, to enable a young maiden at once to assume the profession of arms, to lead her troops to battle, to fight among the foremost, and to subdue with an inferior force an enemy then believed invincible. It is not possible that one who felt herself the puppet of a party, could not have performed these things. The artifices of a court could not have persuaded her that she discovered Charles in disguise; nor could they have prompted her to demand the sword which they might have hidden, without discovering the deceit. The maid, then, was not knowingly an impostor; nor could she have been the instrument of the court; and to say that she believed herself inspired, will neither account for her singling out the king, or prophetically claiming the sword.
>
> After crowning Charles she declared that her mission was accomplished, and demanded leave to retire. Enthusiasm would not have ceased here; and if they who imposed on her, could persuade her to go with their armies, they could still have continued her delusion.
>
> This mysteriousness renders the story of *Joan of Arc* peculiarly fit for poetry. The aid of angels and devils is not necessary to raise her above mankind; she has no gods to lackey her, and inspire with courage, and heal her wounds: the Maid of Orléans acts wholly from the workings of her own mind, from the deep feeling of inspiration. The palpable agency of superior powers would destroy the obscurity of her character, and sink her to the mere heroine of a fairy tale.

Southey's assessment of the political situation in France in the early fifteenth century – and by implication of the one in England in his own time – clearly emerges in Book II. A veteran soldier from Agincourt observes bitterly to Dunois that 'our proud barons in their private broils / Wasted the strength of France.' When Dunois takes Joan to Chinon she responds to the questions of the eminent churchmen by insisting that her inspiration to go to the Dauphin's aid has little or nothing to do with traditional religion but rather with the 'eternal energy' of nature in which God's presence and power can be sensed.

While Southey does not dismiss the established church in the way Voltaire had, his pantheism clearly emerges from Joan's words:

> The forms of worship in mine earlier years
> Waked my young mind to artificial awe,
> And made me fear my GOD. Warm with the glow
> Of health and exercise, whene'er I pass'd
> The threshold of the house of prayer, I felt
> A cold damp chill on me; I beheld the tapers
> That with a pale and feeble light glimmering
> Dimm'd the noon-light; I heard the solemn mass,
> And with strange feelings and mysterious dread
> Telling my beads, gave to the mystic prayers
> Devoutest meaning. Often I saw
> The pictured flames writhe round a penanced soul,
> I knelt in fear before the Crucifix

And wept and pray'd, and trembled and adored
A GOD of Terrors. But in riper years,
When as my soul grew strong in solitude,
I saw the eternal energy pervade
The boundless range of nature, with the sun
Pour life and radiance from his flamey path,
And on the lowliest flowret of the field
The kindly dew-drops shed. And then I felt
That he who form'd this goodly frame of things
Must needs be good, and with a FATHER's name
I call'd on HIM, and from my burthen'd heart
Poured out the yearnings of unmingled love.
Methinks it is not strange then, that I fled
The house of prayer, and made the lonely grove
My temple, at the foot of some old oak
Watching the little tribes that had their world
Within its mossy bark; or laid me down
Beside the rivulet whose murmuring
Was silence to my soul, and mark'd the swarm
Whose light-edged shadows on the bedded sand
Mirror'd their mazy sports, ... the insect hum,
The flow of waters, and the song of birds
Making a holy music to mine ear:
Oh! was it strange, if for such scenes as these,
Such deep devoutness, such intense delight
Of quiet adoration, I forsook
The house of worship? strange that when I felt
How GOD had made my spirit quick to feel
And love whate'er was beautiful and good,
And from aught evil and deform'd to shrink
Even as with instinct; ... father! was it strange
That in my heart I had no thought of sin
And did not need forgiveness?

(Book III, 411–456)

When the elders of the church remain unconvinced, Joan becomes even more impassioned until they finally acknowledge that she is 'indeed, the Delegate of Heaven' (Book III, 563):

True it is
That for long time I have not heard the sound
O mass high-chaunted, nor with trembling lips
Partook the holy wafer: yet the birds
Who to the matin ray prelusive pour'd
Their joyous song, methought did warble forth
Sweeter thanksgiving to Religion's ear
In their wild melody of happiness,
Than ever rung along the high-arch'd roofs
Of man: ... yet never from the bending vine
Pluck'd I its ripen'd clusters thanklessly,

Or that of God unmindful, who bestow'd
The bloodless banquet. Ye have told me, Sirs,
That Nature only teaches man to sin!
If it be sin to seek the wounded lamb,
To bind its wounds, and bathe them with my tears,
This is what Nature taught! No, Fathers, no!
It is not Nature that doth lead to sin:
Nature is all benevolence, all love,
All beauty! In the greenwood's quiet shade
There is no vice that to the indignant cheek
Bids the red current rush; no misery there;
No wretched mother, who with pallid face
And famine-fallen hangs o'er her hungry babes,
With such a look, so wan, so woe-begone,
As shall one day, with damning eloquence,
Against the oppressor plead!... Nature teach sin!
Oh blasphemy against the Holy One,
Who made us in the image of Himself,
Who made us all for happiness and love,
Infinite happiness, infinite love,
Partakers of his own eternity.

(Book III, 483–514)

In like manner, at the end of the poem and after Joan has anointed Charles, Southey uses her to give voice to his views on the responsibility of kings:

I have here this day
Fulfill'd my mission, and anointed thee
King over this great nation. Of this charge,
Or well perform'd or carelessly, that God
Of Whom thou holdest thine authority
Will take account; from Him all power derives.
Their duty is to fear the Lord, and rule,
According to his word and to the laws,
The people thus committed to thy charge:
Theirs is to fear Him and to honour Thee,
And with that fear and honour to obey
In all things lawful; both being thus alike
By duty bound, alike restricted both
From wilful license. If thy heart be set
To do His will and in His ways to walk,
I know no limit to the happiness
Thou may'st create. I do beseech thee, King!'
The Maid exclaim'd , and fell upon the ground
And clasp'd his knees, 'I do beseech thee, King!
By all the thousands that depend on thee,
For weal or woe,.. to consider what thou art,
By Whom appointed! If thou dost oppress
Thy people, if to aggrandize thyself
Thou tear'st them from their homes, and sendest them

> To slaughter, prodigal of misery;
> If when the widow and the orphan groan
> In want and wretchedness, thou turnest thee
> To hear the music of the flatterer's tongue;
> If when thou hear'st of thousands who have fallen,
> Thou say'st, 'I am a King! and fit it is
> That these should perish for me;' ... if thy realm
> Should through the counsels of thy government,
> Be fill'd with woe, and in thy streets be heard
> The voice of mourning and the feeble cry
> Of asking hunger; if in place of Law
> Iniquity prevail; if Avarice grind
> The poor; if discipline be utterly
> Relax'd, Vice charter'd, Wickedness let loose;
> Though in the general ruin all must share,
> Each answer for his own peculiar guilt,
> Yet at the Judgement-day, from those to whom
> The power was given, the Giver of all power
> Will call for righteous and severe account.
> Chuse thou the better part, and rule the land
> In righteousness; in righteousness thy throne
> Shall then be stablish'd, not by foreign foes
> Shaken, nor by domestic enemies,
> But guarded then by loyalty and love,
> True hearts, Good Angels, and All-seeing Heaven.
>
> (Book X, 682–730)

With Southey's poem we have then the first major exploitation of Joan outside France for explicit and positive political ends and it would not be long before she would be found appearing in the same role in her home-land. Meanwhile similar opinions were to be expressed in Burk's *Female Patriotism or The Death of Joan of Arc* (1798), the first play about Joan to be performed in the United States of America, and considered by many to be the 'first really serious imaginative work' about her.[2]

Disguised as a woman, Burk had fled to America from Ireland in 1795 having been expelled from the University of Dublin for his violent anti-English views, his deism and his radical republicanism. (He rejected the University's later offer to take him back.) Published and performed three years later, his play broadly follows the events of fifteenth-century French history, but is fundamentally about America's struggle against England three hundred years later. Like Southey, Burk pays scant attention to the detail and accuracy of historical events. Instead he concentrates on political ideas, with the result that given his own sympathies, Charles is not surprisingly presented as a tyrant. His play as a result is, in Claude Grimal's words, a 'heavy messianic drama promising happiness for all once humanity was delivered from the tyranny of its sovereigns'.[3] Republican democracy is Joan's ambition:

> [...] on the head of every man in France
> To place a crown, and thus at once create
> A new and mighty order of nobility
> To make all free and equal, all men kings
> Subject to justice and laws alone.
> (Act IV, Scene i, 9–13)

Like her English forebear Joan believes in the 'soul of the Universe' (Act II, Scene i, 16) rather than in divine inspiration, which she dismisses as 'a pious fraud'. She admits to having heard no voices nor has she seen angels; she has been moved to act, she says, simply by the sight of her country 'torn by feuds and foul dissensions' (Act III, Scene iii, 17). But Joan is also very human and womanly. She admits to returning the love of Chastel – a character invented by Burk and probably based on d'Alençon – but, like Southey's Joan, she places her duty first and determinedly pushes her personal feelings aside: 'I like thy person and love thy soul / But we must not indulge the thought of love' (Act II, Scene ii).

Burk's play was not particularly successful, due perhaps to the anti-French feelings in America at the time, but his and Southey's work together mark an important shift in the perception of and, more importantly, in the use to which Joan and her story could be put. They also signal the beginning of a serious interest in Joan beyond France. We should not leave the eighteenth century though without reference to a handful of the more traditional treatments of her story and to some of its first musical adaptations. Among the frequent French writings we might note *L'Héroine de la France* (1776) by the Abbé Yart, in which Joan is likened to an angel; the anonymous *La France sauvée ou le siège d'Orléans levé* ('France liberated or the Siege of Orléans raised') (1772) in which the inhabitants of Orléans are severely criticised for their internal wrangling and supine attitude, but are miraculously rescued by a 'simple shepherdess' sent by Heaven; and, last but not least, a poem published in 1776 by one M. de Verdun based on a letter Joan is supposed to have written to Charles moments before her death. In addition to these there was a French pantomime, *Dorothée,* first performed in 1782 and an English ballet. Dorothée had already appeared in Voltaire's poem where she is the object of La Trémouille's passion. In the pantomime she refuses to succumb to the local mayor's advances with the result that he has her imprisoned and sentenced to death by burning. In the third act Dunois arrives, inquires as to what is happening and, as in Voltaire's poem, nobly takes Dorothée's defence and kills the captain of the soldiers guarding her. Meanwhile Dorothée is tied to the stake on the funeral pyre. Her husband – a close friend of Dunois – arrives, snatches her from the flames and together with Dunois throws the mayor onto the fire in her place. What is curious about this poem and what shows how far an author could depart from original material, is that in the list of characters there is no mention of Dorothée's husband. In the closing moments of the play a marginal note alters 'husband' in the text to La Trémouille, and Joan, hitherto completely absent, comes to assist Dunois fight off the local soldiers. In spite of such bizarre changes in the basic plot *Dorothée* none the less retains the theme of an heroic Joan and leaves its audience in no doubt as to its significance.

At the very end of the century the Grand Historical Ballet of Action, *Joan of Arc or The Maid of Orleans* written by Mr Cross with music by Mr Reeve was staged at Covent Garden in London in 1798. Joan's story is again turned on its head but the performance resonates with English patriotism. In spite of her victories Joan has been a 'too daring Maid ... urged on by Daemons to (her) rash design' and the final Air closes with the lines:

> Think not their sons will e'er degrade 'em,
> Gasconade may vaunt its fill,
> The threat'ning foe who dared invade 'em,
> Will find that Britain's Britain still.

Amusingly, however, whatever the intentions of the writer, the audience must have had different and influential sympathies. In the first performance Joan is carried off to hell by a band of devils; audience reaction was hostile with the result that in the second – and much to the audience's approval it would seem – she is accompanied to heaven by a host of angels!

AIRS, DUETS,

AND

CHORUSSES,

IN A NEW

Grand Hiftorical Ballet of Action,

CALLED

JOAN OF ARC:

OR,

THE MAID OF ORLEANS.

Written by Mr Cross

AS PERFORMED AT THE THEATRE-ROYAL, COVENT-GARDEN.

The MUSIC by Mr. REEVE.

LONDON:

PRINTED BY T. WOODFALL, NO. 104, DRURY-LANE; FOR T. N. LONGMAN, PATERNOSTER-ROW.

1798.

(Price 6d.)

86. Cover of Joan of Arc or, The Maid of Orleans *by Cross and Reeve, 1798.*

The Myth Flourishes: The Nineteenth Century.

This kind of popular treatment of Joan would continue throughout the nineteenth century in a variety of forms, but the framework for the huge increase in interest in her – and especially in the ways she could be exploited for political, educational and religious purposes – was built on three events in particular. The first was Napoleon's authorisation in 1804 of the celebration of Joan on 8 May at Orléans; the second and most influential was the publication of Jules Michelet's enthusiastic and nationalistic portrayal of her in his *Histoire de France* (1844) and subsequent essay, to which I have already drawn attention; the third, contemporaneous with Michelet's work, was the publication of the records of Joan's trial and rehabilitation, compiled by Quicherat, between 1841 and 1849. This is not to say that Joan would not still be the subject of countless works of imaginative writing and especially of plays, but many of them are sentimental and naive reactions to Voltaire's poem, imitative of one another and lacking in originality. That this could have been otherwise was voiced by Bernardin de Saint-Pierre, even if he does not mention Voltaire by name:

> If they are properly presented on the stage our national heroes are enough to encourage the spirit of patriotism. What a success and how well received was the heroism of Eustache de Saint-Pierre in the *Siege of Calais*! The death of Joan of Arc would have had an even greater effect if a man of genius had the courage to get rid of the ridicule with which that respectable and unfortunate girl has been covered and in honour of whom Greece would have erected statues.

But Bernardin would not have his wish realised by one of his compatriots; instead it would once more be an author from abroad who, like Southey and Burk before him, could see in Joan a subject fit for serious treatment. Four years before his death in 1805, the German dramatist and poet Friedrich Schiller produced his play *Die Jungfrau von Orleans*. It was translated into French a year later and was arguably the most significant and influential piece of imaginative writing about Joan until those by Péguy a century later or Bernard Shaw's *Saint Joan* in 1924.

If any theme dominates Schiller's works it is the quest for and the importance of personal freedom. His earlier plays had been statements of rebellion against a corrupt society, political systems and petty courts; his later ones embraced the same issues but in a larger context and with greater psychological complexity of character and philosophical weight. His writing also promoted ideal human values – he wrote the *Hymn to Joy* used by Beethoven in the last movement of his *Ninth Symphony* – and developed the idea of a national spirit or soul. To see his *Maid of Orléans*, as some have done, simply as a retort to Voltaire's work, however, is to underestimate it entirely.

Even if Schiller did consider the Frenchman's satire to be lacking in feeling – whatever its entertainment value – his own play is about moral greatness and is full of Romantic passion and dramatic power. It came, he said to Gottfried Körner, 'Straight from my heart, more than anything I've written up to now, particularly my previous plays in which Reason has to battle with the material.' It is also, we should not forget, a play that was written at a time when Germany was divided into a large number of principalities, many of which were under occupation by Napoleon's troops. Whatever the psychological complexities the play may deal with its political message is clear; as Olivier Bouzy has suggested, Schiller's Joan could well be considered the first in a long line of figures of resistance.[4]

A political message from Germany.

Like so many of the plays about Joan, Schiller's takes considerable liberties with history.[5] Joan is not visited by saints, for example, but by the Virgin Mary herself; Joan falls in love with Lionel, an English soldier; Agnes Sorel plays an important supporting role to the supine Charles ('a craven even from [his] birth', says Dunois of him dismissively) and unlike her Voltairean predecessor appears wholly devoted to him. Most noticeable of all Joan, who slaughters her enemies as readily as any of her fellow soldiers, dies in battle and not on the scaffold in Rouen, with the result that the whole trial scene is ignored. Schiller also introduces a mysterious 'Black Knight' to warn Joan of her fate, and has her father, Thibaut, return to Rheims and denounce his daughter as being in league with the Devil. (These are themes that Verdi would use to some effect in his opera and would appear in a number of more fanciful treatments of Joan's story written for the English stage during the nineteenth century.)

But whatever latitude there is in Schiller's treatment of the basic story he makes Joan's ambition clear from the very beginning even though it is not revealed at this stage that she is aware that she is the chosen 'Maid' called to save France. Thus in the Prologue we already have her rallying cry:

> Speak not of treaty! Speak not of surrender!
> The Saviour comes, he arms him for the fight.
> The fortunes of the foe before the walls
> Of Orléans shall be wreck'd!! His hour is come,
> He is now ready for the reaper's hand,
> And with her sickle will the maid appear,
> And mow to earth the harvest of his pride.
> She from the heavens will tear his glory down,
> Which he had hung aloft, among the stars;
> Despair not! Fly not! for ere yonder corn

Assumes its golden hue, or ere the moon
Displays her perfect orb, no English horse
Shall drink the rolling waters of the Loire.
[...] a snow-white dove
Shall fly, and with the eagle's boldness, tear
The birds of prey, which rend her Fatherland.
She shall o'erthrow this haughty Burgundy,
Betrayer of the kingdom; Talbot, too,
The hundred-handed, heaven-defying scourge;
This Sal'sbury, who violates our fanes,
And all these island robbers shall she drive
Before her like a flock of timid lambs.
The Lord will be with her, the God of battle;
A weak and trembling creature he will choose,
And through a tender maid proclaim his power,
For he is the Almighty!
[...]
This realm shall fall! This ancient land of fame,
The fairest that, in his majestic course,
Th' eternal sun surveys – this paradise,
Which, as the apple of his eye, God loves –
Endure the fetters of a foreign yoke?
– Here were the heathen scatter'd, and the cross
And holy image were first planted here;
Here rest Saint Louis' ashes, and from hence
The troops went forth, who set Jerusalem free.
(Prologue, Scene iii)

By Scene ix of the first act, before she appears at Chinon, we learn that Joan has already experienced military action, spurring the French to victory. Raoul, a knight, describes the scene:

We had assembled sixteen regiments
Of Lotharingian troops, to join your host;
And Baudricourt, a Knight of Vaucouleurs,
Was our commander. Having gain'd the heights
By Vermanton, we wound our downward way
Into the valley water'd by the Yonne;
There, in the plain before us, lay the foe,
And when we turn'd, arms glitter'd in our rear,
We saw ourselves surrounded by two hosts,
And could not hope for conquest or for flight.
Then sank the bravest heart, and in despair
We all prepared to lay our weapons down.
The leaders with each other anxiously
Sought counsel and found none, when to our eyes
A spectacle suddenly from forth the thickets' depths
A maiden, on her head a polish'd helm,
Like a war-goddess, issued; terrible
Yet lovely was her aspect, and her hair

In dusky ringlets round her shoulders fell.
A heavenly radiance shone around the height;
When she upraised her voice and thus address'd us:
'Why be dismay'd brave Frenchmen? On the foe!
Were they more numerous than the ocean sands,
God and the holy Maiden lead you on!'
Then quickly from the standard-bearer's hand
She snatch'd the banner, and before our troop
With valiant bearing strode the wondr'ous maid.
Silent with awe, scarce knowing what we did,
The banner and the Maiden we pursue,
And fire with ardour, rush upon the foe,
Who, much amazed, stand motionless and view
The miracle with fix'd and wondering gaze.
Then, as if seized by terror sent from God,
They suddenly betake themselves to flight,
And casting arms and armour to the ground,
Disperse in wild disorder o'er the field.
No leader's call, no signal now avails;
Senseless from terror, without looking back,
Horses and men plunge headlong in the stream,
Where they without resistance are despatch'd.
It was a slaughter rather than a fight!
Two thousand of the foe bestrew'd the field,
Not reckoning numbers swallow'd by the flood,
While of our company not one was slain.

(Act I, Scene ix)

Joan's reputation for both sides is henceforth established. For the English and Burgundians she is, as in Shakespeare's play, a 'witch', a 'sorceress', a 'she-devil', a 'dread-inspiring phantom'. For the French (Schiller's idea of national unity is unambiguous) she is, in Dunois' words, a 'wondrous maiden, sent / By a divine appointment to become / The saviour of this kingdom'. Or, in her own, to Charles, 'The holy maiden sent to thee by God'. True to tradition Schiller has Joan adamantly confirm her vow of virginity: 'I am the soldier of the Lord of Hosts, / And to no mortal man can I be wife'. She rejects declarations of love from Dunois and La Hire, but when she is confronted by Lionel on the battlefield and instantly falls in love with him, she recognises that she has broken her vow to the Virgin Mary and is rendered speechless. The infatuation causes her to be confused. She is unable to discuss it with anyone else and her consequent torn allegiances cause her to fall silent. For a while she is considered to be a witch by her former allies. It is here that, in Lesley Sharpe's words, Schiller shows how Joan's 'public challenge to her divine calling is echoed by her internal guilt'.[6] Joan flees the court and is captured by the English who regather their forces and begin to regain the military advantage. Joan calls on God, miraculously breaks free from her chains, rejoins the French and leads them to victory. Fatally wounded, she is reunited with Charles – who recognises that 'A cloud of error dimm'd our mental sight' – calls on the Virgin and dies. In a sense, of course, this can be seen to echo Joan's rehabilitation:

JOHANNA: (*gazing around her with a joyful smile*)
And am I really, then, among my friends,
And am no more rejected and despised?
They curse me not – kindly they look on me!
– Yes, all around me now seems clear again
That is my King! – the banners these of France!
My banner I behold not – where is it?
Without my banner I dare not appear;
To me it was confided by my Lord,
And before his throne must lay it down;
I there may show it, for I bore it truly.

KING: (*averting his face*).
Give her the banner!

(*It is given to her. She stands quite unsupported, the banner in her hand. The heaven is illumined by a rosy light.*)

JOHANNA: See you the rainbow yonder in the air?
Its golden portals Heaven doth wide unfold,
Amid the angel choir she radiant stands,
The eternal Son she claspeth to her breast,
Her arms stretcheth forth to me in love.
How is it with me? Light clouds bear me up –
My ponderous mail becomes a winged robe;
I mount – I fly – back rolls the dwindling earth –
Brief is my sorrow – endless is my joy!

(*Her banner falls, and she sinks lifeless on the ground. All remain for some time in speechless sorrow. Upon a signal from the King, all the banners are gently placed over her, so that she is entirely concealed by them.*)

(Act V, Scene xiv)

It is tempting to see the end of Schiller's play as an apotheosis of Christian faith, but that would be to take far too limited a view. To be sure Joan is an exemplary figure but she is also complex. Her faith gives her the strength to overcome temptation even though she may (or has to?) die tragically at the end. But as the Prologue makes clear her task is to rid France of an occupying force and at the same time 'heal dissension'. Like Southey's Joan, albeit with different advice and a different political agenda, she lectures Charles on his kingly responsibilities:

Sire, in prosperity be still humane,
As in misfortune thou hast ever been;
– And on the height of greatness ne'er forget
The value of a friend in times of need;
Thou hast approved it in adversity.
Refuse not to the lowest of thy people

> The claims of justice and humanity,
> For their deliv'rer from the fold was call'd.
> Beneath thy royal sceptre, thou shalt gather
> The realm entire of France. Thou shalt become
> The root and ancestor of mighty kings;
> Succeeding monarchs, in their regal state,
> Shall those outshine, who fill'd the throne before.
> Thy stock, in majesty shall bloom so long
> As it stands rooted in the people's love.
> (Act III, Scene iv)

Whatever political dimension Schiller may have had in mind, however, his play presents us with the first psychologically complex portrait of Joan. She has no single dominating characteristic, but is instead made up of various and even contradictory impulses and roles. From the first she is a distant figure, never entirely at one with her natural surroundings – unlike Southey's Joan for example – or with her family. As she becomes aware of and sets out on her mission, she becomes a mixture of prophetess and Amazon-like warrior. She acknowledges that she is drawn to magic and the supernatural. And her reaction when she sees Lionel defies all rational explanation, though, as many critics have argued, it makes her more 'human' and enables her to share and understand the kinds of emotional experiences of those around her. Such is her diverseness that there seems to be no consensus as to the kind of *person* Schiller envisaged, but in his poem *Das Mädchen von Orleans* ('The Girl of Orléans') he insists, not unlike Southey in this instance, that Joan is above all an emotional person, created from the heart. However we interpret her role in the play there is no doubt that Schiller gives his heroine, wittingly or not, a complexity that will not be matched for over a century.

The Maid of Orléans was received in France with enthusiasm and was unquestionably responsible for a number of theatrical ventures during the next decade or so. None have the complexity of Schiller's play and, as we have already noted, many of them resemble one another, choosing on the whole to present Joan as the divinely inspired champion of French patriotism, though the love element that the German play-wright had introduced would become immensely popular. Occasionally the author's imagination seems to take over with (perhaps unintended) comic results. In the first dramatisation of Joan's life in French in the nineteenth century, Cuvelier's pantomime *Jeanne d'Arc ou la Pucelle d'Orléans*, staged on 16 April 1803 at the Théâtre de la Gaïté for example, Dunois appears in the opening act as a young hunter. He is about to be attacked by an enormous wild boar when Joan, who has been helping with the harvest, kills it. They fall in love and by the third and last act, as their wedding is being celebrated by the appearance of cupids and an altar bearing the words 'To love and marriage', there is a clap of thunder and a voice that cries out: 'Joan has perjured herself; she must prepare for heavenly vengeance'.

JEANNE D'ARC,

OU

LA PUCELLE D'ORLÉANS,

PANTOMIME

EN TROIS ACTES ET A GRAND SPECTACLE,

contenant ses exploits, ses amours, son supplice, son apothéose,

MÊLÉE DE MARCHES, CHANTS, COMBATS ET DANSES.

PAR J. G. A. CUVELIER,

associé correspondant de la Société Philotechnique.

Représentée, pour la première fois, sur le théâtre de la Gaîté, le 25 germinal an XI.

16 avril 1803

A PARIS,

SE VEND AU THEATRE DE LA GAITÉ.

AN XI. — 1803.

87. *Cuvelier's pantomime* Jeanne d'Arc ou la Pucelle d'Orléans, *staged in 1803.*

The English reappear, and Dunois and Joan challenge them to a duel. Despite winning they are none the less betrayed; Joan is captured and condemned to die by burning. At this point – and this is a theme that becomes increasingly common – Chandos (Glasdale) promises to save her if she will accept his amorous advances. Joan refuses. No sooner is the fire lit than a dove soars into the air; the pyre disappears and Joan rises in majesty into heaven. In the place of the pyre is an altar and beyond it a triumphal arch with a statue of Joan modelled on the one to be erected in Orléans.

Productions taking similar liberties with tradition appeared in other countries as well. In 1822 a light-hearted 'melodrama in three acts' by Edward Fitz-Ball with music by Mr Nicholson could be seen at the Sadlers' Wells theatre in London. In it Joan is rescued at the last minute from the stake as the French troops pour into Rouen, and three knights – Richemont, Chalons and Beauvais (presumably based on Cauchon) – who have betrayed Charles are arrested. Fitz-Ball again departs completely from the original story when he introduces an extra amorous element into it by having Joan's sister, Lucelle, fall in love with Florine, a young soldier. Fifteen years later Fitz-Ball also wrote the words for 'The New Grand Opera *Joan of Arc*' in which Joan is similarly freed at the last moment and is reunited on this occasion with her childhood sweetheart, Theodore.

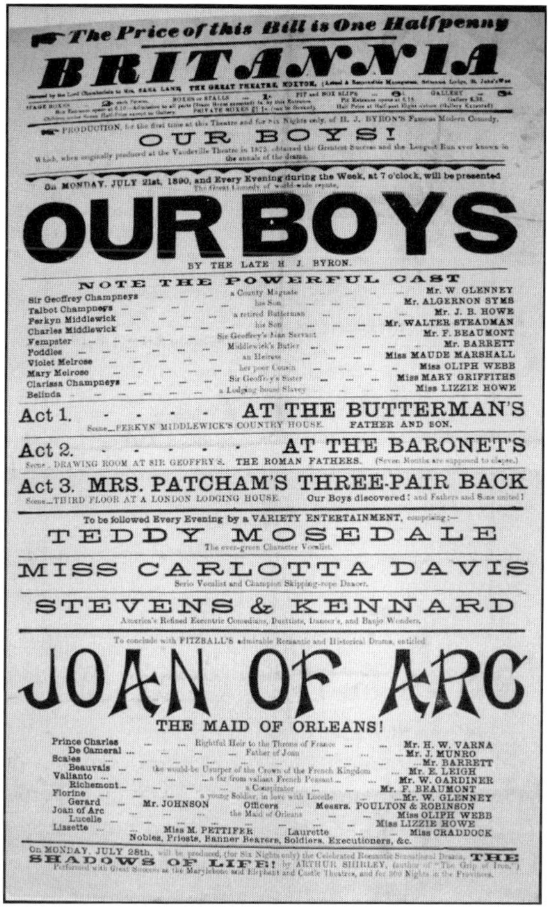

88. *Poster advertising Fitz-Ball's production of* Joan of Arc.

Rather more interesting, especially in terms of its subsequent influence, is Pierre Caze's *La Mort de Jeanne d'Arc ou la Pucelle d'Orléans* ('The Death of Joan of Arc or the Maid of Orléans')(1805) in which Joan is said to be Charles' half-sister, the offspring of an adulterous union between Isabel of Bavaria and Charles' brother Louis, the Duke of Orléans. It is rumoured that she had died at birth but has in fact been fostered by the d'Arc family. The point has already been made that since Louis died in 1407 and Joan was not to be born for another five years, Caze's thesis was already baseless, but this did not stop him from elaborating it further in a two-volume account, *La Vérité sur Jeanne*

LA MORT
DE JEANNE D ARC,
OU
LA PUCELLE D'ORLÉANS,
TRAGÉDIE
EN CINQ ACTES ET EN VERS,
PAR P. CAZE, SOUS-PRÉFET DE BERGERAC.

AN XIII. = 1805.

89. *Pierre Caze's play,* La Mort de Jeanne d'Arc ou la Pucelle d'Orléans, *1805.*

d'Arc ou éclaircissement de son origine ('The Truth about Joan of Arc and her origins') in 1819. Caze was not entirely without precedent of course; in Shakespeare's *Henry VI*, we should recall, Joan not only rejects her father but claims to be of noble birth. Nor, as we have seen in the Introduction, would Caze remain alone in his attempt to provide an alternative account of Joan and her exploits.

However challenging, Caze's idea seems not to have had many if indeed any followers, at least among imaginative writers. Essentially, despite all kinds of fictitious modifications and occasional echoes of earlier works, it was the traditional story of Joan that would hold its own both in France and abroad. Two good theatrical illustrations of this in England are plays by Thomas Serle and one Mrs J. .A. Sargant. In the first of these, *Joan of Arc. The Maid of Orleans*, an historical romance performed at Covent Garden on 23 November 1837, Serle takes as many liberties as Fitz-Ball had done.

Thibaut, Joan's father, is convinced that she has been inspired by the Devil ('Thou has traffick'd with the spirits of evil'), a theme developed by Verdi in his opera. An English soldier, Lionel, has been sheltered by Joan after a raid

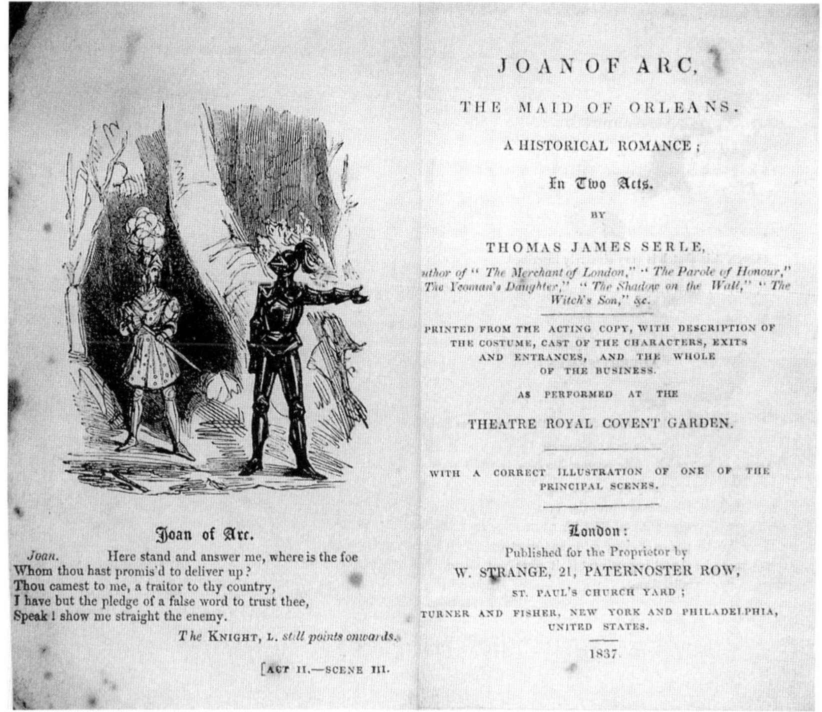

Joan of Arc.

Joan. Here stand and answer me, where is the foe
Whom thou hast promis'd to deliver up?
Thou camest to me, a traitor to thy country,
I have but the pledge of a false word to trust thee,
Speak! show me straight the enemy.

The Knight, L. *still points onwards.*

[Act II.—Scene III.

JOAN OF ARC,

THE MAID OF ORLEANS.

A HISTORICAL ROMANCE;

In Two Acts.

BY

THOMAS JAMES SERLE,

uthor of "*The Merchant of London,*" "*The Parole of Honour,*" *The Yeoman's Daughter,*" "*The Shadow on the Wall,*" "*The Witch's Son,*" &c.

PRINTED FROM THE ACTING COPY, WITH DESCRIPTION OF THE COSTUME, CAST OF THE CHARACTERS, EXITS AND ENTRANCES, AND THE WHOLE OF THE BUSINESS.

AS PERFORMED AT THE

THEATRE ROYAL COVENT GARDEN.

WITH A CORRECT ILLUSTRATION OF ONE OF THE PRINCIPAL SCENES.

London:

Published for the Proprietor by

W. STRANGE, 21, PATERNOSTER ROW,

ST. PAUL'S CHURCH YARD;

TURNER AND FISHER, NEW YORK AND PHILADELPHIA, UNITED STATES.

1837.

90. *Frontispiece and title page of Thomas Serle's* Joan of Arc. The Maid of Orleans, *1837.*

on Domremy. Joan falls in love with him and their lives continue to cross throughout the play. Serle also makes her the object of the affections of Raimond, a village boy, and of Dunois, but Joan remains steadfast in her pledge to deliver France from the English: 'I cast aside / All that could tempt me from the sacred cause / For which my power was given'. Even so, at the end of the play, having been captured by the English, Joan declares her undying love for Lionel who in turn pleads in vain for her release. As the French arrive Talbot fatally stabs her, and with her dying words Joan acknowledges that she has 'falter'd in the task I dar'd assume', but can none the less rejoice in the certainty that her death will not be in vain:

> Fools! slaying me you have destroyed yourselves.
>
> All is accomplished now – My friends! My countrymen!
> Father! you see the event which I foretold!
> King, once more France is free, I was but a woman!
> And falter'd in the task I dar'd assume;
> But now I am forgiven! I am happy!
> My death is the deliverance of France!

JOAN OF ARC.

THE MAID OF ORLEANS.

A HISTORICAL ROMANCE, IN TWO ACTS.—BY THOMAS J. SERLE.

D.H.F

Dramatis Personæ. [See page 11.

First performed at the Theatre Royal, Covent Garden, Tuesday, November 28th, 1837.

Charles, King of France ...	Mr. Serle.
Count Dunois	Mr. Pritchard.
La Hire	Mr. Roberts.
Arnaud	Mr. Tilbury.
Montfort	Mr. Howe.
Thibaut	Mr. G. Bennett.
ravelle	Mr. C. J. Smith.
olbert	Mr. Yarnold.
Raimond	Mr. Diddear.
Talbot	Mr. Waldron.
Lionel	Mr. Anderson.
Officer	Mr. Collett.
Gaoler	Mr. Bender.
Colambert (The Wizard of Chalons)	Mr. Meadows.
The Fiend Knight	Mr. W. H. Payne.
The Abbot	Mr. Holmes.
Isabel (Queen-Mother of France)	Mrs. Clifford.
Joan of Arc	Miss Huddart.
Madelon (her sister)	Mrs. East.
Agnes	Miss. E. Phillips.

No. 347. Dicks' Standard Plays.

91. *Playbill for Thomas Serle's* Joan of Arc. The Maid of Orleans, *1837.*

Mrs Sargant equally exploits the theme of love in a play that is also strongly anti-war, patriotic in message and feminist in tone. The real villains are Charles (despised by Joan) and his courtiers, notably Richemont and Cauchon (Beauvais). The English and especially Warwick and Talbot are dismissive of the French (Burgundians) – 'the false caitiffs' – who betray their own country to side with the enemy. Joan, of course, is the complete opposite. In Act II she gives voice to her resolute, all-consuming patriotism, stirring the French to action:

Oh, hapless country! loved insulted soil!
Birthplace of heroes, martyrs, and of saints!
Land of my sires by kindred blood embued!
Grave of my mother! Altar of my God!
To thee I pledge the life which first thou gavest,
Nor ask a higher, happier boon than this –
To die for thee!

Dunois in particular is moved both by her resolve and by her appearance:

She hath in truth
A charm to make stern hearts most meek, and yet
She is not beautiful, as men count beauty.
[...]
There is a dignity
Withal in her simplicity.

But Dunois, like Valencour later in the play, will not have his love returned. In keeping with her traditional role Joan makes her position clear in Act III:

My lot is cast, and lone
Must I pursue my path till it be ended.
For common love too proud, – too mean, alas!

In France and in England similar treatment is to be found in countless plays and poems throughout the rest of the century. In Banoré Berther's poem *Joan of Arc* (1853), for example, a former soldier of Henry V now recognises that the English were wrong but also how Joan, after her victory, was betrayed by Charles:

Lo! sure 'twas Heaven that sent her aid,
And let her triumph o'er
Those warriors, who to dark defeat
Had never bowed before.
Oh! 'twas a goodly sight to see
Fair England's flower laid low!
And her best and bravest stretched around,
When woman led the foe!
[...]
She saved her country and her king,
And she kept the oaths she swore,
On the cross of her sword, that her sovereign lord
His father's crown should wear.
And then she said that her task was done
Which Heaven bade her do;
But aye he prayed her for his sake
Her glories to renew.
But woe on that perjured coward!
Woe on his blighted faith!

For where shall honour hold her own?
Or where shall truth be safe?
A woman, when all aid seemed past,
Her king from ruin saved;
That woman in bright victory's hour
Was by her king betrayed!

Such was the growing topicality of Joan that she can be discovered in some of the least likely of places. In 1846, for example, she was the subject of the annual poetry competition at Rugby school in England. The winner was one Francis Conington whose deeply romantic and sentimental poem was no doubt in parts influenced by Southey's *Joan of Arc*. After an opening stanza encouraging praise of Joan, Conington evokes her as she becomes aware of her mission:

And there I marked, beside the sparkling stream,
A maiden resting on the forest grass;
All motionless she lay as though a dream
Through the full current of her mind did pass,
Nor did she care to lift her downcast eye,
Lulled by the ceaseless stream that ever murmured by.

Then as I gaze, the heaven grew dark around,
And the red clouds went gathering through the sky,
Then crashed the distant thunder's swelling sound,
Wide glared the flame of heaven's artillery:
The falling raindrops mournful music made,
And the wild sweeping wind went howling down the glade.

Then in the twilight of the roaring wood,
The maid uprose amid the stormy strife,
With hands upraised triumphantly she stood,
Like some old goddess sprung again to life:
And to her lips fast struggling accents rose,
She wailed in anguished tones her bleeding country's woes.

Such examples as these are just a few of the way Joan was typically depicted during the first half of the nineteenth century, and almost exactly at its mid point, in 1852, and in his biography of Joan, the poet and politician, Alphonse de Lamartine, provided a neat summary:

> Dismayed, down-trodden [the French] are plunged into that bottomless pit, where humanity sinks into the horrors of desolation. Into this gulf descended the pure ray of the divine ideal, carrying with it life and salvation. From the profound depths of this hell arose the deliverer, and that deliverer a woman.

Many works, as we have already noted, would continue to promote much the same image of Joan, but there would gradually be a change of tone or at least a new emphasis in France occasioned by a number of significant political and religious events and developments. Not least of these was the defeat of France by Prussia in 1870–71 and the loss of Alsace-Lorraine. This prompted a resurgence of patriotism and led to a growing politicisation of Joan and to her being increasingly, but not wholly, appropriated by groups and parties of the Right. Notable among these was the Assumptionist Order, an anti-republican, deeply conservative movement within the Catholic church for whom the Virgin Mary became the subject of particular veneration. That Joan also should be associated with this movement is hardly surprising and we should not forget that in 1869 Dupanloup had already called for her canonisation. Even if nothing positive would result until 1904, when Pius X would declare her 'venerable', the context for a new, more powerful image of Joan had been created. Lamartine's description of her as 'the pure ray of divine ideal, carrying with it life and salvation' had been prophetic.

One of Joan's staunchest supporters during the last years of the century was, as we know, the republican deputy Joseph Fabre. In the Prologue to his play, *Jeanne d'Arc* (1891), he has her voice a militant patriotism to her feckless relations:

> All parts of France and ours are brothers. Is not France our single mother? Men, how can you think about your fields when there is not the smallest parcel of land in all the kingdom that is not threatened? How can we think of our homes when a foreigner carries off our people? There is something more pressing to do than to cut our corn and make our sheaves, it is to defeat the English. Oh our one idea, our one wish should be to hunt down the foreigner! Let us turn our scythes and forks against him!

And later in the play Fabre has Talbot recognise that Joan is 'sublime' and shows him in despair at not being able to save her from the fire.

In a more concentrated way – the action does not go beyond the raising of the siege of Orléans – the political issues of the day are also reflected in such plays as the Abbé E. Bernard's *Jeanne d'Arc ou la Délivrance d'Orléans* (1896). In the opening scene there is a discussion between two townspeople, Jacomin and his son, Hubert, about duty and commitment. They are joined by Delcour, a treacherous Burgundian, who advises capitulation to the English – Talbot could in this way take the city without bloodshed – and hopes thereby to become mayor. Thus the tone is set and even Joan finds her resolution challenged:

> My God, help me; I feel myself weakening!
> I know what your plans are; I want to fulfil them,
> But what can I do without you? I am weak
> And will give up unless you support me.
> I left everything in order to please you,
> Oh my God, my sole desire was to live in peace.
> I loved my parents so much! Sensing their alarm

I hid my tears from them and wept only in front of you.
You alone God know what I have suffered;
Fears, torments, I have offered everything to you.
It is true that for long I felt my heart full of courage,
But can I struggle for much longer without weakening?

God indeed comes to her aid, but it is La Hire who crystallises the true message of Bernard's play: 'A man without a homeland is the last of men!'

Different, but equally typical of the period, is this physical description of Joan at her uncle's house and anticipating her status as a saint, in a poem by Jules Barbier, *Les Idylles de Jeanne* (1898):

And as the warmth dispersed the mists
The old men could admire this splendid child
With muscles like a man and as beautiful as an angel!
But confronted by so much vigour, grace and beauty
They felt strange,
For in truth it seemed at certain moments
That her words burned with a mysterious fire
And around her head there hovered a halo.

This was not Barbier's only venture into Joan's story, however. In 1873 his five-act play *Jeanne d'Arc* had been immensely popular Like many authors of the period Barbier is free in his interpretation of Joan's story, inventing episodes and details at will. There is, for example a keen rivalry between Joan and Agnès who is jealous of her relationship with Charles; Warwick offers to save her if she will have sex with him and, when she refuses, attempts to rape her, only for her to be saved by the arrival of Ladvenu. But in the aftermath of the defeat by the Prussians two years before it was the portrayal of Joan as an all-conquering leader of men and ardent patriot that mattered. Her words in the final act expressed the hopes of many: 'I know my country: it has given me its soul! / It will rise up again like me when insulted!'

Although a direct reflection of the contemporary political and religious climate in France during the last years of the nineteenth century, such recurring themes and descriptions as these uncannily anticipate those that would dominate so many of the works devoted to Joan by European writers over the next hundred years. But we should not leave the nineteenth century without reference to yet another one, again like Burk's play, from the United states – Mark Twain's novel *Personal Recollections of Joan of Arc*. First serialised anonymously in *Harper's Magazine* in 1895 it appeared as a book a year later.[7] Given his interest in and support for the underprivileged and the socially oppressed, it is perhaps not surprising that Twain should have been drawn to Joan and her story. (He claimed to have spent twelve years studying her.) Like so many he was liberal in his interpretation of the facts, but what is different and particularly fascinating is the way her story is recounted. The novel claims

92. Jeanne d'Arc dite la Pucelle d'Orléans, *illustration after Dumont, from* Harper's Magazine, *1895.*

93. Design by Eugène Grasset for the announcement of the publication of Mark Twain's Joan of Arc, *1895.*

to be the recollections of Louis de Conte 'freely translated from the ancient French into modern English from the original unpublished manuscript in the National Archives of France by Jean François Alden.' Two years older than Joan and a childhood friend, Louis joins her at Vaucouleurs and becomes (as indeed was the case) her page and secretary until her capture. Twain then has him appear as an assistant to the chief recorder, Manchon, at her trial. De Conte is infatuated with Joan, which results in a good deal of hyperbole in descriptions of her and in undisguised hostility to those who pursued her. His description of Cauchon, for example, is typical:

> When I looked again at that obese president, puffing and wheezing there, his great belly descending and receding with each breath (I could see) his three chins [...] his knobby and knotty face and his purple and splotchy complexion, and his repulsive cauliflower nose, and his cold malignant eyes.

But however much he wanted to express his contempt for those in power and who had allowed themselves to be corrupted Twain's main concern is to emphasise Joan's human qualities. She is generous, kind, courageous, sharply intelligent and wise; she is alert too to the political climate of her time. Even at the age of fourteen she is described as a 'hot patriot'. There are no blemishes. She is a perfect being, rising 'above the limitations and infirmities of our human nature', and remains, as De Conte says in his closing words after he has attended the rehabilitation trial, a 'wonderful child', a 'sublime personality', free of 'all alloy of self-seeking, self-interest, personal ambition' and the 'Genius of Patriotism – she was Patriotism embodied, made flesh, and palpable to the touch and visible to the eye.' In the following century this would be exploited in ways Mark Twain could not have foreseen.

Notes

1. References are to *Joan of Arc and Minor Poems*, Routledge, London, 1853.
2. Ingvald Raknem, *Joan of Arc in History, Legend, and Literature.* Oslo: Universitets-forlaget, 1971, 95.
3. 'The American Maid' in Dominique Goy-Blanquet (ed.), *Joan of Arc, a Saint for all Reasons*, Ashgate, Aldershot, 2003, 125 and see below 248–67.
4. Olivier Bouzy, 'Historiographie de Jeanne, du XVe siècle à nos jours', *Jeanne d'Arc, mythes et réalités,* Paris, 1999.
5. Extracts are from the English translation by Anna Swanwick in *The Works of Frederick Schiller*, Henry G. Bohn, London, 1847.
6. Lesley Sharpe, *Friedrich Schiller. Drama, Thought and Politics.* Cambridge: Cambridge University Press, 1991, 273.
7. See *Personal Recollections of Joan of Arc*, Introduced by Justin Kaplan, Oxford University Press, New York and Oxford, 1996.

Chapter Five
Joan Adapted and Adopted

FOR ALL THE ENDLESS RECYCLING of Joan throughout the previous centuries and, in particular, the nineteenth, there were, as we have seen, few individual works (at least in France) of real distinction or originality. This would continue to be the case, but imaginative writers increasingly turned to her in order to explore, and in some cases promote, philosophical, political and, to a lesser degree, religious ends.

Faith, socialism and patriotism: Charles Péguy's Joans

No writings exemplify the first stages of this new tendency better than those of Charles Péguy.[1] We know from Péguy's papers that he had begun to collect material about Joan from 1892. He would return to her and her story during the rest of his life, his portrayal of her at different times reflecting his own political and religious evolution. Most critics are in agreement that in his first trilogy *Jeanne d'Arc* published in 1897 we have an illustration of his fundamental socialist views, while over a decade later in *Le Mystère de la Charité de Jeanne d'Arc* (1910), the focus is much more on the religious aspect of the story as Péguy moved towards a 'rediscovery' of the faith he had rejected in 1895. To be sure, Joan features elsewhere in Péguy's works but it is in these two that he gives us the essence of what she meant to him. At the same time there is also in these two works an overriding preoccupation with Joan as a human being faced with and despairing of the state of France (as was Péguy himself) and of humanity in general. The questions Joan puts to herself are those that Péguy asks; the anguish she felt is his too. Nelly Jussem-Wilson sums this up well:

> To a large extent Joan is of course Péguy. This is most obvious in her angry rejection of the concept of Hell, her compassion for the poor, her revolt against injustice, human and divine. Like Péguy, she bids a sad farewell to her home. She is also proud, intransigent, capable of a rigorous self-discipline, but a rebel against authority imposed by tradition, social position or material wealth.[2]

94. *Poster for Peguy's* Jeanne d'Arc, *Helsinki, 2002.*

In this trilogy Péguy largely follows the traditional chronology of Joan's story but treats it in a completely new way, focussing less directly – if indeed at all – on her exploits than on the inner conflict she experiences as a result of them. In the first of the three plays, *À Domremy* we find Joan, aged thirteen, interacting with her family in a way that Péguy can only have imagined, and with her friends Hauviette, three years younger, and Madame Gervaise who at twenty-five has become a nun. Neither can understand her. Joan despairs of the plight of France and appeals, prophetically, to God to provide a leader:

This is what we need, a leader
Who kneels to pray in the morning
Before going to cut down
The outrageous English in battle.
My God, give him to us.
Oh my God, give us a battle leader
As valiant as an archangel and who knows how to pray
Like the knights who before on the Mountain
Struck down the English.
Let him be a leader in battle and a leader in prayer.
But let him not save one part of the country
Leaving the rest to the English.
Send us a leader, God of France, who will set about
The English and chase them from all of France.
(Act III, 965)

In the second play, *Les Batailles*, events at Orléans are discussed within Jacques Boucher's house where Joan lodged and, as in a classical play, the skirmishes and battles are simply reported. For some reason, while other key historical figures are present, Dunois is missing. Joan despairs of war ('fighting between humans is too ugly') and deliberately refuses to have any communication with her voices. (They never appear in *À Domremy* where Joan merely reports what they have said to her.) She is therefore increasingly alone, abandoned by Charles, by La Hire and by d'Alençon, and she decides to continue her campaign without them. In the final play *Rouen* (in a way that anticipates adaptations of her story half a century later) Péguy continues to emphasise just how isolated Joan is. It is evident that he was familiar with the transcript of the trial but he uses it selectively to show how Joan is the victim of the Church and of the Schoolmen whose repetitive and erudite discussions he heavily satirises. Only in the last scenes when she is shown the instruments of torture or when she is alone with her jailers does she poignantly and despairingly give voice to her feeling of having been abandoned. Envisaging her death she sees her life as a lie for which she will now be damned:

My human death will be on the pyre of wood,
And my body which I had kept pure will burn in pain
As it is consumed by the flames.
The people will be there in the square
Crowding forward, keen to see my living flesh
Consumed by the fire.
Priest and people, massed in the square,

The crowd, mocking, shivering, straining to see,
And the clerics singing the canticles for the dead,
The bells will toll my death.
The flames will devour me in pain
And like this will I pass into the flames of hell.
Pain now before eternal pain.
And in my country people will long talk of Joan the damned.
(Part 1, Act II, 1191)

From this there is no recovery. All she can do in her final prayer as she leaves for the scaffold is to appeal to God to save everyone:

But I know that I did well to serve you,
That we have done well to serve you like this.
My voices did not deceive me.
And yet, my God, try to save all of us,
Jesus, save for us all life everlasting.
(Part 2, Act I, 1204,5)

Whether Péguy could ever have produced a more triumphant or optimistic end to his story of Joan remains unknown. In *Le Mystère de la Charité de Jeanne d'Arc*, published a year after Joan's beatification, of course, he revisits the issues and discussions Joan had with Hauviette and Gervaise in *À Domremy*. On this occasion, however, Hauviette – implausibly for a ten year old – and Gervaise, debate with her in a much fuller and more powerful way. Gervaise in particular has become a form of confessor figure, but they are still incapable of understanding her. Joan's despair is even stronger here. War is not just the conflict between the English and the Burgundians on the one side and the French on the other; it is the manifestation of the opposition between forces that seek to create and those that destroy, between good and evil, between those who follow and fight for Christ and those who have failed him and scorn him. In effect Joan challenges Christ, seeking to emulate him and even do better, and Gervaise quite justifiably warns her against the sin of pride.

Whether, had he continued with the three-part model of *Le Mystère*, Péguy would ever have succeeded in portraying Joan in action as an exemplary militant warrior and in her death almost as a reincarnation of Christ is impossible to say. From the evidence we have Joan does not simply play a larger part but gives passionate voice to ideas that are clearly Péguy's own. Furthermore a stylistic change between the two works is important. The mixture of (predominantly) prose and occasional passages of twelve syllable alexandrines in the first work gives way in the second to free verse which slows the pace and thereby encourages reflection. And this is further accentuated by repetition and the incantatory style of much of what is said. Péguy's writing is powerful, building up, as more than one commentator has observed, like the segments of a Bach fugue. Péguy would be killed in the First World War but his vision of Joan as the embodiment of ordinary people and as a great mystical spirit would live on and influence others of quite different socio-political persuasions from his own.

For all that she was an important rallying figure during the First World War, between *Le Mystère* and Bernard Shaw's *Saint Joan* in 1924 there are relatively few works devoted to Joan, though she would be subtly evoked in the ghost-like figure of Eudoxie who appears to the trench soldiers in Henri Barbusse's magnificent novel *Le Feu (Under Fire)*, published in 1916.

95. A vision of Saint Joan appears to French soldiers by John C. Conacher, Life, *1918.*

Three years later in America a strongly pro-French pageant play by Thomas Stevens should be mentioned. In it Joan clearly stands for France in the immediate post-war years when the country is faced with the immense task of recovery and is surrounded by her former allies, all of whom have their own ambitions:

> Now all her foes, disguised in holiness,
> Ring her about, and torture her bright soul,
> And for the moment, beat her spirit down
> To the chill dust and anguish of defeat.
>
> (Scene, vii)

But Joan would soon be at the forefront of attention again as the drive to canonise her continued with the desired result in 1920. Immediately she became a subject of greater international interest and in Shaw's play we have what many believe still remains one of the most innovative works to be inspired by her.

Bernard Shaw's *Saint Joan*: challenge or inspiration?

'Oh God that madest this beautiful earth, when will it be ready to receive thy saints? How long, O Lord, how long?' With Joan's well-known, plaintive appeal Shaw brings the epilogue and his play to a close. Behind Joan's words, of course, we can find a number of Shaw's political, social and moral preoccupations, explored quite openly in the Preface he provided when the text of the play was published in 1924, just a few months after its first performance in New York on 28 December 1923. In it he discusses justice, intolerance, hypocrisy, modern science, executions, the role of modern doctors, the credulity, vanity and passiveness of the general public and above all the institution of the Catholic Church. Like so many of his plays, *Saint Joan* is fundamentally a play of ideas and in it his heroine is his foil. Shaw makes this quite clear from the very first paragraph of the Preface:

> She is the most notable Warrior saint in the Christian calendar. [...]
> Though a professed and most pious Catholic, and the projector of a crusade against the Husites, she was in fact one of the first Protestant martyrs. She was also one of the first apostles of Nationalism, and the first French practitioner of Napoleonic realism in warfare as distinguished from the sporting ransomgambling chivalry of her time. She was the pioneer of rational dressing for women, and, like Queen Christina of Sweden two centuries later, to say nothing of Catalina de Eranso and innumerable obscure heroines who have disguised themselves as soldiers and sailors, she refused to accept the specific woman's lot, and dressed and fought and lived as men did. [...] She had an unbounded and quite unconcealed contempt for official opinion, judgement, and authority, and for War Office tactics and strategy. [...] As her condition was pure upstart, there were only two opinions about her. One was that she was miraculous: the other was that she was unbearable.

Even though she may have been 'academically ignorant' and full of youthful naivety, Shaw argues that her replies to her judges, the tone of the letters she dictated and her understanding of the political and military situation of her time show her to be intellectually able, astute, quick thinking and a 'born boss'. But she was also more, and Shaw is quite unequivocal. Joan was also a 'genius and a saint', and he underscores her significance by comparing her to Socrates, Napoleon and Christ. Like them she was disquieting and even inspired fear to the point where, like Socrates and Christ, she had to be

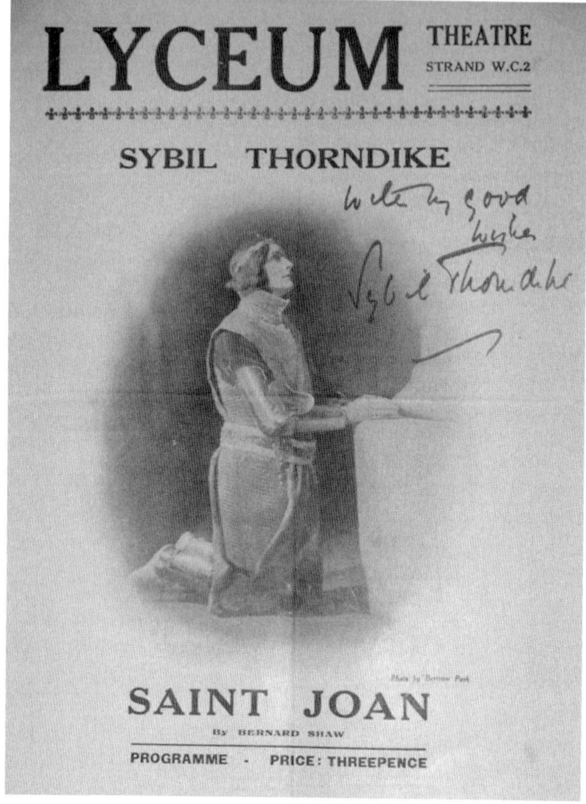

96. *Poster advertising Shaw's* Saint Joan *with Sybil Thorndike in the title role.*

removed. Over the difficult issue of her voices Shaw adopts a position of rational common sense. While he dismisses the idea that these were literally the voices of saints, he willingly acknowledges that for people of powerful imagination or deep conviction, such 'personification' is not unusual.

> I cannot believe, nor, if I could, could I expect all my readers to believe, as Joan did, that three ocularly visible, well-dressed persons, named respectively Saint Catherine, Saint Margaret, and Saint Michael, came down from heaven and gave her certain instructions with which they were charged by God for her. [...] The diverse manners in which our imaginations dramatize the approach of the superpersonal forces is a problem for the psychologist, not for the historian. Only, the historian must understand that visionaries are neither imposters nor lunatics. [...] For us to set up our condition as a standard of sanity, and declare Joan mad because she never condescended to it, is to prove that we are not only lost but irredeemable. Let us then once and for all drop all nonsense about Joan being cracked, and accept her as at least as sane as Florence Nightingale, who also combined a very simple iconography of religious belief with a mind so

LYCEUM THEATRE

STRAND

Under the Management of ... ... WALTER MELVILLE / FREDK. MELVILLE

Licensed by the Lord Chamberlain to Walter and Fredk. Melville, Lyceum Theatre, London, W.C.

EVERY EVENING 7.45 sharp.

MATS.: WED. and SAT. at 2.15 sharp.

SYBIL THORNDIKE

IN

SAINT JOAN

A Chronicle Play in Six Scenes and an Epilogue

By BERNARD SHAW

Characters in order of their appearance

Robert de Baudricourt	HUBERT CARTER
Steward	H. REYNER BARTON
Joan	SYBIL THORNDIKE
Bertrand de Poulengey	VICTOR LEWISOHN
The Archbishop of Rheims	ROBERT CUNNINGHAM
La Tremouille (Chamberlain)	WILLIAM FAZAN
Court Page	SAM PICKLES
Gilles de Rais (Bluebeard)	HENRY TWYFORD
Captain La Hire	MATTHEW FORSYTH
The Dauphin (later Charles VII.)	RUSSELL THORNDIKE
The Duchesse de la Tremouille	BEATRICE SMITH
Dunois (Bastard of Orleans)	DOUGLAS BURBIDGE
Dunois' Page	JACK HAWKINS (By arrangement with Italia Conti.)
Richard de Beauchamp (Earl of Warwick)	E. LYALL SWETE
Chaplain de Stogumber	LEWIS T. CASSON
Peter Cauchon (Bishop of Beauvais)	EUGENE LEAHY
Warwick's Page	WALTER GORE
The Inquisitor	H. R. HIGNETT
D'Estivet (Canon of Bayeux)	H. REYNER BARTON
De Courcelles (Canon of Paris)	WILLIAM FAZAN
Brother Martin Ladvenu	LAWRENCE ANDERSON
The Executioner	VICTOR LEWISOHN
An English Soldier	HUBERT CARTER
A Gentleman	OSBORN ADAIR

Ladies of the Court: Brenda Gordon-Cleather, Iris Baker, Agnes Lauchlan, Gwen Harter, Vere Shopstone.

Courtiers, Monks, Soldiers, etc.: Cyril Hardingham, Michael Logan, Sam Pickles, Chris Walker, Desmond Deane, Carol Reed, Ronald Kerr.

The Curtain will be lowered between the Scenes, but there will be only ONE interval, after Scene Five.

Scene 1	The Castle of Vaucouleurs.	February 23rd, 1429
Scene 2	Antechamber and Throne Room at Chinon.	March 8th, 1429
Scene 3	The bank of the River Loire near Orleans.	May 29th, 1429
Scene 4	The Earl of Warwick's Tent in the English Camp	
Scene 5	The Ambulatory of Rheims Cathedral.	July 17th, 1429

Interval of Ten Minutes.

Scene 6	A Hall in the Castle at Rouen.	May 30th, 1431

EPILOGUE.

Bedroom in the Chateau of Charles VII. June, 1456

(Programme Continued Overleaf)

Extract from the Rules made by the Lord Chamberlain.

(1) The name of the actual and responsible Manager of the Theatre must be printed on every play bill (2) The public can leave the Theatre at the end of the performance by all exit and entrance doors, which must open outwards. (3) Where there is a fireproof screen to the proscenium opening, it must be lowered at least once during every performance to ensure its being in proper working order.

97. Full cast list for the same production.

exceptionally powerful that it kept her in continual trouble with the medical and military panjandrums of her time.

Nonetheless Shaw also reminds us that for people in the fifteenth century, visions and voices of the kind Joan claimed she had or heard were not all that uncommon, and it is this 'contextualisation' that is vital for the ideas he explores and illustrates in the play.

In his Preface Shaw refers to several of the better-known literary treatments of Joan and to some biographies. Only Voltaire's *La Pucelle d'Orléans* emerges with any degree of real credit – hardly surprising in view of the Irishman's liking for the eighteenth-century writer's 'ribald irreverence'. Others are dismissed. Shakespeare's *Henry VI* is 'poor and base in its moral tone'; Schiller's play is 'romantic nonsense'; the biographies by Anatole France and Andrew Lang, and Mark Twain's novel are all too marked by their authors' personal tastes to be of any real value. But at the root of this dismissive treatment is what Shaw sees as the failure of earlier writers to understand

98. Playbill for a New York production of Shaw's Saint Joan.

fully the Middle Ages, a failure that has resulted in a misrepresentation in particular of figures such as Cauchon and Warwick. For similar reasons Joan's trial has been seen as an unfair persecution, but Shaw is at pains to point out – as Thierry Maulnier will be nearly thirty years later – that in essence she would be treated no differently now. Hers is the case of an innocent and ignorant young woman caught between the powers of her time: the Catholic Church and the feudal system. Against them Joan represents, for Shaw, the 'quintessence of Protestantism' and burgeoning nationalism. Joan is the herald of a new freedom.

So weighty are the issues with which *Saint Joan* deals that discussion all too frequently replaces action. All the major events – or at least actions – occur 'off-stage', and many of them are contracted. Shaw's attempts to lighten the tone – Joan speaking like a peasant (Scene ii) or Dunois' interest in a kingfisher (Scene iii) or some of the English Chaplain's behaviour during the trial (Scene

vi) – are unnecessary rather than unsuccessful. It would be wrong, however, to interpret Shaw's play as an attempt to correct earlier representations of Joan and her exploits; rather it is a sober illustration of ideas as important in the early twentieth century as they were in the fifteenth. A good illustration of this can be found in Scene iv in which Shaw has Warwick and Cauchon – both presented as reasonable men even if blinkered by their values and positions – debate the key issues of the play. Present too is the 'bullnecked' English Chaplain whose interventions provide some comedy but more importantly help move the debate on:

CAUCHON: If the Devil wanted to damn a country girl, do you think so easy a task would cost him the winning of half a dozen battles? No, my lord: any trumpery imp could do that much if the girl could be damned at all. The Prince of Darkness does not condescend to such cheap drudgery. When he strikes, he strikes at the Catholic Church, whose realm is the whole spiritual world. When he damns, he damns the souls of the entire human race. Against that dreadful design The Church stands ever on guard. And it is as one of the instruments of that design that I see this girl. She is inspired, but diabolically inspired.

THE CHAPLAIN: I told you she was a witch.

CAUCHON *(fiercely)*: She is not a witch. She is a heretic.

THE CHAPLAIN: What difference does that make?

CAUCHON: You, a priest, ask me that! You English are strangely blunt in the mind. All these things that you call witchcraft are capable of natural explanation. The woman's miracles would not impose on a rabbit: she does not claim them as miracles herself. What do her victories prove but that she has a better head on her shoulders than your swearing Glass-dells and mad bull Talbots, and that the courage of faith, even though it be a false faith, will always outstay the courage of wrath?

THE CHAPLAIN *(hardly able to believe his ears)*: Does your lordship compare Sir John Talbot, the heir to the earldom of Shrewsbury, to a mad bull?!!!

WARWICK: It would not be seemly for you to do so, Messire John, as you are still six removes from a barony. But as I am an earl, and Talbot is only a knight, I may make bold to accept the comparison. *(To the Bishop)* My lord: I wipe the slate as far as witchcraft goes. None the less, we must burn the woman.

CAUCHON: I cannot burn her. The Church cannot take life. And my first duty is to seek this girl's salvation.

WARWICK: No doubt. But you do burn people occasionally.

CAUCHON: No. When the Church cuts off an obstinate heretic as a dead branch from the tree of life, the heretic is handed over to the secular arm. The Church has no part in what the secular may see fit to do.

WARWICK: Precisely. And I shall be the secular arm in this case. Well, my lord, hand over your dead branch; and I will see that the fire is ready for it. If you will answer for the Church's part, I will answer for the secular part.

CAUCHON *(with smouldering anger)*: I can answer for nothing. You great lords are too prone to treat the Church as a mere political convenience.

WARWICK *(smiling and propitiatory)*: Not in England, I assure you.

CAUCHON: In England more than anywhere else. No, my lord: the soul of this village girl is of equal value with yours or your king's before the throne of God; and my first duty is to save it. I will not suffer your lordship to smile at me as if I were repeating a meaningless form of words, and it were well understood between us that I should betray the girl to you. I am no mere political bishop: my faith is to me what your honor is to you; and if there be a loophole through which this baptized child of God can creep to her salvation, I shall guide her to it.

THE CHAPLAIN *(rising in a fury)*: You are a traitor.

CAUCHON *(springing up)*: You lie, priest. *(Trembling with rage)* If you dare do what this woman has done – set your country above the holy Catholic Church – you shall go to the fire with her.

THE CHAPLAIN: My lord: I – I went too far. I – *(he sits down with a submissive gesture)*.

WARWICK *(who has risen apprehensively)* My lord: I apologize to you for the word used by Messire John de Stomburger. It does not mean in England what it does in France. In your language traitor means betrayer: one who is perfidious, unfaithful, disloyal. In our country it means simply one who is not wholly devoted to our English interests.

CAUCHON: I am sorry: I did not understand. *(He subsides into his chair with dignity)*

WARWICK *(resuming his seat, much relieved)*: I must apologize on my own account if I have seemed to take the burning of this poor girl to lightly. When one has seen whole countrysides burn over and over again as mere items in military routine, one has to grow a very thick skin. Otherwise one might go mad: at all events, I should. May I venture to assume that your lordship also, having to see so many heretics burned from time to time, is compelled to take – shall I say a very professional view of what would otherwise be a very horrible incident?

CAUCHON: Yes: it is a painful duty: even, as you say, a horrible one. But in comparison with the horror of heresy it is less than nothing. I am not thinking of this girl's body, which will suffer for a few moments only, and which must in any event die in some more or less painful manner, but of her soul, which may suffer to all eternity.

WARWICK: Just so; and God grant that her soul may be saved! But the practical problem would seem to be how to save her soul without saving her body. For we must face it, my lord: if this cult of the Maid goes on, our cause is lost.

THE CHAPLAIN *(his voice broken like that of a man who has been crying)*: May I speak, my lord?

WARWICK: Really, Messire John, I had rather you did not, unless you can keep your temper.

THE CHAPLAIN: It is only this. I speak under correction; but the Maid is full of deceit: she pretends to be devout. Her prayers and confessions are endless. How can she be accused of heresy when she neglects no observance of a faithful daughter of The Church?

CAUCHON *(flaming up)*: A faithful daughter of The Church! The Pope himself at his proudest dare not presume as this woman presumes. She acts as if she herself were The Church. She brings the message of God to Charles; and The Church must stand aside. She will crown him in the cathedral of Rheims: she, not The Church! She sends letters to the king of England giving him God's command through her to return to his island on pain of God's vengeance, which she will execute. Let me tell you that the writing of such letters was the practice of the accursed Mahomet, the anti-Christ. Has she ever in all her utterances said one word of The Church? Never! It is always God and herself.

WARWICK: What can you expect? A beggar on horseback! Her head is turned.

CAUCHON: Who has turned it? The devil. And for a mighty purpose. He is spreading this heresy everywhere. The man Hus, burnt only thirteen years ago at Constance, infected all Bohemia with it. A man named WcLeef, himself an anointed priest, spread the pestilence in England; and to your shame you let him die in his bed. We have such people here in France too: I know the breed. It is cancerous: if it be not cut out, stamped out, burnt out, it will not stop until it has brought the whole body of human society into sin and corruption, into waste and ruin. By it an Arab camel driver drove Christ and His Church out of Jerusalem, and ravaged his way west like a wild beast until at last there stood only the Pyrenees and God's mercy between France and damnation. Yet what did the camel driver do at the beginning more than this shepherd girl is doing? He had his voices from the angel Gabriel: she has her voices from St Catherine and St Margaret and the Blessed Michael. He declared himself the messenger of God, and wrote in God's name to the kings of the earth. Her letters to them are going forth daily. It is not the Mother of God now to whom we must look for intercession, but to Joan the Maid. What will the world be like when The Church's accumulated wisdom and knowledge and experience, its councils of learned, venerable pious men, are thrust into the kennel by every ignorant laborer or dairymaid whom the devil can puff up with the monstrous self-conceit of being directly inspired from heaven? It will be a world of blood, of fury, of devastation, of each man striving for his own hand: in the end a world wrecked back into barbarism. For now you have only Mahomet and his dupes, and the Maid and her dupes; but what will it be when every girl thinks herself a Joan and every man a Mahomet? I shudder to the very marrow of my bones when I think of it. I have fought it all my life; and I will fight it to the end. Let all this woman's sins be forgiven her except this sin; for it is the sin against the Holy Ghost; and if she does not recant in the dust before the world, and submit herself to the last inch of her soul to her Church, to the fire she shall go if she once falls into my hand.

[...]

CAUCHON *(conciliatory, dropping his polemical tone)*: My lord: we shall not defeat the Maid if we strive against one another. I know well there is a Will to Power in the world. I know that while it lasts there will be a struggle between the Emperor and the Pope, between the dukes and the political cardinals, between the barons and the kings. The devil divides us and governs. I see you are no friend to The Church: you are an earl first and last. But can we not sink our differences in the face of a common enemy? I see now that what is in our mind is not that this girl has never once mentioned The Church, and thinks only of God and herself, but that she has never once mentioned the peerage, and thinks only of the king and herself.

WARWICK: Quite so. These two ideas of hers are the same idea at bottom. It goes deep, my lord. It is the protest of the individual soul against the interference of priest or peer between the private man and his God. I should call it Protestantism if I had to find a name for it.

CAUCHON *(looking hard at him)*: You understand it wonderfully well, my lord. Scratch an Englishman, and find a Protestant.

WARWICK *(playing the pink of courtesy)*: I think you are not entirely void of sympathy with The Maid's secular heresy, my lord. I leave you to find a name for it.

CAUCHON: You mistake me, my lord. I have no sympathy with her political presumptions. But as a priest I have gained a knowledge of the minds of the common people; and there you will find yet another most dangerous idea. I can express it only by such phrases as France for the French, England for the English, Italy for the Italians, Spain for the Spanish, and so forth. It is sometimes so narrow and bitter in country folk that it surprises me that this country girl can rise above the idea of her village for its villagers. But she can. She does. When she threatens to drive the English from the soil of France she is undoubtedly thinking of the whole extent of the country in which French is spoken. To her the French-speaking people are what the Holy Scriptures describe as a nation. Call this side of her heresy Nationalism if you will: I can find no better name for it. I can only tell you that it is essentially anti-Catholic and anti-Christian; for the Catholic Church knows only one realm, and that is the realm of Christ's kingdom. Divide that kingdom into nations, and you dethrone Christ. Dethrone Christ, and who will stand between our throats and the sword? The world will perish in a welter of war.

WARWICK: Well, if you will burn the Protestant, I will burn the Nationalist, though perhaps I shall not carry Messire John with me there. England for the English will appeal to him.

In the following scene Charles has been crowned, Joan is no longer of any use to him. Not unreasonably she is accused of stubbornness and pride, but by depicting her as a young and bewildered girl Shaw ensures that our sympathy for her is retained and prepares us for the final scene in which, as the Inquisitor says, 'it is a terrible thing to see a young and innocent creature crushed between these mighty forces, the Church and the Law'.

Shaw's play was not without its critics, particularly those who considered that the ideas, however powerful, destroyed the play as theatre. Characters were also judged to be too modern, Joan too vulgar and boastful, and Cauchon simply wrong. To such criticism in France, Shaw replied with an open letter in March 1924, which was translated and published in the popular cultural newspaper, *Comœdia*. His sarcasm is not hidden. He accuses previous writers

99. Illustration by Rodolpho del Castillo in an edition of Sainte Jeanne *and* Pygmalion, *Editions Rombaldi, 1962.*

of distorting Joan's story with fanciful interpretations and ridicules the theatre-going public, the 'flaneurs who are interested in nothing but the latest variation on the eternal triangle.' 'I have not belittled Joan', he goes on, 'by turning her history into a melodrama of a wicked bishop and a virtuous maiden. I have taken the tragedy completely outside the taste of the amateurs of such melodrama, and probably beyond their comprehension. They like duels and divorce cases, and cannot conceive any human being taking any interest in the Middle Ages or the Church or the Empire.' In America some audiences had also complained that the play was too long. The director at the Theatre Guild, Theresa Helburn, asked Shaw to shorten it, but he refused and wrote an article in his defence. It remained unpublished at the time, but the scorn he was to heap on average French audiences a few months later is no less apparent:

> *Saint Joan* is not for connaisseurs of the police and divorce drama, or of the languors and lilies and raptures of the cinema; and it is not going to be altered to suit them! It is right over their heads – they must either grow up to it or let it alone. Fortunately for me it interests and even enthralls serious people who would not enter an ordinary theatre if they were paid to and draws novices who have never crossed the threshold of a theatre in their lives – and were taught by their parents that it is the threshold of hell [...] *Saint Joan* must be regarded for the present as an Exceptional play for Exceptional people.[3]

Yet however much Shaw may have shown the way not all dramatists followed his lead. For many the pull of the traditional image of Joan remained strong. In the Foreword to his *Joan of Arc, the Maid of Orléans* (1930) Ymal Oswin is quite explicit that, even without naming him, Shaw has been misguided, and that his own play is a correction:

> It has been a labour of love to endeavour to depict in this play the character of the glorious Maid of Orléans, and to make her live through her own words. In this country [England], writers have too often made her, for example, the patroness of the modern girl, the political woman, and even advanced feminism. It has been our aim to show the strong, simple peasant-girl moulded on heroic lines by her lofty supernatural mission, and her patriotism.

While Oswin follows the chronology of Joan's story faithfully he does introduce some new elements. He has Diane, the wife of La Trémouille, warn Joan's family of the danger their daughter is running in the hope that she will be persuaded to return to Domremy and leave the way clear for her husband's scheming. He also changes relatively minor details of Joan's departure from Domremy – her parents give their consent, she bids Hauviette farewell, her uncle (*sic*) offers her a horse.... Joan is portrayed as diligent but already different, knowing that she is the chosen Maid. Whenever she communes with her saints or reflects on her mission Oswin has her speak in blank verse and not in the laboured, archaic prose that is his norm. Equally laboured in the language used and broadly orthodox in its account of Joan is S. A. Turk's *Joan of Arc: a sacred drama* which had appeared in America two years earlier – possibly another ripost to Shaw's play – under the auspices of the Catholic Dramatic Company whose aim was to publish works 'that conform to our Catholic ideas.' And if outside writing for the theatre any proof were needed for a preference by many for the accepted version of events, we need only to turn to *Joan of Arc or the Story of the Girl Warrior* by Mildred Duff and Noel Hope (pseud.) published in London by the Salvationist Association in 1929. A footnote commenting on Joan's remarkable recovery from her wound at Orléans sets the tone perfectly: 'this wonderful cure proves how healthy her constitution must have been, how sound her nerves, and temperate her habits.' And much later in the book the authors criticise those who 'refuse to believe that for the restoration of the kingdom, Divine power went to fetch out of

100. *Poster advertising Sarah Bernhardt in the role of Joan.*

101. The strange, dream-like world painted by Charles Ricketts in 1922 was used by Shaw for a curtain design for Saint Joan *at the New Theatre in March 1924.*

her cottage, from amidst poor country folk, a girl of seventeen, simple, ignorant, and of humble condition.' Is that not evidence, they ask, of 'the miracle of the conquest of the world by Christianity?'

The making of a political saint

In whatever way Joan was regarded outside France, however, it was inevitable that at home not only would she become once again the subject of wide popular interest but for many would be assigned an increasing political significance, particularly by those whose sympathies lay to the Right. But before this development gathered pace Joan was the subject of two strange books by Joseph Delteil whose interest in her was deeply personal and indeed emotional, and seems to have had nothing to do with the religious fervour that followed her canonisation.

Delteil was a writer of immense lyrical talent who had attracted the attention of André Breton and the Surrealists. His interest in such a 'traditional' subject inevitably caused a rift between them and Delteil met with opposition as well both from those who thought that Joan now had to be seen in a much more serious and patriotic light and from members of the Church who found his treatment of Joan scandalous. Even so *Jeanne d'Arc* (1925) was immensely popular and won the Prix Fémina.[4]

Whatever his detractors might have thought there is no doubt in Delteil's mind that Joan was divinely inspired, but he also portrays her as an instinctive, earthy and sensuous creature with the result that his descriptions can frequently seem extravagant or even absurd. This, for example, is Joan as a baby:

> It will be months before she learns to talk; still, in the language of angels she chatters with the rooster and the sun, two equilateral signs, two spheres of the same rank. With all her body she questions the shining machinery of the world; she questions and gives orders, for today she is the queen of Creation. And she considers her subjects with an air of authority: the fowls and planets, the farm house white as a daisy maid, her little friends the clouds and her retainers the great oaks.

Delteil also frequently dwells on her physical and, above all, sexual presence:

> Joan sank down in the grass, and all her body made contact with the earth. Her breasts against the humus, her eyes on the growing plants, her hands buried to the knuckles in sod, the divine girl was imbibing, from living matter, its infinitesimal saps and essential principles, the scent of flesh and blood. She was lying in a state of relaxation that bordered in mysticism. Her body was half-incorporated in the very text of the Universe. Unspeakedly happy, she sucked an oat-straw. She was all appeal, desire and gift; and every pore of her skin, every orifice of her body seemed immensely open before the mystery life...
>
> [...]
>
> From all her person there emanated a sort of earthy magnetism. She was eighteen at the time and her splendid youth was in all its flower. Tall and robust, noble in bearing, with the features of a drunken angel, a wide sensuous mouth across her sanguine cheeks, the thick nose of Old-Testament mothers, a great mass of red hair on her head, her neck like a tower and her chin like a little child's: she was indeed a lovely girl, and greatly to be desired. There was a hint of malice at the corner of her lips, and a few tiny pimples on her country skin. Two monumental thighs supported the rich harmony of her body. Her ample shoulders seemed destined to support the realm of France in its entirety.

It is not difficult to see why such descriptions would arouse hostility from the Church – as had Voltaire's nearly two centuries earlier – but they did bring a welcome alternative to the seriousness and piety with which the newly canonised Joan was treated. Even if Delteil's decision to write about such a traditional theme caused the Surrealists to disown him, the richness of his writing and his turbulent imagination that had originally attracted him to them were still much in evidence. A final passage that deserves to be quoted is his description of Joan's burning. In it there is the same voyeurism that can be found in many of the films made about Joan, but there is also a power and realistic brutality in his description that leaves the reader in no doubt about the physical horror of such a form of execution:

> A thick, white, heavy smoke was mounting in suffocating columns. Suddenly, the first tongues of fire came licking at Joan's feet. This first contact with the flames, half tickle and half burn, made her hair rise with horror. The tongues of fire, growing longer and longer, more and more numerous, were now prowling about her body, shyly, as a tiger circles round a goat before it springs. Sparks were falling on her face, on her belly. Her feet were roasting. A horrible odour of burned flesh, of burned human flesh, caught Joan by the throat, and this odour was stronger than any pain. Already her kirtle was in flames. The placard with its strings glowing fell into the fire. Her shift was now burning up to the knees. Suddenly Joan perceived her bare knees, bare in the sight of 10,000 men. Her thighs were showing already. Then, the real torture began. Forgetting fire, torture and death, Joan thought only of her modesty, her virgin modesty. She was afraid of the fire because it was baring her body. A spark fell on her throat. The cloth caught fire and her breast slipped out, the lovely breast of a tall country girl. Below her the soldiers were nudging one another. 'Look, look!'. They began to chuckle. And the foul crowd was staring, with swinish eyes, at this spectacle of a virgin laid bare. Horrors! The thighs are naked to the waist. A spark set fire to her hair, and the high mass of it flamed up magnificently, then crumbled about her ears and shoulders, fell in black ashes across her bosom. Now her other breast was laid bare. All the old men in the crowd were feasting their eyes on these pink breasts, pricked with black burns. Joan grew desperate. Her eyes rolled emptily in their burned lashes. Ah, ah, she was naked before 10,000 men, 10,000 peeping Toms! Making a supreme effort she broke the cords which bound her arms. With her free hands, ah! those poor roasted hands, reddened with blood and fire, she struggled against the flames; no, against her nakedness. She hid her legs with fragments of cloth, plastered her breasts with bits of cord. But the flame was stealing it all, rag by rag, thread by thread. Obstinately she covered herself with morsels of burned fabric, with blackened embers; in spite of her efforts the flame swallowed everything. Then, she crossed her long arms over her body in a final attitude.... But now it was physical agony, the agonies of hell, which submerged this woman, submerged everything. She tried once more to cross her legs; the fire relaxed muscles and members. She was twisting in convulsive spasms. Little by little she was losing all strength, all feeling. Her thighs were burning, her breasts were burning. Her ears were burning. Her arms were burning. The white virgin was now only a black torch. She repeated, by starts, in the midst of great sighs 'Jesus... Mary... My God... My God...'. At this moment the last cord which bound her to the stake fell into the ashes. Joan tottered as if drunk, a sort of charred bacchante, naked and flayed, clawed by the nails of Satan. In a wild relaxation of her nerves she stretched out her arms; they were rigid and terrible. One fearfully unstable moment she remained in this position. Then she crumbled into the glowing coals. (pp. 257–261)

Delteil would return to Joan in 1927 with *La Passion de Jeanne d'Arc* in which his own love for her becomes very clear. In the Preface to this second book he writes: 'I love Joan of Arc. This is my principal reason for writing her life, and there is none other required. [...] Neither the dust of history nor the desiccating breath of Time can steal her living colours and her smile of flesh. No, she is not a legend, she is not a mummy.'

Interestingly enough Delteil's works do not appear to have prompted others of a similar kind. While Joan's youth and human qualities would continue to be underlined by some she now became appropriated by right-wing writers and intellectuals in various ways. As we have already seen Maurice Barrès had successfully promoted her as a national icon and called for an official holiday, but she was now acclaimed much more widely. One of the first voices to be heard was that of the Catholic novelist Georges Bernanos who published the first serious piece on Joan – and perhaps as a reaction to Delteil's extravagance – in the right-wing periodical, *La Revue hebdomadaire*, in 1928. (The essay would reappear as a book in 1934.) Before the War and up to the mid 1920s Bernanos was a staunch supporter of the Action française and while his views on the state of France and on ways in which it could be improved were less aggressive than those of Maurras and his political colleagues, he shared with them a nostalgia for 'la vieille France', in his case a kind of ideal feudal society in which a militant Christianity had a central place.

Jeanne, relapse et sainte is a powerful polemical piece in which, as in several other essays he wrote during his life, Bernanos deplores the loss of strict conservative and Catholic values. For him the answer to the growing mediocrity afflicting France was through a renewal of what he termed 'the spirit of childhood'. His essay opens with a tribute to Péguy, whose spiritualism he greatly admired, and a plea that henceforth Joan should 'belong only to children'. He sees her trial, condemnation and death as having been a victory for mediocre and self-protecting men; nor, he claims, is there anything to be admired in the rehabilitation. By recognising its earlier errors the Church was merely acting out of self-interest once again and not for France. Joan presented a challenge and a threat; despite becoming 'more feeble than a small child' under the pressure of interrogation, she remained true to what she believed in and was rewarded by God. Sainthood involves risk and struggle but is based essentially on innocence, by which Bernanos means that quality, inherent in a child, that resists compromise and corruption whatever the consequences and has been exemplified across the ages from St Bernard and St Francis to St Theresa of the Infant Jesus. Bernanos would soon break with the Action française, which as we know was condemned by the Pope Pius XI for not respecting true Catholic values, but his belief in Joan as the incarnation of those qualities that would restore France to her former greatness would never change. In his best-known novel, *Journal d'un curé de campagne* (1936), for example, two of the characters – Torcy, a priest, and Olivier – both express their belief in a militant Christianity and look to the Middle Ages as a time when it flourished and to Joan as its most perfect expression. Like some before him as well, Bernanos links Joan in this novel with the Virgin Mary.

Bernanos would soon be followed by others whose sympathy for right-wing values would be far more extreme and who, in some cases, would embrace the fascism that swept across much of Europe in the 1930s and welcome the Nazi presence in France after 1940. Of these the first to turn to Joan was Robert Brasillach when in 1932 – possibly inspired by performances of Shaw's play in Paris in 1929 and 1931 – he wrote a four-act play, *Domrémy*, on which he would continue to work for the next eleven years, finally producing in 1943 a revised version in which France is referred to as an occupied and divided country. In 1932 Brasillach was still a relatively minor if talented literary critic and essayist. Over the next decade he would become a major figure on the literary stage and also evolve politically, to become increasingly and violently anti-Semitic and embrace Nazism with enthusiasm. In February 1945, despite an appeal to De Gaulle for clemency by a number of major writers and intellectuals, he was tried and shot for his collaboration. But little of Brasillach's political or ideological persuasions colour his writing about Joan – any more in fact than they colour most of his fiction. In *Domrémy* Brasillach follows the traditional story and only in the last additions allows allusions to the contemporary situation to appear. For him, Joan, to quote Hauviette, is simply a 'great and marvellous person' whose freshness, gay personality and insolence he liked to think he shared, and given what he knew during the last months of his life was likely to be his fate, it is not surprising that he saw her as the victim of an 'ignoble farce'.

Joan five centuries later.

For many, however, the parallel that could be drawn between the fifteenth century and France in the 1940s was more explicit. The Vichy government presented Joan as the model spiritual child of rural France; Péguy's writings were recommended reading in schools, Shaw's *Saint Joan* enjoyed a season in the winter of 1941–2, and the oratorio *Jeanne d'Arc au bûcher*, with music by Arthur Honneger and words by Paul Claudel, toured the country in the summer of 1941. The figure of Joan and the values she represented also featured in or were clearly alluded to in much of the propaganda issued by Pétain's government. Even when it was clear that the Germans would be defeated many continued to see in her the only possible way forward. Alphonse de Chateaubriant, for example, would write in his pro-fascist newspaper *La Gerbe* as late as May 1944:

> The difficult times we live in now, in this very month, this very week, even today, draw us closer to her. A people who possess Joan of Arc are for ever protected against death.
>
> Everything about her was crystal clear. It is easy to see what it was like for this

> girl from the soil of France against the English – hard, self-centred people. She was like a gentle thought, she brought with her an atmosphere of freshness and grace, the light of Domremy.

And yet there was an obvious ambiguity in such use of Joan. In the fifteenth century she had after all defeated an occupying power but now being a perfect foil for Pétain's anglophobia, she became what Gabriel Jacobs has called 'an important double figure'.[5] The circumstances of those belonging to Resistance groups meant that any major exploitation of Joan as an anti-Nazi symbol was difficult. But with either the naivety or unconcern of both the Vichy authorities and more significantly the Nazi censors – evident too in the way both Anouilh's *Antigone* ('Antigone') (1942,3) and Sartre's *Les Mouches* ('The Flies') (1944) were allowed to have extended runs – an alternative interpretation of Joan produced some limited but interesting results.

The first example is Claude Vermorel's play *Jeanne avec nous* ('Joan with us'), which ran in Paris from January to August 1942, when the Nazi authorities finally decided to ban it. That it should enjoy a run even as long as this is a little surprising. Certainly the English (with the exception of Bedfort [*sic*]) are portrayed as brutal and bloodthirsty, but the French Church, with the exception of Ladvenu, is calculatingly self-seeking and willing to cooperate with them. (The parallel with the general collaborationist sympathies of the French Catholic Church in the 1940s is obvious.) The Inquisitor, the 'calculating policeman of faith', authorises and delights in the most horrendous tortures behind a mask of deep faith and humility. But Vermorel had written his play in 1938 and, as some reviewers pointed out, since the members of the Church address one another as 'comrades', it is possible that he had the Communists in his sights. 'Jeanne avec nous' had been the rallying cry of Blum's Popular Front government in the mid 1930s whose policies the Communists had refused on more than one occasion to ratify. A hardening of their position could also be reflected in such remarks as, for example, Cauchon's: 'In troubled times, comrades, the Church has had to take surgical action. When the anger has passed it can be more lenient.' Even if this had been Vermorel's original intention it is not difficult to see how his play could be adapted to the circumstances of 1942; in fact his director, George Douking had the actors playing the English soldiers click their heels Nazi fashion!

Whatever motivated Vermorel, his Joan is direct, fearless and witty; she is also aware of her own importance and is momentarily tempted by Bedfort when he offers her the command of the English army – an offer she quickly rejects however, such is her belief in freedom:

JEANNE: Don't think for a moment that I despise the people. I know them and I love them. All of them who want France to exist wherever French blood flows through the veins reject you.

BEDFORT *(ironically)*: The people of France? Do you think that they are so willing to take risks? These little shopkeepers who pull down their blinds at the slightest demonstration, these middle-class stay at homes already in mourning for their youth at the age of twenty-five, these stubborn, striking peasants shut in behind their fences, picking up bits of string, hating any kind of adventure. What France means is peace, carefulness, anarchy and egoism.

JEANNE: And these peasants who grab hold of their scythes as soon as anyone threatens their patch of land, these stubborn stay at homes who rise up in a crusade against slavery and injustice are a defeated, exhausted, uncertain people who at an order turn round and win the battle? France – that means, nerve, pride, heroism and brutality in the name of God.

BEDFORT: Jeanne, I came here unbeknown to my advisors and full of brotherly feelings. I still am like that. My offer is a sincere one. Accept it; I can change my mind you know.

JEANNE: That's just what I'm afraid of. You can display them like fruit you have to sell – you put those with the fewest worms at the front. (BEDFORT *tries to speak, his attitude hardening)* Would I trust those who deal with a prisoner illegally? (BEDFORT, *now violent, tries to speak again).* Are you really simple enough to think that I would accept? That I would tear myself away from my country to cling to yours? That my victories should be those at Crécy and Agincourt? That I would destroy my harvest before it had ripened? That I could suffer this double insult – jeers from my own people and your praise at the same time? There will only ever be one cause for me – the one I serve. I'll say it again and again – freedom. And again – freedom. And I will be free.

(Act III, 99, 100)

When, in 1945, *Jeanne avec nous* reopened it was immediately hailed as a 'resistance' play, but it remains something of a puzzle. Whether or not originally anti-Communist its ending suggests that Vermorel had a more ambitious purpose. By the last scene Joan is dead and the discussion of her death is accompanied by a storm. Bedfort recognises that her image will continue to develop in unforeseen ways. Who or what she was remains a mystery: 'Fifty years from now, if people talk about you, what kind of image will they give of you? Who were you? Did you even know yourself?' are the questions asked. At this point 'Joan' appears 'with flowers falling around her, her eyes closed, her hands clasped in prayer, wearing a straight dress and a helmet. She is all in white.' 'Joan' is a statue and to Bedfort's question 'Who is this woman?' the sculptor replies: 'She is Faith. I have carved her wearing this pure white dress like a stalk that is growing strongly. But she also wears a helmet: she represents true faith, warrior faith.' But to the Inquisitor's question: 'What did you think about Joan?', he replies: 'Which Joan? Which Joan of Arc?' There appears to be more than a hint of the ending to Shaw's play here. Joan has escaped from her role to become a symbol both of faith and of freedom. She is refusing to be browbeaten by authority, Communist or Nazi. It is hardly surprising that the 1945 production was well received, but it is a pity that *Jeanne avec nous* is not more widely known today.

Equally disappointing is the absence of any reference to Louis Auppegard's *Le Retour de la Sainte* first published in 1945 by Penguin in their French series but conceived and written much earlier. In 1940 Auppegard, a pseudonym for Louis Roché, was working at the French Embassy in Dublin, hoping to be transferred to London. This would eventually happen but meanwhile the idea for the play had already taken shape. In a letter to a friend he describes how this occurred:

> It was in August 1940, on my way back from London, that I had the idea for this play. I came back to Dublin, more sickened and more dispirited than ever by what I had just learned about the attitude of the ministers at Vichy and of the various French bishops. [...] On the boat from Holyhead to Kingston I was taken by the idea of preparing a broadcast [...] more or less on the following theme: if Joan of Arc were to appear in the unoccupied zone Pétain would have her arrested and Baudrillart would send her to the stake. I remembered later that Dostoievski in the *Brothers Karamazov* describes how Christ comes back to earth and is condemned by the Grand Inquisitor. But it was less originality that I was interested in than a truth that was both cruel and moving.

Roché wrote various drafts of his play during the next two years. There were three main characters: Jeanne Martin (Joan), the Connétable (Pétain) and the Cardinal Archbishop of Gergovie (Baudrillart). As he revised his text Joan became less overtly religious and the Connétable disappeared from the action to become an'off-stage' unseen authority referred to by his supporters or whose voice is heard on the radio. By 1942 the play was in its final version and there was talk of its being printed 'en petit format' (small format), but the project was dropped. (It is possible that this could have been a reference to the clandestine Editions de Minuit books of which the first, also appearing in 1942, was the celebrated *Le Silence de la mer* by Vercors.) In any event Roché's work remained unpublished until 1945, but when it appeared it contained a Preface written four years earlier and of which the final paragraph is a clear statement of his intent: 'the author has not sought to depict accurately circumstances which from exile he can only picture in his imagination. [The play] is rather a statement of faith in the French people expressed through a series of dialogues and short scenes.' With echoes of Péguy, the key words here are 'faith' and 'people'.

With its relatively fragmented form it is perhaps unlikely that it could have been successfully staged, though it seems that there was talk of its being made into a film. But what is remarkable about *Le Retour de la Sainte* is the way it champions and glorifies resistance almost before it had begun to be organised and Roché includes a Dedication to his fellow countrymen whose lives had been sacrificed:

> Victims of a ferocious enemy, you will be avenged! And when the day of Liberation comes we will go silently and with our children to the place of your execution [...] Glory be to those who refused to give in. Glory to those who faced torture and execution! Glory to those who sacrificed themselves so that men could be free in their souls and bodies, and about what they could see, hear, say and feel.

Jeanne Martin, the play's heroine, a 'young anarchist primary school teacher' arrives in the southern unoccupied zone from the industrial town of Roubaix in the north of France. Although it is never made absolutely explicit she is clearly the reincarnation of Joan that Roché had intended. (We learn in Scene xi that the real Jeanne Martin was killed as she left the north after the German invasion and is buried in the cemetery at Saumur.) She inspires the spirit of rebellion in those around her, has two 'miracles' attributed to her, is captured, sentenced to death, has the opportunity to recant but refuses and is shot. Those already with her and others who are encouraged by her to resist the occupying powers are never named; they are simply representatives of the true people of France – a labourer, a tax collector, a priest, a garage mechanic, a sewage worker, a peasant, a farmer's wife and so on. Similarly those who support the Connétable and his government are designated by their occupations – army officers, a civil servant, the cardinal's assistant, a policeman. The first scene, set in a small restaurant, opens with a broadcast by the Connétable:

> Citizens! Ever since I assumed control I have made myself convince you by all means possible that you have been utterly defeated. Having given up the period of rest to which I was fully entitled I have patiently sought ways of making you understand that you can only save yourselves by surrendering to the clemency of our conquerors. This gleam of light shines through our misfortune: full of generosity they have accepted to make you work. No longer can you waste time or stand around chatting. Your duty, for the sake of the nation, is to follow my advice. Accept this magnanimous offer. Overcome all your prejudices and preferences. Remember that you have been beaten and that those who have been beaten are not in a position to be difficult. Once again I give you this advice which, I regret to say, has not been followed up to now. Accept our conqueror's offer. Goodnight my friends.

A woman in the restaurant reacts immediately:

> What you have just heard is an act of treason. You will not follow the advice of this senile leader. You will not allow yourselves to become slaves. You will not allow yourselves to become contaminated by the rubbish that comes from this fake, deceitful sadness. You will not be beaten by the assurances of this old man who is proud because he had always believed in our defeat. You will not sink into despair. You will not accept despair as the only suitable attitude. Believe me! Don't

> believe our government. This government is full of the enemy's prisoners. It gives you orders based on decisions made in shame and it hasn't the courage to admit that it has given into and is obeying those who are stronger. Never before in our history, not even five hundred years ago has the French government sunk to such a low point.
>
> You know what your duty is. You must struggle against our enemy and our government at every moment and with all possible means in order to free France.

People in the restaurant applaud, with the exception of the civil servant who is indignant: 'It is shameful to speak of France in this way. That's how to bring even more misfortune. If we refuse to reconcile ourselves with the enemy we will be treated even worse.'

This is the scene in which Jeanne first appears and in which the debate is clearly laid out. The official government position is defended by the Cardinal Archbishop and in particular the commonly held view that the Occupation is a kind of punishment:

> It is precisely because France failed in its Christian mission that the world trembled. All the fine speaking in the world can't hide this fact. What?, you ask, what has France, that great nation done? France has been defeated! The music of pipes and drums sounds beneath her triumphal arches. Foreign soldiers contemplate the tombs of her former glory. France has been defeated because her ministers were cowards and her people unconcerned. France is gradually coming out of the grave where she was lying. Her face is covered in mud and the palms of her hands still bear the marks of stones. From her mouth there come neither cries of pride nor of demands. She looks for God and implores his pity. 'Lord, Lord', she cries, 'Do not look upon me!', because in her humiliation she is embarrassed. No, Jeanne Martin, France will not be saved and brought back to life by a few unscrupulous dynamiters.

By the end of Scene ix in conversation with a priest he is showing signs of doubt, however:

THE CARDINAL:	Do you remember, Father, there was a strange passion in that schoolteacher. We didn't pay enough attention to it. The way she stood up to me with such assurance exasperated me. I only saw a plan in the way she talked of God. I was wrong.
THE PRIEST:	There could be no doubt about her cunning though.
THE CARDINAL:	There is a much bigger problem. Everything you tell me shows that this woman has some kind of mystical hold over our people and especially the common people....
THE PRIEST:	Does your Eminence really believe that we have a religious problem?
THE CARDINAL:	Yes, I think so. That is why I'm asking you to say to the Connétable that I'm very sorry but I won't be able to go and see him until after tomorrow. I want to give myself time to think. Since he is keen to re-establish order he wants to be sure that he has the support of a Church dignitary.

THE PRIEST: The government will probably ask for a quick and spectacular intervention.
THE CARDINAL: That's what I'm afraid of.
THE PRIEST: I don't understand.
THE CARDINAL: It's not been proved after all that Jeanne Martin boasts that she is a reincarnation of Joan of Arc. Perhaps she is being manipulated by some clever propagandists. Perhaps she is a little mad. Ideas like this create problems that are not solved by the heavy-footed police and army.... I don't know whether you have thought of the most serious possibility, Father?
THE PRIEST: What is that?
THE CARDINAL: Who is to say whether one way or another Jeanne Martin isn't sincere?

In the final scene he attempts to persuade Jeanne to abjure: 'I can save you but on one condition. You must sign a paper recognising that you are an impostor and not St Joan, and that you regret having led so many good Catholic French people astray. Here is the paper! Sign it and you will be spared. You will have your name changed and you will leave for the colonies.' Unlike Joan, however, Jeanne refuses to sign and is so noble in her refusal that the Cardinal acknowledges that he could almost be persuaded to believe her; only his sense of position prevents him: 'If I were not careful Jeanne Martin, I'd end up believing that there is little more needed for you to achieve a kind of sainthood...'. He leaves and the play closes with a conversation between Jeanne and her gaoler and the prison almoner, before she is taken away to be executed. Like Joan's death five centuries earlier, hers is a confirmation of her inspiration and her sanctity:

THE GAOLER: Madame Martin, people don't make up stories to tell an old gaoler like me. It's not anarchists but patriots the government is rounding up.
JEANNE: You're right.
THE GAOLER: It's a sad thing for the country that they are going to shoot you.
JEANNE: No, there are thousands of men and women to take my place. In any case the Cardinal tried to save me at the government's request. Naturally I refused.
THE GAOLER: You refused! You were wrong. Nobody has ever seen a woman with as much courage as you have. What's more you're very intelligent. Yes, what you've done is very intelligent – to pass yourself off for Joan of Arc who has come back on earth.
JEANNE (*surprised*): Really?
THE GAOLER: Yes, because it got people excited and it was a bit of a mystery. Of course, it wasn't just anyone who could pass herself off for Joan of Arc. It had to be you. No one is like you. But with respect you ought to have listened to the Cardinal. Your arrest and condemnation haven't frightened anybody. In fact things are getting worse.
JEANNE: Thank you for saying that – it's what the Cardinal said to me. They

will carry on. My God, if there are any who have doubts about the victory make a strong wind blow across France after my death! It will be like a pack of wolves attacking robbers who think they are protected by darkness. It will be like a song of freedom that will sweep across France from door to door.

THE GAOLER: Madame Martin, you've got plenty of guts.

JEANNE: See how God has organised everything. Fate is against the Connétable.

THE GAOLER: I would have liked him to change your death sentence for life imprisonment. You could have seen what happened then. Who knows?

JEANNE: That was impossible though. The government knew it. And even if they had shut me up away from towns in a deserted place surrounded by barbed wire and guarded by several police units, the French would have found a way of seeing the edge of a roof, the end of a lightening conductor or smoke rising above the trees or the crest of a hill. So it's better they kill me as quickly as possible even without knowing who I am. The government would have preferred to avoid the problem but couldn't. My death was like a forced card and has been played. The end is coming.

THE GAOLER: Don't speak to me about it any more!

JEANNE: You must only think about freedom. The patriots will win. Think about the great wind that will blow across all France.

THE GAOLER: Madame Martin, I'm not particularly religious but I think you are a kind of saint. (*He listens.*) I can hear steps. I'll go and look. (*He leaves. The door opens a moment later and the prison chaplain appears.*)

THE CHAPLAIN: Madam Martin, I fear the moment is not far off.... (*He stops at the entrance to her cell.*) I am the prison chaplain. I've often helped those condemned to death – they said they were your friends – with what little help I could give them. If I can be usful to you in any way I'll be happy to do so.

JEANNE: Come in, Father.

THE CHAPLAIN: Don't call me 'Father'.

JEANNE: Isn't that the way you speak to a confessor?

THE CHAPLAIN: I haven't come to hear your confession.

JEANNE: Don't I have the right to confess?

THE CHAPLAIN: It's not for me to hear the confession of a saint.

JEANNE: What, you?

THE CHAPLAIN: Yes, I know you are a saint.

JEANNE: You believe in this criminal adventurer, this anarchist schoolteacher?

THE CHAPLAIN: You are a saint.

JEANNE: But you, a priest, you think that...

THE CHAPLAIN: Of course you're not what people have said you are, Joan of Arc reincarnated. That's impossible. But just as Christ inspired saints throughout the world, Joan can inspire sainthood in the heart of a young French woman. In you there is something of the spirit of Joan.

JEANNE: Sometimes I've believed that. But don't deceive yourself. I'm not a saint. I'm only a woman who loves her country.

THE CHAPLAIN: No, I've been there when your friends have died and only a saint could have inspired that faith. And they have given it to me.

JEANNE: Oh! your faith touches me.

THE CHAPLAIN (*kneeling*): I believe that you will free France just as Joan of Arc did five hundred years ago.

JEANNE: Little priest, how many times have I followed you on your bicycle? With your cassock badly tucked up you struggled up the hills in summer. The horse flies clung to your clothes and the sun beat down cruelly on your neck. Or in winter in an icy wind you would run to see the sick. Or again, you would travel on the wooden seats of third-class carriages, holding you bag close to you and taking your well-worn rosary out.

THE CHAPLAIN: Jeanne Martin, deliver us!

JEANNE: Little priest of France, son of the people, I have followed you in all your difficulties. It's not easy being a priest in this country. It's not a job you take on because you're interested or can't think of anything else. You have to have a real vocation. How many times have I seen you go through the working-class areas with the roofers and builders calling you names or imitating the cries of rooks? How many times have I seen you speaking nicely about the wine harvest or the apple crop to peasants whose suspicion you could sense. How many times have I seen you knock timidly at the door of the chateau or the lawyer's. You had to ask for money and people weren't polite to you but rather protective. And you never dared say how much you needed. And they gave you less than the last time. And you know that when the door was shut they would talk about the savings made in your parish and lavish hypocritical approval on your holiness.

Little priest of France, how simply you told the children about the saint who was burned alive. With children it was easy, but there were others who called themselves free thinkers, the schoolmaster who never set foot in the church and all those coarse noisy men in their mourning clothes who, at burial services, stayed outside the church while their wives went in for the absolution alone.

THE CHAPLAIN: None of that's important... (*embarrassed*) Don't talk about that at the moment when....

JEANNE: The moment when I'm about to die! But, yes! It does me good to talk about it.

THE CHAPLAIN: Up to the last moment you think about others more than about yourself. You really are a saint.

JEANNE: Not long ago I was terribly afraid of dying. It was in vain that I showed courage in front of the Cardinal or the gaoler. I was horribly afraid. But now I feel stronger. I'm still afraid, like an animal who is going to be killed, but I know that what I have done will not die with me.

THE CHAPLAIN: No, the patriots will continue to follow you.

JEANNE: You are the last person I can talk to. You represent all those who have followed me from the start or who have been inspired by feelings rather than by calculations. I seem to see them all from my cell – Rémy, Big Mouth, the mechanic, the Latin teacher, the tax collector... I am leaving all of them! I will never see them again....

THE CHAPLAIN: Saint Jeanne, I can't stand the idea that...

JEANNE: Don't despair, little priest! You believed in me. (*She stands up.*) You believed in me before you saw me. You have the faith of those simple people who entrust you with their last regrets and their last enthusiasms. It's that faith that will count. Stand up and be brave! Your faith has helped me.

THE CHAPLAIN: Saint Jeanne, may God bless you and satisfy all your wishes.

JEANNE: The day will come. (*They hear steps.*)

THE CHAPLAIN: I'm afraid.... (*The door opens.*)

JEANNE: Yes, they are coming for me.

THE GAOLER (*very emotional*): Madame Martin, I don't know what to say... but you understand...

JEANNE: Yes, I understand.

(*A number of officials and gaolers come into the cell silently.*)

THE GAOLER (*in a low voice*): Look, I'm not the only one who is sad.

JEANNE (*turning round*): May God keep you! (*The chaplain wants to follow her. Joan stops him.*)

JEANNE: No, stay here. They have more need of you. (*To the gaolers.*) The day will come! (*She goes out. The gaolers do not move, looking towards the open door. The old gaoler leans on the table. The sound of steps fades away, and then there is silence. The chaplain kneels. Suddenly there is the sound of a shot.*)

THE GAOLERS (*with a heavy voice*): Long live France! Long live Jeanne Martin!

THE CHAPLAIN: Saint Jeanne! Saint Jeanne! (*The gaolers look at the chaplain in astonishment. Then a strong wind blows through the prison. Doors bang and locks whistle. There is the sound of a widow being broken.*)

A GAOLER: What a wind!

JEANNE'S GAOLER: The wind!... The wind!... (*shouting*) She said so... The wind! The wind! Saint Joan of Arc! Ah! I thought so, she was a real saint!

Notes

1. See *Œuvres Poétiques complètes*, Pléiade, Gallimard, Paris, 1941.
2. *Charles Péguy*, Bowes and Bowes, London, 1965, 17.
3. Copy held in the Centre Jeanne d'Arc.
4. The translation of Delteil's book is by Malcolm Cowley (Allen and Unwin, London, 1926). Several small passages have been omitted.
5. 'The Role of Joan of Arc on the Stage of Occupied Paris' in Roderick Kedward and Roger Austin (eds), *Vichy France and the Resistance*, Croom Helm, London and Sydney, 1985, 106.

Chapter Six

Retrials . . . and a Myth Renewed

When, after the Liberation, courts were set up across France to put on trial those who had been guilty of collaboration, Joan's story again became popular. The period known as the *épuration* ('purging') saw persecutions sometimes as bad as those witnessed under the Nazis, as people settled old scores or sought revenge. Writers who had published in periodicals and newspapers sympathetic to Nazism or who had been openly in favour of the regime were blacklisted by the Communist dominated Comité national des écrivains (National committee of writers); publishing houses that had produced their works were boycotted and eminent publishers like Bernard Grasset or Gaston Gallimard put on trial. By 1952 an official truce was declared by parliament but trust had been betrayed and much bitterness inevitably remained, and for many of those who suffered, a sense of acute victimisation. Furthermore this was the period when existentialism came to dominate French intellectual life with popular books like Camus's novel *La Peste* ('The Plague') (1947) and his essay *L'Homme révolté* ('The Rebel') (1951) examining the lot of the individual alone and responsible for his actions in a hostile world. No play better exemplifies this than *Jeanne et ses juges* ('Joan and her judges') by Thierry Maulnier written in January 1949 and performed in May in front of Rouen cathedral.

Maulnier originally intended to write a chronicle of Joan's exploits from Domremy to Rouen but, as he explains in a preface written two years later, he had to abandon this when faced by a number of material concerns - budget, space, time available and so on. Instead he concentrates on the crucial moment of Joan's trial - her recantation and subsequent volte-face - and the result is a remarkably dense work which, whatever its limitations as drama, not only takes us to the heart of Joan's personal dilemma but raises as well substantial political and philosophical issues. 'It is certain', writes Maulnier, 'that of all the episodes in an extraordinary life which begins as a fairy tale, develops into a national epic and finishes with as complete an imitation of Christ's passion as a human being has ever been asked to bear, it is the trial, the sublime and hideous trial that provides us with the dramatic action of the most vital and present kind.' Already the title provides us with a clue. Although Maulnier makes it clear that Joan's judges are men of the Catholic Church but in the pay of the English, to refer to them as '*the* judges' and not '*her* judges', and moreover for them to remain anonymous, gives them a timeless quality. The fact too that he reduces their number to just three is not just a convenience for the production. It focuses our attention on Joan as an individual and on the sense of justice much more sharply. What Maulnier sets out to present is 'quite simply the mechanism of justice or of injustice in all its quasi-abstract bareness' whose aim is either 'to crush the solitary, cornered individual or to get him to deny himself and what he believes in.' With a barely concealed reference to the courts of the *épuration*, Maulnier goes on to compare Joan's trial with those of Antigone, Socrates and Jesus:

> It is always the same trial in which society sets out to stifle in an unusual and hence dangerous individual any glimmer of freedom, of charity, of courage or of love perceived as a threat. Joan had to appear not only in front of 'her' judges but 'the' judges, in front of the judges who today force submission from revolt, an acknowledgement of unworthiness from honour, of error from innocence, lies from truth. Joan had to appear in front of the judges who might judge us tomorrow, and today pass judgement while we remain silent, indifferent, complicitous or terrorised. Joan had to appear in front of the tribunal responsible for eternal injustice. [...] There would be no point in enacting Joan's trial yet again unless at the moment when she is crushed, the cry of the rebellious and imprisoned child cuts through the comfortable silence in which we wrap ourselves, to remind us to the point of anguish that this silence is not comfortable, that Joan's sentence, her resistance and her torture are taking place near us and matter to us, just as if she were being killed tonight under our windows. We must not sleep. We must not sleep....
>
> [...]
>
> We should not forget that in Rouen there were not only the full public hearings. We see too much of these. We do not see enough of the prosecution office, of the police interrogations, of the interminable days and nights the accused spends within four walls, utterly alone with only himself to rely on, driven into a corner by tiredness, insomnia and close to seeing any distinction between what is true and what is false disappear. He has to confront the small team of specialists whose task it is to get him to surrender his freedom and turn him into a docile beast ready to confess and to repent in public.

Maulnier goes on to point out that while Joan may not have been tortured physically, she was submitted to interrogation techniques that have barely changed over five centuries, and for the purposes of comparison makes a specific point of targeting the trials taking place in the Communist block:

> If we can judge by the major political trials taking place in the East, there are physical, chemical, biological and psychological means of getting the accused to say whatever you want him to say, without causing him any obvious damage. Apart from that Joan's judges behaved just like modern ones. Their technique is based

> on harassment, unending repetition and monotony. They ask her hundreds of questions that are often pointless and absurd [...] Everything invites us to think that the apparent incoherence of the way the trial was conducted was in fact quite deliberate and similar to those today where the police carries out its tasks in the ordinary way: namely to harass the person who has been arrested until he gives in.

What Maulnier sets out to show in his play therefore is how Joan is worn down by her trial, how gradually her conviction that her voices have truly come from God is shaken. The real Joan is not the courageous, unshakeable heroine and model 'for pious statues, for the Place des Pyramides, for national holidays.' Joan is not superhuman but human; a normal young woman who is tired, confused and above all afraid. If she clings to her belief that 'my voices told the truth. My mission came from God. The king I serve is the true king', it is only in increasing desperation, and in turn this belief will crumble before the sheer horror of being burned alive. And Joan recants. This takes us to the heart of the play, both for its portrayal of Joan and for its relevance for Maulnier's discussions in the Preface of trials, justice and injustice. Whoever their paymasters were, the judges also represent the Catholic Church. To have Joan recant therefore means that their conscience is clear. What they thought

> as they slipped between the sheets was probably not "The humiliation of that slut was good to see", nor even "We've done what we were ordered to do. Will we be paid for our soft attitude?", nor above all else "It's a pity we haven't had the pleasure of seeing her burn", but rather: "The poor child. We've saved her from the ultimate peril. May God take note of that." And they fell asleep in the bliss of knowing they had performed a good deed.
>
> But the judges were not the principal actors. For those who truly pulled the strings what was important was not that Joan should repent but that she should acknowledge she had not been telling the truth. Christian contrition does not, in any case, call for so much fuss to be made about the repentance of criminals and witches. [...] The trial was as politically motivated as any could be and if there had ever been any doubt, that quickly became clear. But more than being specifically a political trial, it was one of propaganda and to be exploited as such – and if we are to appreciate that more clearly we need to look at it from a modern perspective.
>
> Today we have trials aiming at recantation and we know that it is not so easy not to recant. The aim of these trials is to make those accused, by persuasion, by threats, by torture, by tiredness, by drugs – or by all of them together – to deny what he has believed in, to dishonour himself by renouncing the cause he has served and to become a weapon to be used by those accusing him against others who will be accused later. [...] Political prisoners today are not killed. I mean they are only killed later and the murder becomes part of the propaganda: it has no purpose other than to prove that a confession was made freely, that it was not bought, that there was no promise of being allowed to live, that there was no collusion between the accusers and the accused. What is important is that the cause being persecuted does not acquire martyrs, that there are no heroes to produce more heroes and that every blow given to those it is wished to silence

> discourages them a little more, makes them feel ashamed. Joan's trial is the forerunner of our modern political ones. Her judges' objective was not so much that Joan should disappear but that she should deny herself.

Given this unremitting pressure what is all the more remarkable about Joan therefore is that she should suddenly reject her recantation. Yet her readopting of male garments has nothing to do with her being tricked by her persecutors, says Maulnier, rather it is an act of free will, emblematic of 'that reassertion of oneself that the non-believer will perhaps call the ultimate expression of human freedom and the believer, the revelation of God's grace.' (In the play Joan will claim that she alone is responsible: 'What I have done, I have done freely'(Part 2, Scene xii).) Here Maulnier moves from his bitter indictment of politically motivated trials to the psychological and philosophical dimensions of Joan's decision, refusing to allow anything external to aid her – even her voices. Having stressed how utterly abandoned Joan has been during her trial, he now questions her repeated claim that she was being guided by her voices. The only evidence we have for this is Joan's word and to accept it unquestioningly provides too easy an explanation and, moreover, is a weakness in terms of dramatic tension:

> For the ending of this unbelievable story I will not be satisfied with a rather obvious *deus ex machina*, with this poor theatrical device whereby three heavenly counsellors arrive in front of the downcast Joan on a sunbeam in order to reproach her for having recanted and to give her courage. It is important for me that Joan discovers the strength to remain unbending inside herself and not in three supernatural tutors.

In the play we see the saints and we hear them speak, but whatever pity they feel for Joan on Saint Michael's orders they do not respond to her cries for help. She must be shown to be – or at least to feel – utterly abandoned. God, if God exists, has left her to make her decision alone:

> Who cannot see that the extraordinary effort by which she rises from the depths of despair to the highest point in the legend of human achievement must be attributable to her and to her alone, and that God has left her free to choose or refuse death? Who cannot see that she is only what she is if she has been privileged to experience not the greatest security but the greatest possible anguish, and that if God chose her he made this test for her as hard as possible.

All Joan has to rely on therefore is her certainty in the divine nature of her mission, in other words her faith: 'God's presence has to be seen as God's absence. God has to be with Joan and yet as if he were not. She alone must choose her way.' In this she reminds us strongly of Anouilh's Antigone:

> Thus it is only in the hours following the recantation, and because there has been the recantation, that we get to the core of this tragedy which is, if we may

call it so, a perfect emptiness. Defeated, abandoned by her king and his companions in arms, forgotten by her people and left by her heavenly counsellors, prisoner of the English, overwhelmed by fear and by fatigue so weak is her body, and overwhelmed in her ignorance by her judges' language, Joan still had within her the strength not to yield. She struggled and from that struggle, mysteriously, came hope; "I've not denied anything yet. That's another day gained. They want that of me and they won't get it. Right up to the fire." The passionate determination not to change is the most basic and profound affirmation of oneself, a strength that is cunning and almost animal-like which scorns life and is essential for the armed and unarmed soldier alike and without which there can be no heroism on the battlefield or martyrdom. Obstinacy – the obstinacy of this hardy little peasant, of this stubborn girl from the east of France was enough to keep her from capitulating. But her public repentance in the Saint-Ouen cemetery broke this determination and her last reason for resisting. Joan was no longer simply abandoned; she had abandoned herself, Joan had abandoned Joan. (In the play Maulnier has Joan come to this decision, not in a monologue but in conversation with her double, 'the other Joan' (Part 2, Scene xi).) From that moment on the condemned girl was separated from her past, from everything that had driven her on: she had no goal to aim for, no path to follow, no freedom to claim, no dignity to save, no reason to be this rather than that. Emptiness was not only all around her, it was inside her and had absorbed her. She was nothing any more [...] and it is precisely from this nothing, from this dead, cold, dark world that the flash of revolt bursts out. A divine miracle? Perhaps. But the miracle is only worthy of God if first and foremost it has been worked by the person herself, if she has it within her to decide in an instant, alone and without help, to climb back up the path she has come down.

As a believer himself, Maulnier appears tacitly to accept that ultimately Joan was divinely inspired but, as we have seen, refuses to allow her any help other than what she can draw from the resources, spiritual and psychological, that she possesses within herself. Only at the very end of the play as she is being taken through the streets of Rouen, does Saint Michael finally agree that the saints may go to support her. This results in a scene in which Maulnier brings Joan's crisis to breaking point and interiorises it completely.

SAINT CATHERINE, SAINT MARGUERITE, SAINT MICHAEL

CATHERINE: We should go to her. That's intolerable.

MARGUERITE: She's been waiting for us at night, alone and unable to sleep, and we don't answer her. Look at her. Questions fly around her and daze her. Sometimes she is threatened, sometimes traps are laid for her. She is confused with theological argument, she hesitates, she pulls herself together again, she weakens and only with difficulty picks herself up again. She no longer knows what she is saying or what she should say. She looks around her, looking for us. Look at her!

CATHERINE: We were there for her in her father's garden to show her the difficult path she had to follow. We were there when she first went to the king. We didn't fail her at Poitiers with the Doctors, nor in the councils when it was difficult to distinguish between good and bad advice, nor in battle, nor at the coronation, nor when things went wrong at Compiègne, nor in the tower at Beaurevoir. And now she has been alone for eighty-six days, alone in front of this powerful and relentless court united against her. Alone in the middle of this town inhabited by her enemies, abandoned by the king she loves, by the country she has served. And the entire Church is united against her. Here she is harassed and tormented, her forehead damp with anguish, no longer knowing whether she is right. We are her last hope, the hope she despairs of, and she can only resist because of this hope and it is slipping through her fingers. Why, at the last and when the worse is just beginning, does the hardest blow have to come from us?

MARGUERITE: She is struggling. She is struggling and lying boldly. Listen to her: 'Yes, I can hear my saints. Yes, they come to me in prison every night. I'll take their advice this evening so that I can answer you.' To make them believe it she almost believes it herself. She carries this lie in her heart like a mother carries her dead child so that it doesn't become cold too quickly: 'I can hear them. I hear them almost every hour.' But are we going to let her go to her death for a king who has forgotten her, for a people who insult her, for a mission that no-one else will take on and for her voices that have fallen silent?

CATHERINE: Archangel, you must help her!

MARGUERITE: Archangel, let us go to her.

MICHAEL: You will not go near her.

MARGUERITE: She is only a child of the earth, surrounded by evil and we love her.

MICHAEL: There was a child of the earth who was the son of God, and God let him be taken by soldiers to the scaffold where he was nailed limb by limb. He made no sign and he loved him.

CATHERINE: Have you no pity for her?

MICHAEL: You are just women! I pity her.

MARGUERITE: Does she have to suffer to this degree?

MICHAEL: I pity her but she must face her pursuers who have tracked her down and have cornered her. Her heart has to tremble like a bird that is being squeezed to death. She must wring her hands, cry in the night and call and call and call and get no answer. She has to see the last glimmer of hope disappear. I pity her. But she must die horribly, her body bitten all over by the snake-like flames. I do pity her.

CATHERINE: That's a hard kind of pity.

[...]

MICHAEL: For what has still to be done she must be responsible. This is the moment when she is to be weighed on earth for heaven. It must be her weight alone. Don't upset the scales.

CATHERINE: What can a poor human creature do without heaven's help?

MICHAEL: Why would free will have been given to man if he never used it? There are moments in every man's life when the hand on his shoulder is taken away, when all voices cease, when he has to take a decision and without God's help. He doesn't know but God is weighing him up. Everything would be too easy if we were always there to say: 'Go right, go left, go on, stop'. That moment has come for Joan when she is wholly responsible for herself and it is as though

God were not there. We have helped her. We helped her at Domremy, at Orléans, from Orléans to the coronation, and our help was in keeping with the prodigious task for which she had been selected. For what remains to be done she alone, hear me well, she alone is responsible; the merit or the fault will be hers. Everything that now concerns her rests in her poor, shackled hands. She will be worthy or unworthy, she will bear it or be a coward. Be quiet, you are no longer part of the game. Now is the time for human free will and we can do nothing for her. We can't relieve her of her burden without damaging her. God is simply an onlooker.

(Part 2, Scenes iv and ix)

L'AUTRE JEANNE: When will you stop moaning and looking for help? No one is going to come; you've nothing to wait for. You are the one people are waiting for. Don't think about what is supporting you but what you carry. If you fall everything will fall. Man stands firm because of the burden he bears.

JEANNE: So much misfortune is on me...

L'AUTRE JEANNE: Use it to become stronger.

JEANNE: So much tiredness...

L'AUTRE JEANNE: Use it to become stronger.

JEANNE: So much shame.

L'AUTRE JEANNE: Use it to become stronger. (She goes to her to help her stand. Jeanne weakly tries to resist.) Do you think you can resist me? I can see you – bruised, beaten down, your eyes dimmed, your cheeks salt with tears. You poor human creature overwhelmed by tiredness, sleep and fear. Come on now, you can't struggle with me as Jacob did with the angel because you know you would be thrown down.

JEANNE: What do you want of me?

L'AUTRE JEANNE: You went straight to your king who didn't know that he was king, and you recognised him so that he would recognise himself. I came to you who didn't know that you were Jeanne and you recognised yourself.

JEANNE: I'll say what my king said then: "What do I have to do?"

L'AUTRE JEANNE: You led your king to Rheims so that he could be crowned. I am going to lead you to your coronation. He had his in Rheims, you will have yours in Rouen.

JEANNE: What coronation can a poor girl like me have?

L'AUTRE JEANNE: One more brilliant than the finest royal one. What flames will illuminate it! You will be queen, Jeanne, and take your place with the martyred saints. Queen for all those, alone and distraught, who are summoned before the judges for political reasons or out of revenge. Queen for all those people being killed across the world. Queen of the gagged, defeated and oppressed people. Queen of those tortured or in prison [...]

(Part 2, Scene xi)

Taken together, Maulnier's Preface and play make almost as powerful a statement as Shaw's had done thirty years earlier. While the play may lack the Irish writer's wit and while the characters are often too wooden and little more than declaimers of their creator's ideas, the play was a success. From the opposite end of the political spectrum and six years after *Jeanne et les juges*, Janine Bouissounouse – in ignorance or defiance of Maulnier's play? – produced her *Jeanne et ses juges*, published by the Communist funded Les Éditeurs français réunis. While the play follows Joan's story faithfully, Bouissounouse's 'Avant-propos' spells out its political intention unambiguously:

> The last war, the occupation and the armed uprising of the people give an immediate relevance to Joan's struggle and her martyrdom. Never has the story of the young peasant girl who obeys her voices and leaves her village to crown her king and chase the foreigner from the land been so meaningful to us who also lived in a France swamped by invasion, abandoned by those whose duty it was to defend her, and handed over to the enemy. Is the similarity not striking? The suffering and anger of the people, the treachery of our leaders, the actions of the partisans, the maquis, repression, torture, executions, a willingness to slander and dishonour our patriots and their cause....

In 1955 the political weight of the French Communist Party was declining rapidly as it became politically outmanoeuvred internally and as the Cold War gained momentum. Whether Bouissounouse wrote her play to help revive the Party's reputation by reminding people of the heroic role many of its members had played during the resistance, or whether it is simply a celebration of Joan, is impossible to say. Whatever her reasons, it would be one of if not the last play to take inspiration quite so directly from recent political events, but unlike Maulnier's it fails to develop any serious philosophical dimension, with the result that all too frequently it reads like a work driven by the Party's directives on art and literature that had been in place for the best part of the previous decade.[1]

Nonetheless eminently suitable as it was for adaptation to the immediate circumstances in France during the post-Liberation years, it is hardly surprising that Joan's story should have been used to reflect them. Even Jean Anouilh, arguably the leading French playwright of the time, who in 1953 produced his play, *L'Alouette*, would not be able – or would not choose – to avoid this. But there was one important exception. In 1950 Jacques Audiberti had written a different and certainly one of the most inventive plays about Joan in which he focuses less on the historical details and more on how such a story is regenerated across the ages.

Pucelle has three sections (*tableaux*) and a Prologue. Joan is projected through two characters: as Jeannette, a peasant girl courted by and eventually married to Mathieu and as Joannine who is to become the legendary Joan who *already* exists. When she is not sitting silently Jeannette leads the simple life Joan would have known as a child; Joannine is loud, strong and familiar with her social superiors and given to manic laughter. Within the play set ten years after Joan's death – and what we can call the 'frame play' – there is to be a representation of Joan's life written by one of the characters of the 'frame play', Gilbert de Nugy, and performed by a troop of strolling players. His – and Audiberti's – brief explanation is revealing: 'Gradually people have believed that she was condemned and burnt. [...] I have accepted this and adapted it for the mystery play by these strolling players. [...] The past must re-emerge. Now perhaps I'll understand the past and finish it.' One of Audiberti's concerns therefore appears to be the way in which historical legends are conceived and developed. At the same time, in the 'frame play', he has Joannine herself reflect on this and on the way she has, as a result, become utterly alone: 'When I am all alone I call myself the 'late Joan'. None the less I'm immortal because I am already dead.' At this point in the second *tableau* she is about to leave, presumably for Chinon, and she remarks to De Nugy:

> I'm leaving. Your words and then those of officers, Dominicans and artists have refined the image of me. You have built up a picture of me. I have no resistance left. I'm going off to be like myself. I'm leaving in glory to become that great blue and golden slut you pestered me into becoming. [...] I'm only a puppet created by those chasing after me.

Immediately following this Jeannette and Joannine fall into conversation:

JEANNETTE:	Wait a minute. I'm you. Every time your friends are not there to look after you I'm you. I'm the daughter of this small peasant household. I'm you. And you are me.
JOANNINE:	I don't dispute that. I'm the daughter of this small peasant household. I'm you. And you're me.

And when Joannine threatens to kill Jeannette the latter is quick to point out: 'Don't you see, if I die, you die.'

The third *tableau* returns to the performance of the De Nugy's mystery play, observed by Jeannette and Mathieu. The actors due to interpret the parts of Joan and the Executioner have inexplicably disappeared and Jeannette is chosen as a substitute, a move that immediately reintroduces the issue of truth and legend. One spectator asks:

> If this woman is really the one who fought at Orléans and yet as everything indicates she has never left her village, how could she have been both here and far away? And what is more, if she was burned ten years ago how is it that we see her in flesh and blood now?

The play begins but gets out of hand; theatre becomes reality and Jeannette is burned alive. De Nugy is powerless to stop it: the legend has been created out of history, but it has suddenly become real. 'The execution is taking place before my eyes and for me,' he observes. But while Jeannette may have died, Joannine – or her image – descends from the scaffold and instantly becomes statuesque, as the stage directions indicate: 'She stretches out. The bells sound. She becomes transfixed.' She has become the image of the legend that will develop over the next five centuries. And at the very end of the play the directions send the spectator/reader back to the beginning for the process to start again.

The creation, then, and the regenerative, cyclical nature of legends – a subject Audiberti treats in other plays such as *La Fourmi dans le corps* (1962) or *La Guillotine* (1964) – appear to be his central concerns. But *Pucelle* also has a sinister dimension. In the Prologue, the play within the play is awaited by Joan's former squire who lost both his arms during battles ten years earlier. That incident will be infinitely repeated; like all other aspects of the Joan legend, escape or change is impossible.

For all its originality Audiberti's play enjoyed no great success – no doubt at least in part a reflection of unwillingness on the part of the French to have one of their greatest stories or their own conservatism challenged. But with Anouilh things would be quite different.

Already with *Antigone* (1944) he had exploited an equally well-known mythological story to produce a deeply moving play in which unyielding integrity and human dignity confront compromise and opportunism. (He would explore similar themes in plays like *Pauvre Bitos ou le dîner de têtes* (1956) and *Becket ou l'honneur de Dieu* (1960).) Translated into English in 1955 by Christopher Fry as *The Lark*, *L'Alouette* bears traces of a number of earlier 'Joan' plays, notably those by Shaw (which Anouilh had translated) and Vermorel.[2] It has a clear comment to make about recent trials both in France and abroad, and is not without traces of Audiberti's work. But as his title suggests Anouilh also aims to provide something different – fresh, natural, ethereal. Like Shaw's play in particular, but also in a way like Audiberti's, *L'Alouette* begins with the outcome already known. It differs fundamentally from *Saint Joan* though by its depiction of episodes of Joan's life that are more usually simply alluded to – her home life and her relationship with her father or her meeting with Baudricourt, for example. She does not leave home because she told to do so by divine voices, but in order to avoid being forced into marriage. The effect of this is to emphasise early on that Joan is an ordinary creature of flesh and blood. Her greeting to La Hire, for example, is one of earthy comradeship, but in which there is a strong hint of sexuality: 'You smell good La Hire, you smell like an animal, like a man.' Throughout the play Anouilh refrains from depicting her – or even suggesting that she is – spiritually superior or marked out already for sainthood, even if we know that she is one of his noble beings who refuse compromise. But in no way does this diminish the tragic inevitability of the play. The events of Joan's life are 're-enacted' in the courtroom; we know what will happen to her and as Cauchon observes: 'We can only take our turn to play our parts be they good or bad as they have been written for us'; nothing can be altered and it is vital that Joan should be seen – as in the plays by Vermorel and Maulnier – as a simple individual conscience struggling against blinkered ideology and all-powerful institutions. In this way Anouilh too is reflecting on the events of the previous decade of French history (as he will in *Pauvre Bitos*), only less precisely than his predecessors. A conversation between Cauchon and Warwick illustrates this well:

> CAUCHON: Although we collaborated wholeheartedly with the English regime it seemed, given the chaos, the only reasonable solution at the time. We could have saved some of our poor honour by attempting to do the impossible against you, living off your money and with your eight hundred soldiers outside the courtroom. It was all very well for those in Bourges, protected by the French army, to say we had sold out! We were in occupied Rouen!
>
> WARWICK (*irritated*): I don't like the word 'occupied'. You forget the Treaty of Troyes. Quite simply you were on his majesty's lands.
>
> CAUCHON: Surrounded by his Majesty's soldiers and with his Majesty's hostages being executed, obliged to observe a curfew and subject to his Majesty's rationing.... We were men and fondly imagined we could live and try to save Joan as well. It was a sorry state of affairs for us in any case.

We hear a similar echo of the past in Cauchon's words to Joan:

> Joan, listen to me and try to understand. Your king is not our king. A proper and correct treaty has made Henry VI of Lancaster King of France and England. This trial is not a political matter... All we are doing with all our strength and faith is to bring a stray sheep back into the fold of our Mother Church. But even so Joan, we are men and consider ourselves to be the subjects of King Henry, and our love for France – which is as great and as sincere as yours – make us recognise him as our lord so that France will rise from her ruins, dress her wounds and finally get out of this dreadful, never-ending war that has been draining her of blood. The vain resistance of the Armagnac clan and the ridiculous ambition of the one you call your king to have a throne that is not his – all of this is an act of rebellion and terrorism against a peace that was almost certain. The puppet you have served is not our lord, understand that.

Like Shaw, Anouilh endeavours to make Cauchon sympathetic, but less to justify the Church's position in the fifteenth century in the way the Irish playwright had done, than to throw into sharp relief the bigoted and hysterical Promoteur and sinister Inquisitor, determined to discover heresy at all costs. (Not only can this be read as an allusion to the anti-Semitic purges of the Occupation and to the trials of the *épuration*, but also to the anti-Communist witch-hunts that were gathering pace in America in the early 1950s.) Against them all, however, Joan expresses a faith in the fundamental goodness of man:

PROMOTEUR: What have you given your prince in Chinon for him suddenly to take courage? Does it have a Hebrew name? The Devil speaks every language but has a soft spot for Hebrew.

JOAN (*smiling*): No, sir, it has a French name and you have just used it yourself. I gave him courage, that's all.

CAUCHON: And you think that God, or the power you think is God's, has nothing to do with it?

JOAN (*radiant*): I think God is there all the time, my lord Bishop. When a young girl speaks two words of good sense and people listen, it's because God is there. God is cautious. When two words of good sense are enough he's not going to the expense of a miracle.

LADVENU (*gently*): That is a good and humble reply Monsignor and can't be held against her.

PROMOTEUR (*suddenly spiteful*): Indeed! Don't you believe in the miracles as the Bible teaches them? Do you deny what our Lord Jesus did at Cana, do you deny that he brought Lazarus back to life?

JOAN: No, sir. Our Lord certainly did all that since it is written in His books. He changed water into wine just as he created the water and the wine. He brought Lazarus back to life. But for Him, who has total control over life and death, that's no more difficult than threading a distaff for me.

PROMOTEUR (*screeching*): Listen to her, listen to her. She says there are no miracles!

JOAN: Oh there are, sir. It's simply that real miracles are not conjuring tricks or amusing acts. Gypsies did those in my village square. Real miracles that cause God to smile with pleasure in Heaven are those that men do on their own, with the courage and intelligence He has given them.

CAUCHON: Do you realise how serious what you are saying is, Joan? You're quietly telling us that the real miracle performed by God on earth is man and nothing else. Man is sinful, full of error, awkwardness and impotence.

JOAN: Yes, but of strength and courage as well, and vision when he is at his nastiest. I've seen them in battle...

LADVENU: Monsignor, in her own inadequate but sincere way Joan has expressed certain intuitions that may be wrong but are naive. Her thoughts are not sufficiently formed to be part of our debate. Perhaps by pressing her with questions we risk making her say more or something other than she intended.

CAUCHON: Brother Ladvenu, we will try to understand the awkwardness of her replies as honestly as possible. But our duty is to keep questioning her to the end. Don't forget that we are not absolutely sure that we are dealing with Joan, and only Joan. And so, Joan, you will make excuses for man? You believe him to be one of God's great miracles, if not the greatest of them all?

JOAN: Yes, sir.

PROMOTEUR (*screeching and beside himself*): You blaspheme! Man is full of impurities, debauchery, obscene thoughts. He twists and turns on his bed at night, prey to all bestial obsessions.

JOAN: Yes, sir. He is disgusting and he sins. And then suddenly and for what reason (this pig who liked to enjoy himself so much) he throws himself in front of a runaway horse as he leaves his house and debauchery and saves an unknown child. And with all his bones broken he dies peacefully, the same man who had taken so much trouble to prepare his night

PROMOTEUR: He dies like a beast, in sin, damned without a priest.

JOAN: No, sir. Rather glowing and clean, with God waiting for him, smiling. He has acted like a man, once badly and once well. And God has created him precisely with that contradiction.

Eventually, of course, Joan is persuaded to abjure and it is at this point that Anouilh begins to give the story his unique twist. Warwick, who throughout the play within the courtroom has the role of a commentator and stage director (not unlike De Nugy in Audiberti's *Pucelle*) congratulates Joan on her decision, even though he is fully aware of the danger of her becoming a martyr and even though he also knows (as do we) what will inevitably happen to her. But when he describes the life she can look forward to as a prisoner Joan changes her mind and preparations are made for her execution. At this point, however, Beaudricourt [*sic*] rushes onto the stage to remind everyone that the coronation scene – Joan's moment of triumph – has been forgotten! The pyre has to be removed therefore and an altar erected in its place. Warwick withdraws. He *knows* that Joan will be burned, but the closing image remains that of a radiant Joan with her banner, as Charles is crowned. In the closing – and surely not without irony – words of the stage directions, she has become the 'magnificent image that adorns prize books.'

BEAUDRICOURT: We can't stop there, Monsignor, we haven't had the coronation. We said we would act out everything. It's not fair. Joan can expect to have the coronation scene; it's part of her story.

CAUCHON: That's true! We were about to commit an injustice.

CHARLES: You see! I was sure my coronation would be forgotten. People never think about it. But it cost me a lot of money.

WARWICK (*appalled*): Oh well, now the coronation. That's bad taste. It wouldn't be right for me to be at this ceremony, Monsignor. I'm going to slip away. Anyway, as far as I'm concerned it's over, she's burned. His majesty's government has got what it wanted.

CAUCHON (*shouting to the executioner*): You there, take down the pyre. Unfasten Joan. Bring her her sword and standard. (*Everyone rushes happily to the pyre. Charles, who is being dressed for his coronation addresses the audience, smiling.*)

CHARLES: That man's right. There will never be a real end to Joan's story. The one that people will talk about when names will have been forgotten or confused is not the one with her being pursued in Rouen like some miserable beast, it's of Joan in all her glory at Rheims. The true end to Joan's story is a joyful one. Joan of Arc is a story with a happy ending.

Joan in Germany again.

With the exception of the plays by Bouissounouse and Audiberti, and a handful of references to her in some poems by the Communist writer Louis Aragon, Joan in France at least, belonged in essence to those whose sympathies lay to the Right. In Germany the situation was completely and interestingly different. Between 1929 and 1931 Bertolt Brecht had written *Die Heilige Johanna der Schlachthöfe* ('Saint Joan of the Stockyards'), a didactic play inspired by the Marxist theories to which he had been converted in 1928, though it would not be performed for another twenty-eight years by which time Brecht had established himself as a revolutionary writer with plays like *Mother Courage* (1939) or *The Caucasian Chalk Circle* (1949). *Die Heilige Johanna* is set in the slaughterhouses of Chicago and deals with the epic struggle between the capitalist owners, bankers and the exploited workers.[3] (We should note in passing that the English translation of *schlacht* by 'stock' is inadequate. *Schlacht* means 'slaughter', and the play refers not only to that of the animals but of the workers as well.) The play also shows, however, that even the most noble-minded defenders of the workers – here the Black Straw Hats (The Salvation Army) with Joan as their principal spokesman – are ineffective. This is not simply because the system is too powerful, but because their idealism no longer has any relevance for the real world. Joan may indeed represent goodness, but her attempts to encourage the workers to think differently are out of touch and hopelessly inadequate:

JOAN: Well, anyone who really cares for God's word and what He says and not just what the ticker tape says, and there must be some people here that are respectable and conduct their business in a God-fearing way, we have nothing against that – he's welcome to visit our Divine Services on Lincoln Street, Sunday at two, music after three, admission free.

By the end of the play, however, Joan comes to realise that to believe that there is a God who will eventually provide comfort for the workers is not enough. She offers a new militant, revolutionary message but it is drowned by the cacophony of capitalists' and workers' voices and she dies:

JOAN: So anyone down here who says there is a God although there's none to be seen and He can be invisible and help them all the same should have his head banged on the pavement until he croaks.

SLIFT: Listen, you've got to say something to shut that girl up. You must speak – anything at all, but loud!

SNYDER: Joan Dark, 25 years old, laid low by pneumonia in the stockyards of Chicago, in the service of God, a fighter and a sacrifice!

JOAN: And as for the ones that tell them they may be raised in spirit and still be stuck in the mud, they too should be tossed out heads down.

> It's not like that! Only force helps where force rules, and only men help where men are. (*All sing the first verse of the chorale, to keep Joan's speeches from being heard.*)

Die Heilige Johanna clearly conforms to Brecht's ideas about epic theatre and alienation. The struggle he depicts is fundamental to human experience. His audience is expected to recognise the inequalities and exploitation involved, but is given no final answer; instead it is encouraged to think how, otherwise and by continuing the struggle, society can be improved as it inevitably evolves.

Beyond upholding the cause of the oppressed, Joan in this play bears little resemblance to her fifteenth-century forerunner. In a second, *Die Gesichte der Simone Machard* ('The Visions of Simone Machard') – begun in 1941 and finished in 1946 – Brecht remains close to several of the key episodes in the original story.[4] It is situated in June 1940 at a small town called Saint Martin in central as yet unoccupied France where many of the local people can think only of themselves and their safety. Simone works at the hotel and is given a book about Joan by her teacher. She begins to dream that she is Joan. An angel, who appears on the roof of the town garage, tells her she has been chosen to save France and gives her an invisible drum symbolising the soil of France. In an emergency the drum will sound calling people to come together to fight for their country. Gradually Simone confuses dream with reality; local dignitaries become those of Joan's story; the hotel owner is the *connétable*, the spineless mayor, Charles. In her dreams Simone manages to unite all French people and in reality makes the hotel owners dispense food to refugees fleeing from the north. When the Germans arrive Joan wants the town's stores of petrol destroyed, and when her request is refused (the petrol supplies would be a way of establishing good relations with the Germans) she is sacked. She therefore sets light to them herself, is arrested, handed over to the Germans and condemned to death. But the Germans, realising that to execute someone so young might be an unwise move, hand her back to the French, agreeing that the charges should be changed. At a court manned by people she knows, Simone is accused not of an unpatriotic act but of one of revenge for having been dismissed from her job and she is sentenced to a corrective spell in a remand home. As she is being led away there is a bombing attack – the drum – and we can assume that the majority of people of the village who have left in disgust at the court's verdict, have gone to fight for their country. Unlike *Die Heilige Johanna* with its relatively narrow focus the play is complex and deals with a range of issues as real in France in the early 1940s as they were in the fifteenth century – patriotism, idealism, opportunism, treachery, victimisation for example. Brecht insisted that a young girl should play the part of Simone, even though he recognised the limitations this could create for the character's psychological development. On 8th December 1942 he wrote: 'originally I saw her as a somewhat ungainly, mentally retarded and inhibited person; then it seemed more practical to use a child, so I'm left with the bare functions and nothing to offset them with in the way of individuality.' While there is obviously some truth in this, Simone's young age makes the way she is victimised and forced into the hands of brutal sadistic nuns of the Disciplinary Order of Saint Ursula for her corrective treatment all the more poignant. As she is led away the angel appears for the last time and offers the final patriotic message:

> France's daughter don't be afraid
> Each hand lifted to do you harm
> Soon must wither away on its arm.
> No matter where they may send you to
> France will always go with you.
> And before much time has passed
> Glorious she will rise at last.

And this is followed by the sight of the sky reddening with fire – not that of any pyre but as the result of sabotage or English bombs.

The Trial
The fourth Dream of Simone Machard
Night of 21–2 June

A jumble of music. In the courtyard stands the Hauptmann in armour and Simone as Maid of Orléans, surrounded by soldiers in black chain-mail decorated with swastikas; one of whom, identifiable as the Hauptmann's batman, holds a swastika banner.

Hauptmann: We've got you now, Joan of Orléans, and you are going to be handed over to a court that will decide why we should condemn you to die at the stake. *(Exeunt all except Simone and the standard bearer).*
Simone: What kind of court is that?
Standard Bearer: Not the ordinary kind. It's ecclesiastical.
Simone: I'm admitting nothing.
Standard Bearer: That's fine, but the trial seems to be already over.
Simone: You mean they sentence you before examining you?
Standard Bearer: Of course.

People who have apparently been attending the trial leave the hostelry and cross the yard into the street.

Père Gustave *(as he crosses the yard, to Thérèse)*: Death! At her age!
Thérèse: Who'd have expected that, even two days back?
Simone *(pulling her by the sleeve)*: Did Hitler come himself?

Thérèse *seems not to notice her and leaves with* Père Gustave. Simone*'s parents cross the yard, the father in uniform, the mother in black.*

Madame Machard *(sobbing)*: She was always very obstinate even as a little girl. Just like her brother. It's a terrible blow for Monsieur Machard. Now that he's working for the council, too! What a disgrace! *(Both exeunt. The brothers* Maurice *and* Robert *cross the yard).*
Robert: She didn't look at all bad.

MAURICE: Especially in that frilly blue dress.
SIMONE *(pulling Robert by the sleeve)*: Did you see the judges?
ROBERT *(casually)*: Yes, of course.
SIMONE: Shall I see them too?
ROBERT: Sure to. They'll come out here and sentence you to death. E*xeunt both.*
A LOUD VOICE: Pray silence for the Cardinals and Archbishops of the Ecclesiastical Court of Rouen! Sentence on the Maid of Orléans will now be pronounced. First the staff will be broken over the Maid.

Out of the hostelry steps one of the judges, adorned in magnificent cardinal's robes. He hides his identity behind a breviary, and crosses the yard. He stops behind a bronze tripod with a kettle on it, turns his back, claps the breviary shut, takes a small staff out of his sleeve, solemnly breaks it, and throws the pieces into the kettle.

THE LOUD VOICE: His Eminence the Bishop of Beauvais. For liberating the city of Orléans: death. *(Before moving on he looks back indifferently over his shoulder. It is the Colonel.)*
SIMONE: Monsieur le Capitaine! (A *third judge steps from the hostelry and repeats the procedure.)*
THE LOUD VOICE: For launching an attack on the city of Paris and the black market petrol: death. (*The third judge is the* PATRON)
SIMONE: But Monsieur Henri, it's me you're sentencing!

The PATRON *makes his usual gesture of helplessness, and a fourth judge steps out of the hostelry and repeats the procedure.*

THE LOUD VOICE: For uniting all Frenchmen: death.

The fourth judge grips his breviary too convulsively, and drops it. He tries to pick it up quickly, and is recognised: it is the MAYOR.

SIMONE: The Mayor himself! Oh, Monsieur Chavez!
THE LOUD VOICE: Your supreme judges have spoken, Joan.
SIMONE: But they're all Frenchmen. *To the standard bearer:* There must be some mistake.
STANDARD BEARER: No, Mademoiselle, this is a French court. (*The four judges have stopped at the entrance to the yard.)*
MAYOR: You must know that from your book. Of course the Maid is sentenced by French judges, and rightly so since she is French.
SIMONE *(confused)*: That's true. I know from the book that I'll be sentenced to death. But I would like to know why. I never really understood that part.
MAYOR *(to the judges)*: She is asking for a trial.
CAPITAINE: What's the point if she's already been sentenced?
MAYOR: Well, at least the case would have been examined, the defendant interrogated, and everything discussed and weighed up.
COLONEL: And found inadequate. *(Shrugging his shoulders)* But very well then, if *you* insist on it.
PATRON: We're not prepared, you know. (*They put their heads together and confer in whispers. Père Gustave carries out a table and puts plates and candles on it. The judges sit down at it.)*
PÈRE GUSTAVE: The refugees from the hall are outside. They're asking to be admitted to the trial.

Patron: Out of the question. I'm expecting my mother, and she doesn't like the way they smell.

Capitaine *(calling into the background)*: The trial will be held in camera. In the interests of the state.

Patron: Where are the papers? Probably gone astray again, like everything else in this country.

Mayor: Where is the plaintiff? *(The other judges look at each other.)*

Mayor: Without a plaintiff it can't be official.

Patron: Père Gustave, go and get us a plaintiff from the store room.

Père Gustave *(calls from the gate towards the street)*: The High Ecclesiastical Court of Rouen calls on anybody who has a complaint to bring against the Maid. – Nobody? *(He repeats his challenge. Then to the judges)*: Here comes the plaintiff: Isabeau the Queen Mother, supporter of the treacherous Duke of Burgundy and of the hereditary enemy.

Madame Soupeau *(in armour comes out of the hostelry and greets the judges, who bow low before her. With the routine amiability of a great hôtelière)*: Good evening, mon Capitaine. Don't get up. Don't let me disturb you. *(Over her shoulder into the hostelry)*: One portion of Alsace-Lorraine for Monsieur le Capitaine, well done! How would you like your peasants, Connétable? I hope you are satisfied with the service this time, mon Colonel. *(Pointing to* Simone*)*: Everything would have been saved if this Maid of Orléans hadn't interfered in the negotiations. Everything: France and the brickworks too. You are too weak, gentlemen. Who makes the decisions here, the Church or a servant in the hostelry? *(Starts shouting like one possessed)*: I demand and insist that this person be put to death immediately for heresy and disobedience, not to say obstinacy. Heads must roll. Blood must flow. She must be bodily exterminated. She must serve as a bloody example. *(Exhausted)*: My smelling-salts.

Capitaine: A chair for the Queen Mother. *(*Père Gustave *brings her a chair.)*

Patron: Isn't your armour rather tight, Maman? Why are you wearing it, anyhow?

Madame Soupeau: Well, I'm at war too, aren't I?

Patron: At war? What war?

Madame Soupeau: My war. Against this rebellious Maid who has been stirring up the people in the village hall.

Capitaine *(sharply)*: Shh! *(To Simone)*: What right had you to lead the French to war, Maid?

Simone: An angel told me to, venerable Bishop of Beauvais. *(The judges look at each other).*

Patron: I see, an angel. What sort of angel?

Simone: From the church. The one top the left of the altar.

Capitaine: Never set eyes on him.

Mayor *(friendlily)*: What did this angel look like? Describe him.

Simone: He was very young and had a beautiful voice, honourable sirs. He told me I must...

Colonel *(interrupting)*: What he told you is of no interest to us. What sort of accent did he have? Was it an educated one? Or the other kind?

Simone: I don't know. He just spoke.

Capitaine: Aha.

PATRON: What sort of clothes did this angel wear?

SIMONE: He was beautifully dressed. His robe was made of stuff you'd pay twenty or thirty francs a yard for in Tours.

CAPITAINE: Do I understand you correctly, Simone or Joan, as the case may be? So he wasn't one of those great magnificent angels whose robes cost perhaps as much as two or three hundred francs a yard?

SIMONE: I don't know.

COLONEL: What condition was the robe in? Quite worn?

SIMONE: The angel was just a bit chipped, around the sleeve.

COLONEL: I see. Chipped around the sleeve. As if he had to wear it to work too? Was it torn?

SIMONE: No, not torn.

CAPITAINE: All the same, it was chipped. And at the place where it had been chipped, the sleeve could quite well have got torn with all that work. Perhaps the reason why you didn't see it was that it was exactly where the colour had been rubbed off. But it could have been, couldn't it? (SIMONE *does not reply).*

COLONEL: Did the angel say anything that a person of quality might have said? Think that over.

SIMONE: General things, mostly.

MAYOR: Did the angel resemble anyone you knew?

SIMONE *(quietly)*: My brother André.

COLONEL: Ah, a private soldier. Private Machard. Gentlemen, now it's out. A most peculiar angel, I must say.

MADAME SOUPEAU: A real public-bar angel, a gutter seraph! In any case now we know where those 'Voices' come from. From the taverns and the sewage farms.

SIMONE: You shouldn't run down the angel, Reverend Sirs.

PATRON: If you look on page 124 of your book you will see that we are the Ecclesiastical Court, in fact the highest authority on earth.

COLONEL: Don't you think that we, the high Cardinals of France, know the will of God better than some jumped-up angel?

CAPITAINE: Where does God dwell, Joan? Below or above? And where did your so-called angel come from? From below. So who sent him? God? Or could it have been the Devil?

MADAME SOUPEAU: The Devil! Joan of Orléans, the voices you heard came from the Devil.

SIMONE *(strongly)*: No, no! Not from the Devil!

CAPITAINE: Call him, call your angel! Perhaps he'll defend you, great Maid of Orléans. Usher, do your duty.

PÈRE GUSTAVE *(calls)*: The Supreme Ecclesiastical Court of Rouen calls upon the angel, name unknown, who, so the Maid alleges, has appeared to her on several occasions, to come and bear witness on her behalf.

> SIMONE *looks at the garage roof. It remains empty.* PÈRE GUSTAVE *repeats his summons.* SIMONE, *in great anguish, looks at the smiling judges. Then she crouches down and in her confusion begins to drum on the ground. However, there is no sound and the garage roof remains empty.*

SIMONE: It does not sound here. What has happened? It doesn't resound. French soil no longer resounds. It doesn't resound here.

MADAME SOUPEAU *(stepping towards her)*: Are you in the least aware who *is* France?

As in *Die Heilige Johanna* Brecht does not offer any solutions, nor is the play specifically about France either in the fifteenth century or the 1940s. Despite being a little confused it is, like virtually everything he wrote, a highly politically charged play. With her concern for and support of the people Joan clearly belongs to the Left and as in the earlier work – and indeed in many others – Brecht's targets are once again the forces of conservatism and the establishment that so easily crush individual and selfless actions and ambitions. But the play takes us beyond mere politics to raise more general questions about human selfishness and stupidity, and the victimisation of the weak, and the 'mad-hatter's tea party' style in which much of it is written only serves to make this more apparent.

Beyond politics?

While these plays are the last literary attempts in the twentieth century to make use of Joan's story either to reflect directly contemporaneous political events or to convey a particular message, it was not neglected, however, especially beyond France. Plays, novels, poems and comic strips would continue to exploit it in a variety of ways. Of these one of the most interesting is Maxwell Anderson's play *Joan of Lorraine*, produced in New York in 1946. Maxwell uses the technique of a play within a play to explore the way the actors – and in particular Mary Grey who is due to take the part of Joan — come to understand the psychology of the people they represent. As she studies and works at her part, Grey gradually realises that Joan had to deal with men who were essentially corrupt and in the end had only her faith to keep her strong. At the same time, through her discussions with Masters, the 'director' of the play, Anderson uses her to consider how a story such as Joan's can be manipulated (corrupted) to ensure success at the box office:

MARY: You want the play to mean that Joan had to work with dishonest people to put a kingdom together, just as we have to work with dishonest people to put on this play. And it's not true! It's never been true! You can refuse to work with thieves. [...] The meaning of Joan is not a small thing for me. She was clear and clean and honest and I want her shown the way she was. [...] An actress is held responsible for the plays she chooses, remember. And this play was different when I chose it.

The 'play' is modified in the light of her observations and by the end her integrity is maintained: 'Some of the new lines in this scene are Joan's own words. I could feel them turning and living. [...] And it doesn't matter what we say about her. Nobody can use her for an alien purpose. Her own meaning will always come through, and all the rest will be forgiven.' Although it is not generally thought to be one of Anderson's better plays, *Joan of Lorraine* enjoyed considerable success and not without a hint of irony in view of its fundamental theme, was adapted two years later for the screen by Victor Fleming, with Ingrid Bergman in the title role. Joan's integrity is also the subject of a play, *Let Man Live*, by the Norwegian writer Pär Lagerkvist in 1949. In it she is one of fourteen martyrs, including Socrates and Christ, who through a series of monologues reflect on their responsibility and motivation. In New York, two years later, a long poem by Sarah Larkin *Joan of Arc* follows the conventional story emphasising how Joan's divine inspiration sustained her to the end. And in France in 1956 René Char published, in a limited edition of seventy-two copies, a prose poem entitled *Jeanne qu'on brûla verte*. In it Joan begins as green wood (walnut, apple...) but finishes as dust. Warner sees in Char's short description of Joan 'the fundamental pattern of Christian sacrifice',[5] but what strikes the reader most of all is the natural, even pagan depiction of her and her fate. Joan's ashes will blend with the French soil from which new life will spring. Joan also made her appearance in Australia in 1973 with Thomas Keneally's novel *Blood Red, Sister Rose*. Keneally creates a powerful picture of fifteenth-century rural France with its violence and squalor and of a court that is full of double dealing and vicious treachery. Joan is at first depicted as a simple and ordinary village girl: 'She was sure she wanted to grow up to be like Zabillet [her mother], ironic and fertile towards some warm oaf. That seemed enviable.' (She is later described by Gilles de Rais as 'squat and plain'.) She also takes part in semi-demonic, sexual village rituals in which people play the parts of saints and the devil. All this is presumably so that Keneally (like Besson in his film, *The Messenger*, 1999) can play down the spiritual or supernatural explanation of Joan's voices or visions, and as Joan gradually assumes her role he also shows her to have 'natural' reactions. She is sexually attracted to De Metz and later to D'Alençon. At Orléans she has to suppress a feeling of blood lust and experiences 'a delirium of amateur soldiering', even if (true to tradition) she never strikes a blow. After the coronation Joan, who knows her fate, has a strong sense of being discarded and Keneally summarises the last months of her life before she is captured, 'pulled from her horse by a Burgundian Bastard in a skirmish outside Compiègne', in a single page. He then deals with the trial and Joan's death in an Epilogue in the form of a letter written by her father to 'all (my) dear relatives in the region of the Meuse and in Sermaize and in the surrounding districts of Champagne'. If *Blood Red, Sister Rose* is unusual in not taking the last months of Joan's life into account more fully, this forces us to concentrate on her as someone who gradually comes to realise she has been chosen to do God's will but is never fully aware of what is happening to her. Keneally cleverly conveys this by having his narrative a mixture of an omniscient narrator who can describe and explain ('She couldn't even die by accident; the day for her blood had been arranged') and a series of extended dramatic exchanges in which Joan can appear witty, innocent, baffled, frightened or angry as the moment dictates.

Even from this brief description we can see that Keneally's novel is one of the more unusual treatments of Joan's story of all time, but we cannot leave the twentieth century without recalling two other quite different innovative pieces from France and Japan. The first is Michel Tournier's *Gilles et Jeanne* (1983) in which he focuses in particular on Gilles de Rais who meets Joan for the first time at Chinon, and on the bond that forms between them. Already in a marriage of convenience with a cousin ('a fat, lazy girl') Gilles is instantly struck by Joan, seeing in her 'everything he likes and has always been waiting for – a young boy, someone who would be his companion in arms and with whom he could play, and at the same time a woman, and above all a saint bathed in light.' As Tournier adds, it is miraculous that such 'rare and incorruptible qualities should be found in the same being.' For Gilles, Joan is his saviour: 'Joan, you are a saint' [...] Make me a saint as well.' Gilles remains with Joan up to her failure to take Paris. As she lies wounded in her tent he confesses his love for her in a way that anticipates the rest of the story and one of Tournier's preferred themes – the negative or malignant inversion of seemingly positive values: 'There is a fire in you' observes Gilles, 'I think it comes from God but maybe it is from hell. Good and evil are always close to one another. Of all God's creatures, Lucifer was the one who was most like Him.' He kisses Joan's wound, communing with her: ' "I've communed with your blood. I'm one with you for ever. From now on I'll follow you wherever you go – to heaven or to hell."' When Gilles hears of Joan's capture and sentence he goes to Rouen with La Hire in an attempt to save her, but is helpless and can only watch her burn. The shock is traumatic and he changes; his face now bears 'Signs of the devil.' He withdraws to his estates in the Vendée in western France from where 'once the evil transformation has taken place, he will re-emerge and like an angel from hell will spread his wings.' From this point on Tournier tells the story of Gilles and his slaughter of children in all its horror up to his trial and execution by burning when he calls on Joan just as she had called on Jesus. Provocatively, through Gilles' diabolic mentor Prelati, Tournier wonders whether the fire will have cleansed him of his crimes and allow him one day to be canonised like Joan. In his use of Joan's story Tournier follows several before him in attacking the church and the sanctimonious and self-seeking clergy for whom the mysteries of good and evil remain impenetrable. But it is also part of the challenge he always offers his readers. In a way that is entirely typical of his work as a whole he invites us to discover what is hidden behind the surface of familiarity and convention and in particular how the slightest modification of circumstances can lead to an entirely different – and often more sinister – interpretation or significance. He is not directly undermining the value Joan has had for previous generations but he does raise questions about the way her story has been recorded and even more about how precisely good and evil are to be assessed.

102. Yoshikazu Yasuhiko's comic strip, Joan, *Tokyo 1995, vol. 1.*

Even further removed from the precise details of the fifteenth century but raising a number of interesting questions is Yoshikazu Yasuhiko's three-volume comic strip – described as a 'graphic novel' – *Joan*, published in Tokyo in 1995 and 1996 with the English translation four years later.[6] The story is related by Emily, the seventeen-year old illegitimate daughter of the Duke of Lorraine and Alison Dune. After the Duke's death, his wife persecutes Alison and has her killed. Now an orphan, Emily is cared for by Baudricourt (the same Duke

Yoshikazu Yasuhiko's comic strip, Joan, Tokyo 1995, vol.2.

to whom Joan had gone) and raised by him as a boy, Emil. Emil had already seen Joan at her father's chateau and, projected back in time by twelve years, has a vision of her spinning and subsequently setting off for Chinon. Emil's destiny is set; she will follow Joan's order – 'Protect the king no matter what happens' – and she leaves with Baudricourt to fight for Charles against his own son, Louis.

Although the Hundred Years' War is almost at an end there is opposition to Charles, perceived as a weak king, led by Louis and several of the knights who had hitherto fought with Joan – Dunois, La Hire, d'Alençon. Emil has a series of adventures and Joan appears to her on a number of occasions either to protect her or to offer advice. In some cases Emil's experiences cast light on what had happened ten years previously. At one point, for example, she is

Yoshikazu Yasuhiko's comic strip, Joan, *Tokyo 1995, vol.2.*

taken by La Hire who has been devastated by Joan's fate and under the influence of Prelati has (as in Tournier's story) turned to a life of debauchery, devil-worship and twisted sexual practices. Knowing nothing of this Emil goes to him to raise money for the king's army under the command of Richemont. Prelati sees her as an ideal sacrificial victim but just as they are about to take her, Joan appears. La Hire collapses, dreams of his childhood and of his time with Joan, confesses his sins to Emil and gives her the money that will enable the king's army to be reinforced, trained in modern battle techniques and be victorious. When Emil is later taken by d'Alençon he has her imprisoned, so guilty does he feel at having abandoned Joan and because he is convinced that Emil is a 'stupid puppet of the king (who has) defamed Joan.' Finally Emil becomes the prisoner of Louis, seventeen years of age like her, and married to

Yoshikazu Yasuhiko's comic strip, Joan, *Tokyo 1995, vol. 3.*

Margaret of Scotland who is four year younger. Unaware of Emil's sex, Margaret falls passionately in love with her and manages to save her from the torture chamber, but she is powerless to stop her sadistic and vicious young husband deciding to burn Emil. Laven (*sic*) appears as her confessor and prays for a miracle. As the fire is lit a huge storm breaks and douses everything, but there is also a vision of Joan at the stake. Like La Hire, Louis is overcome with remorse and is ready to make peace with his father.

The third volume closes with the 1456 rehabilitation examination (wrongly dated as having taken place ten years earlier to fit with the rest of the book's chronolgy). Joan appears once more to Emil, now elegantly dressed as a young woman, to thank her and announce that at last she can return to Domremy. But we are left with a question:

Yoshikazu Yasuhiko's comic strip, Joan, *Tokyo 1995, vol. 3, p.218.*

Each of the three volumes has a brief account of events in France during the years following Joan's execution and a glossary containing a selection of names and dates. No doubt these are intended to be informative for a Japanese audience and give the story authenticity. But the questions raised also take the reader further. In a postscript Chojun Otani claims that *Joan* is less about history than the 'inner dramas of us human beings'; all of us, he argues, are torn between an acceptance of reality 'and the self that whispers that it is not the only way.' One reading of this would appear to be an appeal for peaceful

Yoshikazu Yasuhiko's comic strip, Joan, *Tokyo 1995, vol. 3, p.218.*

solutions to all conflictual situations. Did France have to suffer the ravages of the Hundred Years' War? Did so much blood have to be shed? Did Joan have to die? And in this way the book can be seen to have as much relevance for the late twentieth century as for the fifteenth, when despite treaties and negotiations solutions were reached only after conflict and then frequently not respected for long. Otani – or rather the book – also raises the matter of individual decision-making and private debate, not unlike that explored somewhat more pedantically by Maulnier. While Joan had her voices to inspire and guide her, Emil has her sense of mission and Joan as her model. Like some others before him, by cutting out the divine element altogether, Yasuhiko could have turned Emil's adventure into a truly existential one. But Joan's interventions to save Emil from certain sacrifice at the hands of La Hire and

Prelati or from death make this impossible. Even so *Joan* is more than a racy reworking of the traditional story. Yasuhiko's message is a plea for peace, yet he seems to recognise that no matter what sacrifice may be made to achieve it there is no foreseeable end to violence.

Notes

1. See David Caute, *Communism and the French Intellectuals*, André Deutsch, London, 1964 and my *Literature and the Left in France*, Macmillan and Methuen, London, 1983.
2. *L'Alouette* is performed regularly in Parisian and provincial theatres in France. When it opened in New York, *The Lark*, with Julie Harris as Joan, enjoyed a run of 229 performances.
3. The translation of *Die Heilige Johanna der Schlachthöfe* is by Frank Jones (*Bertolt Brecht. Plays*, Vol. 2, Methuen, London, 1962).
4. The translation of *Die Gesichte der Simone Machard* is by Ralph Manheim (*Bertolt Brecht, Collected Plays*, Vol. VII, Vintage Books, New York, 1975). In 1959 Brecht also wrote *Der Prozess der Jeanne d'Arc zu Rouen, 1431* ('The Trial of Joan of Arc at Rouen, 1431'). This is an adaptation of a radio play by Anna Seghers, first broadcast in Belgium in 1935. Seghers plays down the divine source of Joan's voices and instead implies – by using the noise of a crowd – that they are those of the people. This must have appealed to Brecht and he develops it by adding three new crowd scenes to Seghers' text. The play has been translated by Ralph Manheim and Wolfgang Sauerlander in *Bertolt Brecht, Collected Plays*, Vol. IX, Vintage Books, New York, 1979.
5. See Warner, *op.cit.* 30.
6. The English translation by Reiko Terui, Kate Bundy and Sandra Zalman was published by Comics One Corporation in 2000.

Chapter Seven

From Silent Movie via the Big Screen to Television Soap

GIVEN THE IMMENSE POPULARITY of Joan's story by the late nineteenth century it is hardly surprising that the new art of the cinema should have been immediately attracted to it. During the course of the next hundred years directors from no less than eight countries would turn their attention to it and produce around fifty feature, documentary, educational and television films; some embrace Joan's career in its entirety, others concentrate on the last months or even hours of her life, others again merely use her story as a model or point of reference. As in literature, too, though to a lesser extent, 'external' events and situations have their influence – the political climate, the taste for large-scale spectaculars, the perception of women and their role in a male dominated world, mere escapist entertainment and so on – but only at the time the film is made. In this the cinema differs from the theatre. Films are frequently contrasted to plays, especially if the subject is the same. But while the basic raw material – that is, the original script and scenario – will always remain the same, once we move to a production and performance at least two fundamental differences become evident. The first concerns location. While early silent filmmakers had only the most primitive conditions in which to produce their work, increasingly and often benefiting from lavish budgets directors would enjoy a virtually unlimited choice of location and complex technological resources. By contrast, despite significant improvements to all aspects of theatrical production, directors are only rarely able to escape completely from the physical constraints imposed by the stage, no matter how large and open. The second difference is that of interpretation. Like a painting or a photographic print, a film may lend itself to multiple analyses and interpretations by critics and its audience, but once it has been finished and committed to celluloid it is, like these other art forms, fixed; it is no longer live. A play by its very nature is different. Like an opera or a piece of music it continues through performance to renew itself. In so doing it provokes the audience to consider a range of possible interpretations that, in addition to those arising from the subject and its treatment, may depend on anything from the size of the theatre to a change of cast, the mood of the performers or the whim of the director. A further layer of complication is added when the subject of the film or play is, like Joan, well known. Some adaptations or interpretations will concentrate on the general and popular aspects of her life with an emphasis on whatever particular one the director considers to be significant. In Joan's case these tend, inevitably, to be her sanctity, her patriotism and her victimisation. As we have seen, literary accounts of Joan's exploits may vary depending on the time they were written and to the intentions of the author at that time. But such accounts and especially those written for the theatre may be read and performed at different times and more importantly in different ways, with a purpose and result that were not part of the author's original intention. Films do not have this flexibility. The director like the playwright may set out to reflect contemporaneous issues or preoccupations, but while on screening his film may provoke intense critical debate it remains the same film; it cannot be re-performed or reworked. A

103. Poster for an exhibition in Orléans celebrating the adaptations of Joan's story for the cinema. Note the absence of a shot from the German film directed by Ucicky in 1935.

different interpretation of the same subject would require a new film which, as is often the case will be heralded by its director as an improvement on and corrective of earlier ones.

According to the leading Joan film scholar Robin Blaetz, there were at least eight films made about Joan between the late 1890s and the outbreak of the First World War.[1] Most of these are lost but a fragment from what is probably the earliest (1895?),*Orléans glorifie la Pucelle* ('Orleans celebrates the Maid') by Thomas Edison, depicts the market place in Rouen with Joan, having had a plea for mercy rejected, placed on a neatly stacked pile of logs that appears dangerously close to the surrounding timber framed medieval houses. Nothing here suggests anything other than a faithful reflection of the standard story, but within five years George Melies' carefully researched, hand-tinted *Jeanne d'Arc* contains barely disguised socio-political comment. While the depiction of Robert de Baudricourt's castle with a grotesquely fat friar quaffing ale amid scenes of bawdy entertainment may be no more that a cliché of medieval life, the white-hooded figures at Joan's trial and execution bear a sinister resemblance to members of the notoriously reactionary and racist Ku Klux Klan. They would reappear, with much greater relevance, in Cecil B. DeMille's film *Joan the Woman* that would be made in America in 1916, a year after the Klan had regrouped and become increasingly active. Not surprisingly the Church was hostile in its reaction.

Four other films were made between *Jeanne d'Arc* and 1914, two of them in Italy by Mario Caserini. According to Blaetz, the second, based as Tchaikovsky's opera had been on Schiller's play, has Caserini's opera singer wife Maria Gasperini in the title role and is probably the first attempt to use Joan's story to create an 'exotic spectacle'. A second opera star, Maria Jacobin, was also to appear, with much success it seems, in yet another Italian film Nino Oxilia's *Giovanna d'Arco* (1913). Oxilia's script relied heavily on the recent biographies of Joan by Anatole France and Andrew Lang and was by all accounts a powerful visual spectacle.

The first film that can legitimately be considered to provide the kind of spectacle that would dominate so many of the later films, however, was DeMille's *Joan the Woman.* Once again Joan was played by an opera singer, on this occasion by the thirty-four year old Geraldine Farrar, who brought to the role a sense of real life and struggle, or even though physically she could hardly be said to resemble a battle-honed nineteen-year-old girl Be that as it may DeMille himself wanted his film to be 'an absorbing personal story [set] against a background of great historical events', and his scriptwriter, Jeanne MacPherson projected Joan as 'a woman of flesh and blood, whose heroism was as much a victory over herself as [...] over the English',[2] underlining her humanity rather than her saintly qualities. Shooting took place throughout France and in his search for authenticity DeMille gave careful attention to dress, armour and weaponry. But the film is not simply impressive on account of its visual qualities.

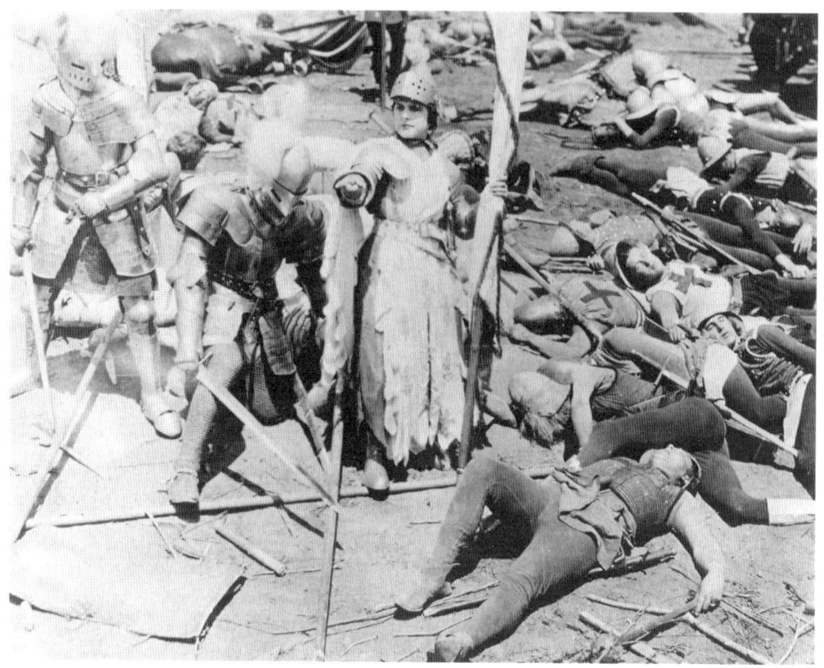

104. Geraldine Farrar in Joan the Woman *(DeMille, 1916). By courtesy of the British Film Institute.*

It was premiered on Christmas day 1916 at the moment when America was about to enter the conflict in Europe, and the first and full version of the film portrays Joan symbolizing an endangered France to be helped at a crucial moment. DeMille develops an ingenious double plot through the character of a young soldier, Eric Trent, both a fifteenth-century knight and a young twentieth-century British officer. Joan and Trent fall in love, recalling Schiller's Joan and Lionel. Torn between her infatuation for Trent and her love of France, Joan eventually and melodramatically chooses the latter. Like Lionel, Trent fails to save her and in this version Joan is burned. Five centuries later and visited by Joan's ghost Trent expiates his earlier failure and the evils committed by the English by volunteering to blow up a German trench, knowing that he will be killed in the process. Joan's image hovers over the explosion. In a shorter version of the film – no doubt due to cuts made by the censors to all films imported to France from America at the time – the love element has been removed with the result that Joan appears more as the traditional unwavering heroine, the embodiment of what Blaetz has termed 'national pride and universal self-sacrifice'. Although she was not well received by the French critics who would have preferred a more spiritual (and no doubt physically more attractive) Joan, Farrar's sheer physical presence is impressive. The opening shots of her spinning and then 'crucified' against and image of the *fleur de lys* set the tone for her interpretation of the role, and her actions as leader of her troops or as she goes to her death are full of a melodrama that remains powerful.

105. Geraldine Farrar in Joan the Woman *(DeMille, 1916).*
By courtesy of the British Film Institute.

It is hardly surprising that after her canonisation Joan should once again become the focus of attention of a number of directors, and the 1920s are marked by two contrasting but remarkable films which appeared in 1928: *La Passion de Jeanne d'Arc* ('The Passion of Joan of Arc') by the Danish director Carl Dreyer, and *La Vie merveilleuse de Jeanne d'Arc* ('The marvellous life of Joan of Arc') by Marc de Gastyne. Both initially intended to produce large-scale accounts of all Joan's life, but when he learned that Gastyne was already embarked on his version Dreyer decided instead to concentrate on her trial and death, basing his scenario on the records of the trial compiled by Quicherat and enlisting the help of Joseph Delteil.[3]

... Jeanne d'Arc est française. Elle fut la première Française. Son épopée courte et magnifique est la plus belle de notre histoire, la plus pure, la plus glorieuse. C'est Jeanne la Pucelle qui créa vraiment la France. Elle est à nous. Si l'on veut dignement, noblement, raconter par le cinématographe cette admirable et rapide existence, montrer à l'écran cette pure et radieuse figure devant laquelle le monde entier s'est incliné, il faut le faire non seulement avec toute la piété, tout le respect désirables, mais encore avec une grande foi française. Pour bien comprendre Jeanne d'Arc, il faut être Français, pour sentir tout ce qu'il y a de français dans son bon sens souvent malicieux, dans sa bonne humeur, dans sa gaité, tout autant que dans sa dévotion gallicane, il faut être Français, Français de père en fils, Français de toujours.

Or, voici qu'une grande firme cinématographique française annonce qu'elle va faire tourner en France, une "Jeanne d'Arc" par un metteur en scène danois, avec une artiste américaine ! Cela est proprement inadmissible !

Quel que soit le talent de ce metteur en scène (et il est très grand), quelle que soit sa déférence, quel que soit son désir de ne nous choquer en rien, il ne peut pas nous donner une Jeanne d'Arc dans la vraie tradition française. Et la "star" américaine, dont on dit le nom dans la coulisse, ne peut pas tourner notre Jeanne, fille saine, enjouée, rayonnante de pureté, de foi, de courage et de patriotisme.

Laisser faire cela chez nous serait une abdication scandaleuse.(...)

Jean-José Frappa, <u>CHANTECLER</u> Ier janvier 1927

106. *Extract from an article in* Chantecler, *1st January 1927 deploring the choice of a Danish director to make a film about Joan: it is 'completely unacceptable'. To understand Joan, one has to be 'French, French by descent and for ever French'.*

Joseph Delteil   20.5.73

LA TUILERIE DE MASSANE
34 · GRABELS (PRÈS MONTPELLIER)
TÉL. [illegible]

Chère Madame,

Je vous remercie infiniment pour votre aimable lettre, qui me touche beaucoup.

J'ai en effet collaboré avec Carl Dreyer, en 1927 je crois, pour le scénario <u>La Passion de Jeanne d'Arc</u>. Je me souviens que nous avons travaillé ensemble pendant tout un mois, et que nous avons fait beaucoup de recherches dans beaucoup de directions. Dreyer était un homme froid et positif, un peu lent. J'apportais de mon côté à l'envi idées et images, avec enthousiasme. Et Dreyer choisissait.

Je regrette de ne pouvoir, à cette distance, vous préciser davantage les détails de cette collaboration. Mais finalement le film est plutôt l'œuvre de Dreyer.

Veuillez agréer, chère Madame, l'assurance de mes sentiments les meilleurs

Delteil

107. *Letter from Joseph Delteil outlining his contribution to Dreyer's film.*

The result is a film that is remarkable in its intensity of emotion and which, by its title, draws an explicit comparison with the life of Christ and sets a bench mark against which all subsequent films would in some ways be measured. In one famous scene shot in her cell, Joan contemplates and puts on what we are clearly intended to take for a crown of thorns.

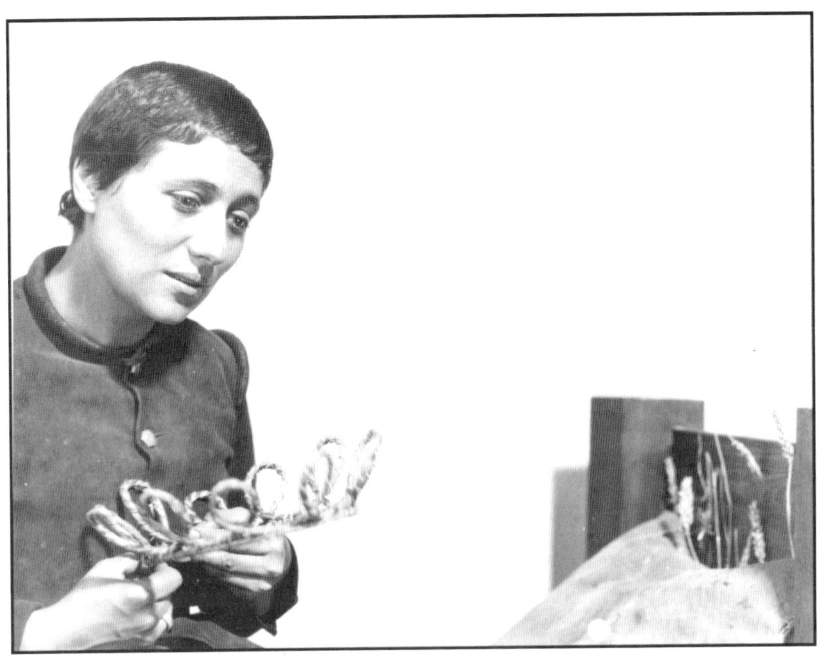

108. Renée Falconetti as Joan in La Passion de Jeanne d'Arc *(Dreyer, 1928).*
By courtesy of the British Film Institute.

In another, as she stumbles towards the funeral pyre, an elderly woman comes from the crowd and offers her some water. We also frequently see her with her head slightly inclined to her right as is Christ's in so many images.

Renée Falconetti, who played Joan and would never again perform on film, is utterly convincing in her displays of despair, panic, terror and fear, especially when her head is shaved in preparation for the execution. Valentine Hugo, the wife of one of the film's artistic advisors Jean Hugo, poignantly recalls the scene in her memoirs:

> The silence was like that in an operating theatre. In the cold light that accompanies morning executions and with our feelings full of prejudices, we were moved as though the mark of shame was being applied to this woman for real. Electricians and technicians held their breath, eyes were full of tears. With all the flowers that had been sent the atmosphere at this simple hair-cutting scene was funereal.[4]

Dreyer builds up the tension by concentrating all Joan's interrogations into one day and to convey it on film he chose to deploy close-ups that frequently fill the whole screen. We see Joan's judges just as she does as they glare down at her or smirk between themselves as they attempt to trap her. The camera sweeps round them in a dizzying circle underlying the claustrophobia of the court room and their faces are shot almost as though they are unaware of being filmed, as in a modern documentary. As Dreyer himself explained:

> The records give a shattering impression of the ways in which the trial was a conspiracy of judges against a solitary Jeanne, bravely defending herself against men who displayed a devilish cunning to trap her in their net. This conspiracy could be conveyed on the screen only through the huge close-ups that exposed, with merciless realism, the callous cynicism of the judges hidden behind hypocritical compassion.[5]

And as they torment her in her cell, her brutal, gloating gaolers are filmed in the same way.

Once the film takes us out of the courtroom or Joan's cell the technique and pace change. Joan's humiliation and suffering are contrasted with scenes of the market place in Rouen in which people appear to have gathered for entertainment; there are contortionists, acrobats, sword-swallowers, and swings on which children play. The result is a disturbing mix of carnival and tragedy, and in some of the scenes in the closing sequences the camera appears to flip over giving the impression that the world (and hence its values) is upside down. As Joan slowly burns the local people turn on the English who retaliate in the most brutal fashion, beating them with flails and hurling spears as they retreat into the safety of their castle. All this sequence of scenes is shot through clouds of swirling smoke and flames with Joan's silhouette hanging from the stake. As an individual she has become almost insignificant, but while initially she may have been just one more attraction for the crowd, at the close she can only be seen as a victim – like Dreyfus – of the systems of Church and State that have followed their self interested paths relentlessly, and to have triggered popular unrest. Dreyer's stark and emotionally charged film marked a significant change in the way Joan – or the image of Joan – could be used in film. Though severely pruned of some details the story is still unmistakeably hers, but Dreyer's approach takes us beyond it in order to concentrate on the innermost struggle of an individual faced with overwhelming odds. The spiritual dimension is in no way reduced, rather it is underlined by the intolerable psychological struggle Joan is obliged to undergo, reflected in her facial expressions. Although almost permanently tearful, her face frequently registers frustration, incomprehension and terror, but there are moments of sublime happiness when she realises that she has not lost contact with God or with her saints. There is no doubt that the black and white print adds to

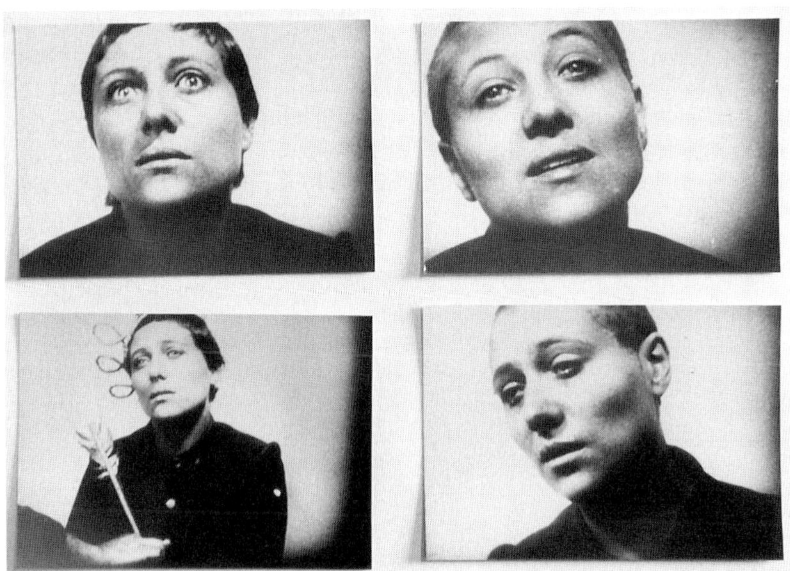

109. Four close-ups of Renée Falconetti as Joan .

the starkness of Dreyer's portrayal of Joan and it is interesting that thirty years later, while full colour would be available to him, Robert Bresson decided not to use it for his *Le Procès de Jeanne d'Arc* (1962).

110. Publicity for Marc de Gastyne's film.

111. Simone Genevoix in one of the prison scenes.

Quite what he would have produced had Dreyer continued with his original plan to make a large-scale version of Joan's life is impossible to say, but it is difficult to imagine that at the time it could have bettered or been more enthusiastically received than Gastyne's film. Thanks to improved technology this can be seen as the precursor of the epic treatments given to Joan in the latter half of the twentieth century. For the first time too the film portrays Joan – played by the seventeen year old Simone Genevoix – as an androgynous figure.

112. Publicity flyer for de Gastyne's film with Simone Genevoix as Joan.

Like DeMille and possibly influenced by Schiller's play as well, Gastyne also introduces a love element through the character of a childhood friend, Rémy Loiseau, whose offer of marriage she refuses.

113. Simone Genevoix as Joan calling on La Hire to renounce swearing.
By courtesy of the British Film Institute.

The film is impressive in countless different ways: the pace of the opening scenes with their haunting shots of horsemen against a magnificent skyscape; the close-ups of Joan when she hears her voices for the first time; a shot of her offering thanks to God after the victory at Orléans, kneeling by a stake with chains attached to it that grimly anticipates what is to come; the expression on Cauchon's face at her trial which gradually shifts from being benign to angry and cruel. And Genevoix's reactions at the moments of abjuration and subsequently on condemnation are as powerful as anything achieved by Falconetti. But the highlight of the large-scale dimension of the film is the attack on Les Tourelles that was actually filmed at Carcassonne with hundreds of extras drawn from the French army in uniforms of the First World War, giving the film more of a patriotic flavour than a religious one. Although carefully planned, the attack rapidly became out of the director's control. In his memoirs Gastyne relates what happened:

> The wave of horsemen set off with the frail figure of Joan brandishing her banner leading them. As though it were a kind of fantasia the Arabs threw themselves forward shouting savagely. Simone's horse panicked took the bit between its teeth and charged into the tumult with its rider courageously hanging on to her banner. But her bolting horse was too much for her. It was a sight that shook us all.

> The soldiers charged the English defences but instead of stopping as I had told them the horses leaped over the barriers erected in front of them, wrecking everything in their path. Fearing the worst the officers whistled in an attempt to stop them but in vain. Surprised by this unscripted attack the soldiers playing the parts of the English became angry and began to fight seriously, trying to knock the riders off their mounts. It was an amazing mess. My cameramen kept on filming. Only with a lot of difficulty did the officers manage to stop the fighting but we expected the worse. Fortunately less harm was done than we feared. But Simone, carried away by her powerful beast, shot off into the countryside and finished her crazy ride by falling headfirst into a pile of dung on a nearby farm. When we came to her aid she got up, more dead than alive, but without any injuries and in her tiny child's voice asked, 'Was it good?' When she learned that the scene had been more successful than we had ever hoped she clapped her hands and said, 'That's great!', and still crying burst into laughter.[6]

Another twenty years would have to pass before the first of a number of films made on a similar scale would appear. But Joan was now beginning to attract the attention of directors elsewhere and in 1935 Gustav Ucicky's *Das Mädchen Johanna* appeared in Germany at the time when Hitler was already in power, when National Socialism was rapidly gaining ground and Germany was striving to establish herself as a major cultural nation in Europe.

This all had an impact on Ucicky's interpretation. Certainly Joan is successful at Orléans (we see her swordless urging on her soldiers from the battlements), she is tried, will recant and be burned, believing that 'I must die so that my fatherland will be free'. Played by Angela Salloker, Joan comes across as a wide-eyed innocent with none of the doughty spirit and conviction that are generally associated with her nor any of the intensity displayed by earlier actresses. Ucicky's Joan is shallow, longs for beautiful things and looks forward to the time when she can return home. But above all she is out manoeuvred and manipulated by a Machiavellian Charles and a vicious La Trémouille who persuades the king that she is a witch. Her only support comes from a fictional character, Maillezais, Charles' half-brother and intended perhaps to take the place of Dunois, but he is powerless to help her. What is more, the French lords and barons who had rallied around Joan are depicted as drunken louts who, at the banquet after Charles' coronation, call for her to be burned as a witch. The fact that she is the complete victim is no better illustrated, as various critics have observed, than by frequent shots of her and Charles together showing him in a superior position.

After the victory at Orléans Charles quickly realises that not only is Joan less of a popular threat to him dead but that from her death and martyrdom he will be able to draw the power he requires to unite his people: 'She is a thousand times stronger dead.' Not only does Ucicky depict Charles quite differently from earlier directors – and indeed later ones – he is also effectively saying that treachery in the nation's interest is justifiable. The film finishes with Joan's retrial and with scenes of the market square where she was burned

114. *Gustav Ucicky's* Das Mädchen Johanna, *1935, with Angela Salloker as Joan. By courtesy of the British Film Institute.*

being blessed, of lilies and of boys and girls unambiguously intended to represent the healthy, pure youth (the boys swing censers) of the National Socialist society. Such details as these indicate the stamp of Nazi approval and it is not impossible that Josef Goebbels, as Hitler's minister responsible for culture, had an influence in the film's production. Put into the historical context of the fifteenth century the film can be said to illustrate how France found national unity after the humiliation of the Hundred Years' War; put into that of the late 1930s it carries a far different meaning. In his eulogy of Hitler in 1945 Goebbels found occasion to quote one of Charles' lines: '(Joan's) death will give people faith in a divine mission, under the sign of which the people will defeat the enemy.'[7]

With the outbreak of the Second World War interest in Joan would again find its focus in France with, as we have seen, both sides – Resistance and Collaboration – appropriating her for their propaganda and political ends. No film depicting her was made there, but in America Robert Stevenson directed *Joan of Paris* in 1942. In it the French actress Michèle Morgan plays the part of a French girl, Joan, who enables a group of English fighter pilots to escape from occupied France but at the expense of her own life. Other than this film the only other two made during the war years and in the same year and in America appear to have been a musical comedy *Joan of Ozmark* and *Between us Girls*. In neither does Joan's story have a significant part to play and only in the latter is there the suggestion that women could make an heroic contribution to the war effort.

115. Michèle Morgan gazes heavenwards for guidance. By courtesy of the British Film Institute.

Nine years after the end of the War in 1954 a Franco-Italian production directed by Jean Delannoy entitled *Destinées* appeared, once again starring Michèle Morgan. The film has three episodes each focussing on a particular incident in the lives of Joan, Elisabeth I and Lysistrata. The one concerning

Joan deals with the episode at Lagny (not included as far as I know by any other director) when Joan is supposed to have brought a dead child briefly back to life. Morgan is too sedate and almost regal for the role, but fragments of the ten-minute film suggest that the much larger version planned by Delannoy could have been successful. As Joan leaves Lagny, for example, we have a glimpse of a fence in the shape of a cross burning.

In 1947 Delannoy had indeed produced a full-length version together with the writer Pierre Bost but it seems that the reason for this project's not having been realised was the announcement in America of Victor Fleming's high-budget *Joan of Arc* with Ingrid Bergman in the title role, based on the play by Maxwell Anderson in which Bergman had also starred. Screened in 1948 to immense publicity the film's message and structure are traditional and simple. As ever Joan 'is France' as d'Alençon says at one point, and in her own words she will 'be guided by God and by the people'. Perhaps inevitably at a time when anti-American feelings in France were beginning to be expressed, especially on the Left, the film was badly received. But on most counts it fails. While for the period the colour is magnificent Bergman is often ill served by the props. (We only have to compare, for example, the battle scenes and those

116. Poster for the opening of Fleming's film in France.

117. Further publicity to stimulate interest in Fleming's Joan of Arc.

in Gastyne's film, or 'Orléans' with its plastic walls and Carcassonne.) Magnificently dressed at *all* times and immaculately made up whether in the heat of battle or after months in prison (we only see a trace of sweat on her brow at the stake) Bergman and her stilted, self-preening performance do not ring true.

118. Ingrid Bergman as Joan. By courtesy of the British Film Institute.

Bergman had another chance to play the part of Joan six years later in *Giovanna d'Arco al Togo* ('Joan at the stake'), directed by Roberto Rossellini and closely based on the oratorio by Paul Claudel and Arthur Honneger that takes the form of a spiritual meditation with Joan in conversation with her confessor Brother Domenico. Throughout she remains chained to her stake as she recalls episodes from her life – depicted in a series of flashbacks – and as she comes to understand them so she prepares herself for ascent into heaven. All earthly matters are cast aside. The Church and royal court are mocked. Cauchon, for example, is depicted (as Claudel intended and as he is in the earlier oratorio) as a prancing, self-important pig; members of the court are sheep; court scenes emphasise superficiality and greed. By comparison when in the triumphant closing moments Joan breaks free from her chains and rises to heaven, an angelic choir sings: 'There is no greater love to give than to give your life for those you love.' Rossellini's images successfully capture Claudel's emphasis on the resurrection of Christ and on eternal life.

119. Bergman still immaculately made up but genuinely intense. By courtesy of the British Film Institute.

Although not widely shown or known since it first appeared the film prompted considerable debate, mainly about the ability of Rossellini to treat such a subject with conviction and about the film's technical qualities, but as a film about Joan and about what truly motivated her it (like the oratorio) is strikingly unusual and effective. Only parts of the films by Dreyer and Robert Bresson match it in spiritual intensity.

Before Bresson embarked on his film in the early 1960s, however, Hollywood's attention was drawn to Joan once again.

The story is well known of how, in 1957, Otto Preminger canvassed extensively throughout the United States in an attempt to find a young girl with no acting experience, in order, so he hoped, to be able to come up with a fresh interpretation of the role of Joan. Eventually he recruited Jean Seberg (a

120. Jean Seberg as Joan. By courtesy of the British Film Institute.

young farm girl from Iowa chosen from 18,000 hopeful applicants) for the title role. Seberg was kept as much as possible in isolation so that her reactions to people and events around her might appear genuine. But her lack of experience told and she comes across – not surprisingly – as altogether immature and incapable of meeting the demands of a role that had challenged some of the best and most experienced actresses of the previous half-century. The only time a sense of real drama appears to grip Seberg is during the trial scenes (known to have necessitated much extra rehearsal time) when her terror, as she learns she is to be burned, is convincing. As it is also during the scene of the execution when, so it is rumoured, her costume accidentally caught on fire! But in spite of these few moments the film was still a failure. In France, where anti-American feelings were running high and where, in any case, no unknown young actress from Iowa could possibly capture the spirit of Joan, it was severely criticised, but even in America box-office takings were hugely disappointing.

Preminger had wanted the script of his film to be based on the text of Shaw's play, but the playwright refused. (Shaw had in fact written a screen play in 1933 but Preminger seems to have been unaware of this and Shaw does not appear to have enlightened him.) The script that he eventually used was an adaptation of Shaw's play by Graham Greene, but with changes in emphasis. As Preminger wanted, Joan has to be seen to be correct and the subtleties Shaw had introduced in the dialogues between Warwick and Cauchon, for example, or his insistence on the correctness of Joan's trial, are missed.

Another four decades would pass before similar large-scale treatments of Joan would attract directors' attention, but her story was not forgotten. In 1962 Robert Bresson's black and white *Le Procès de Jeanne d'Arc* ('The Trial of Joan of Arc') was produced to much acclaim. In several respects it recalls Dreyer's film and has, as we have already observed, some of the spiritual intensity of Rosellinni's. Like Dreyer, Bresson concentrates on Joan's trial and execution, with the result that his film has the kind of minimalist power that is typical of much of his work. As Jean Guitton has claimed 'images have been paired down to their most basic ingredients, they are strained, pure.' While Dreyer's Joan is tearful, cautious, even slow, and treated brutally by the judges, Bresson's – played by Florence Carrez (better known as the novelist Florence Delay) – is confident, sharp and spiky in her answers to their boring and repetitive questioning. She comes across as a modern young woman but one who also has privileged access to the life of the spirit. Bresson observed that 'She combines her five senses in a new way. She sees her voices. She convinces us that there is a world beyond the one we are aware of. She steps into this supernatural world but closes the door behind her.' Technically the films have a number of similarities, especially in the use of close-ups and insistence on enclosed spaces and use of detail at the expense of large overviews. Bresson's technique of filming over shoulders or through doorways, windows and spy holes also has the effect of drawing us into the action as though we were present, though, as Kevin Harty has commented, there is something distinctly voyeuristic about this.

121. Florence Carrez contemplates her forthcoming trial and fate.
By courtesy of the British Film Institute.

But perhaps the most moving and powerful moment in the film is when the smoke from the pyre clears and all we see is a charred stake. Joan's body has gone and birds fly overhead. We do not, indeed we cannot understand; the power of grace is beyond our comprehension. Whatever the historical circumstances of Joan's life, it seems that Bresson is saying that her uniqueness is ultimately unfathomable. With this ending it is almost as though the last word about Joan had been said and indeed it would be more than thirty years before another attempt to treat her in film would be seen in her own country.

Meanwhile one of the more unusual adaptations of her story came from the Soviet Union in 1970. *Nachalo* ('The Beginning') directed by Gleb Panfilov tells the story of a young Soviet factory worker who is spotted in an amateur pantomime and invited to take the part of Joan in a film.

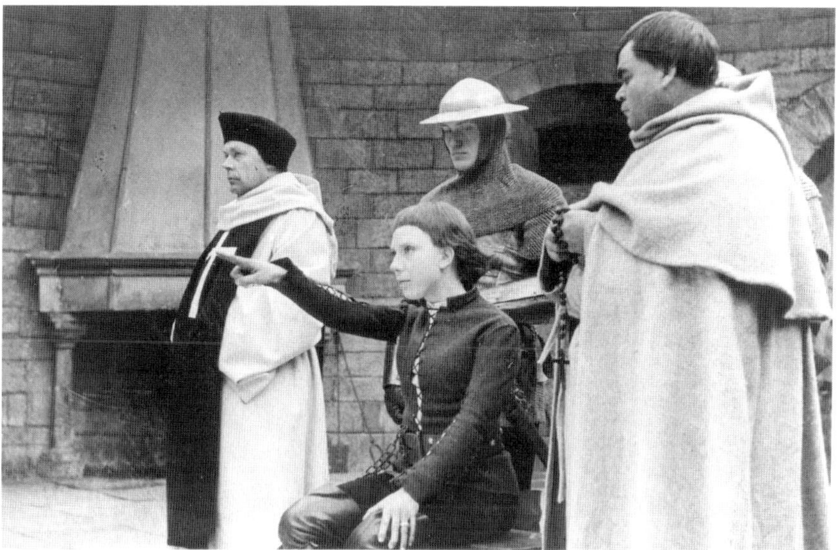

122. Inna Tchournikova defiantly responds to questioning.
By courtesy of the British Film Institute.

In a way that may remind us a little of Anderson's *Joan of Lorraine* we switch back and forth from the film to rehearsal and the 'real' world. Once the film has been made and released to great acclaim, Joan (played by Inna Tchournikova) is informed by the agency that there is no more work for her. 'You are special', the receptionist tells her. Interwoven with the 'Joan' theme of the film is the account of an affair she has with Arkadia, one of the factory managers that also lifts her out of the routine of her normal existence. But this too is fated not to last. Their final meeting before the release of the film ends in tears, at which point we cut to the scene of Joan's execution, accompanied by the sound of crackling fire. The parallel is clear. Just as she has been 'special' as an actress so has her brief idyllic time with Arkadia; only memories are left.

The public would have to wait for nearly a quarter of a century before the first of the latest clutch of major films about Joan appeared. Despite certain limitations they all try to introduce a new element or suggest a slightly different reading from those that had been screened before. The first to appear in 1994 was Jacques Rivette's *Jeanne la Pucelle*, a massive six-hour feature that has two parts. The first, *Les Batailles*, ends with the battle at Orléans; the second, *Les Prisons* begins with the coronation. Rivette chose to follow the strict chronological pattern of Joan's exploits and aimed at as realistic a portrayal of fifteenth-century France as possible. Time passes slowly, people are clad in worn and dirty clothes, colours are muted. Joan is a simple peasant girl who acts not because of some mystical inspiration (she hears no voices) but on her own initiative. Sandrine Bonnaire who plays the part of Joan has talked of how she attempted to interpret Joan as normal a human being as possible. 'I wanted to make her human', Bonnaire has said. 'For me all heroes are human beings. In this sense the fire really is the end. We need to know whether she is human or not. She suffers; she feels the fire like any other woman. She is a creature of flesh and bones.' At times she is bewildered and uncomprehending. She cries when she is wounded, is taught to write her name, and does not know how to take the rough humour of the knights around her. Rivette is not the first, as we have seen, to play down the spiritual dimension of Joan, but what is especially interesting about his depiction of her is that it came at a time when, as Blaetz rightly reminds us, Joan's image had been appropriated by the Right. His heroine, she writes, 'is a striking contrast to the one parading in armour on the saint's feast day with the leader of the Front National.' No doubt because of its length and slow pace Rivette's film has not had the impact or even distribution that it deserves. But even apart from its political statement it is a remarkable achievement. It may not have the harrowing intensity of the films by Dreyer or Bresson or the vivid excitement of Gastyne's, but it far surpasses the Holywood features of the 1940s and 1950s. Moreover it provides as authentic an impression as possible on film of what life was like in France five hundred years ago.

Five years later, in 1999, Luc Besson directed in English the last major film devoted to her in France, *The Messenger; The Story of Joan of Arc* starring Milla Jovovich.

If Rivette's main concerns were authenticity and an attempt to remind his viewers that Joan did not belong automatically to the extreme Right, Besson chose to focus on her inner self. In a film of standard length he concentrates on the well-known, major episodes of her life – the recognition scene at Chinon, the battle at Orléans, the coronation, her trial, abjuration and death. Like Rivette, Besson plays down the question of divine inspiration. While Joan may tell Charles about her voices there is no earlier scene depicting her communing with them; indeed she may have imagined them and it is precisely what motivated her that Besson appears to be primarily interested in.

The key to this appears to lie in the first major scene of the film. As a ten-year-old girl Joan witnesses the savage looting and destruction of her village by a troop of marauding English soldiers and the brutal rape and murder of her sister, Catherine. There is no doubting Joan's deep if immature faith, but what motivates her, Besson would have us believe, is the repressed hatred and passionate desire for revenge triggered by what she has witnessed and he replaces the more usual encouragement given to Joan by her saints with a series of hallucinations. In these a character simply called 'The Conscience' – a mixture of tempter and consoler – gradually explains what is happening to

123. Milla Jovovich rallies her troops at the battle of Les Tourelles. By courtesy of the British Film Institute.

her and eventually absolves her. Quite what Besson wants us to make of Joan, however, is not clear. In many respects she is simply and perhaps not unsurprisingly unstable – even mad — but her instability has a strange sexual dimension to it. In one scene towards the end of the battle at Orléans that several critics remarked upon, Joan hallucinates a Christ-like figure who strokes her face while she – a virgin we should remember – has blood pouring down her face. Reviewing the film for *The New Yorker* Joan Acocella observed that as a result of her childhood experience, sex and a passion for Christ are far from purely spiritual.

While the directors of both these films ensure that the realism of fifteenth-century France is not lost, we have the impression that they may also be attempting to detach Joan and her story from the conventional and well-trodden paths of previous accounts and relate her to the climate and preoccupations of the modern world.

At the same time it is difficult to imagine how much further any director might go without losing all sense of the original story. In Canada, Christian Duguay's television and feature film *Joan of* Arc, also produced in 1999, takes considerable liberties with history. Cauchon appears for the first time at Chinon, for example, Joan sets out on her mission in an attempt to take revenge on the English for having caused the death of a handicapped friend,

Raymond, and she has Glasdale butchered by her archers. Played by the very plain Leelee Sobieski, Joan does not believe in her role until she is convinced of it by an angel who descends from the sky like a fairy-tale princess in a cartoon film. Ultimately, however, there is a serious statement; once again Joan is depicted as being the innocent victim of the combined powers of the Church and State, but the film fails to convey any sense of anguish or tragedy.

Since this spate of feature films two quite different approaches to Joan and her story should be mentioned. 2000 saw the production of an experimental film *Wired Angel,* directed in black and white by Sam Wells. Wells is less concerned with the story of Joan than with the creation of a medieval world full of ritual and mystery through a clever use of lighting and unusual camera angles. And since 2003 another Joan has appeared on American television screens in the popular teenage soap, *Joan of Arcadia.* Set in the town of Arcadia, this is the story of the bright high-school daughter of the Girardi family. The father, a police chief, has moved his family to Arcadia where, as its Classical name suggests he should, he hopes to find a peaceful neighbourhood, but an unexpected outbreak of crime provides a challenge and causes tensions within the family to rise. But more particularly Joan also begins to act strangely. Unbeknown to her family she finds that quite ordinary people – a cleaner, an electrician, a beggar, for example – introduce themselves to her as God, to advise her on how she should behave in a particular situation or to give her specific instructions and problems to solve. This she manages to deal with – though not without difficulties – by a mixture of common sense, intuition and growing faith. Each episode is a kind of self-contained moral tale and clearly struck a rich vein of interest.

While in literature the image of Joan has shifted in many ways usually on account of the religious or political climate and the tastes of the author, in film it has in most cases been the basic story and the spectacle that it has been possible to generate from it that have been dominant. There are to be sure exceptions, notably the films by Dreyer, Rossellini and Bresson, but what catches the popular imagination remains the sight of stirring battle scenes and the execution. The enigma of Joan remains of course. A woman in a man's world who accomplishes what had hitherto seemed impossible and is punished by a male dominated society for having done so. And Besson's film goes even farther when it suggests that there is something fundamentally unstable in the female psyche. But whatever modern interpretations a director may try to impose or introduce into a portrayal of Joan the bare facts of her story form a framework from which it is difficult to escape. One possibility, already suggested by films such as *The Beginning* or even *Joan of Paris,* is for the story to be transposed in time completely. It would not be impossible, for example, to imagine a future space age Joan of Arc whose heroics in the face of invading alien forces lead to her sacrificial death and martyrdom in a nuclear conflagration.... Various directors, including Stephen Spielberg, have been rumoured to be turning their attention to Joan, but unless something quite as radical as this is considered, it is difficult to see what might emerge, and in any event the basic story remains.

Notes

1. Details of Blaetz's works are found in the Bibliography. Her article in *Joan of Arc, A Saint for all Reasons* edited by Dominique Goy-Blanquet contains the most complete filmography of Joan to date.
2. Quoted in Blaetz, *Joan of Arc, A Saint for all Reasons, op. cit.*, 147.
3. Much has been written about the loss of the negative of Dreyer's film, accidentally destroyed in a fire at Universum Film A. G. in Germany in 1928. Fortunately one nitrate copy had been sent to Dr Harald Arnesen in Oslo and was found sixty years later. See Blaetz, *op. cit.* 149, note 18.
4. Manuscript held in the Centre Jeanne d'Arc.
5. Quoted by Harty, 'Jeanne au cinéma', from Ib Monty in *The International Dictionary of Films and Filmmakers* , Chicago, 1990, edited by Nicholas Thomas, Vol. I, 691.
6. Manuscript held in the Centre Jeanne d'Arc.
7. Quoted by Blaetz in *Joan of Arc, op. cit.*, 153, from Heinz Steinberg in '*Das Mädchen Johanna* de Gustav Ucicky ou Jeanne et Goebbels', in *Etudes cinématographiques*, 18–19.

Chapter Eight

Joan in Music and Song: From Ballad to Rock Opera and Musical

Across the centuries, song has always been one of the most popular and instant ways of marking events of national importance, and it is interesting to speculate how the French in taverns and army camps must have celebrated Joan's feats across France and how a rather different view might have been voiced by the English and Burgundians. Unfortunately from the years of her campaign and even beyond her retrial nothing seems to have survived. The earliest musical tribute we have to her appears to be a song by Eloy d'Amerval, written, it is thought, sometime in the mid-fifteenth century, calling on the citizens of Orléans to celebrate the raising of the siege:

In answer to the sweet prayer
Uttered by the King to God
Came a chaste shepherdess
To fight on our behalf.
Inspired by God
She so harmed the English
That they were put to flight
And the siege was raised.
Sing, members of the clergy and you town's people,
And you, noble merchants, join us.
Let all the people of Orléans raise their voices
To thank God and the Sacred Virgin
Who on that eighth day of this month
Looked at them with pity
And so hunted down the English enemy
That the duchy was set free with great joy.

But this seems to be a lone example and it remains again unfortunate and equally strange that nothing should have survived from the following three hundred years. Only in the late eighteenth century do we begin to find references to a number of different musical pieces. In France there were two pantomimes, *Fameux Siège* ('The Celebrated Siege'), presented to the king at

PROGRAME

DU

FAMEUX SIEGE,

PANTOMIME.

Repréſentée devant leurs MAJESTÉS, à Marly-le 5 Juin 1778.

DE L'IMPRIMERIE

De P. R. C. BALLARD, ſeul Imprimeur de la Muſique du ROI, des Menus Plaiſirs, de SA MAJESTÉ, & de Monſeigneur & Madame la Comteſſe D'ARTOIS.

Par exprès Commandement de SA MAJESTÉ,

124. Official programme for Le Fameux Siège.

Marly in 1778 and successfully performed thereafter at the Théâtre de Nicolet in Paris and *Dorothée* (1782), a comic opera by the prolific Rodolphe Kreutzer staged at the Théâtre des Italiens in Paris in May 1790. In Italy Gaetano Andeozzi's four-act opera could be seen in Venice in 1793 and a year later in London, I. C. Cross's *Joan of Arc or the Maid of Orléans*.

125. Opening bars of the piano reduction of the duet 'Lie still my trembling heart'.

We also have fragments of a song by the popular singer Poirier written probably around 1790, *L'Histoire admirable de Jeanne d'Arque*:

Seeing our misfortune
God in his mercy
Sends to France
To put an end to our pain
The Maid of Orléans
Who with a new spirit

Defeats the English
And gives the towns back
To the august person
Charles, king of the French.

By comparison with the range of literary material devoted to Joan, by the end of the eighteenth century musical offerings were clearly scarce even if we allow that some have been lost. But from the beginning of the next century there was to be a change. Joan would be celebrated in ballads, cantatas, hymns, masses, operas, musicals and instrumental pieces of various kinds. Much of the vocal material, like so much of the literature about Joan at this time, is repetitive and predictable; well-known melodies were frequently re-used and in general there appears to have been little in the way of musical originality. Not surprisingly perhaps pieces were provoked by events, especially in Orléans, and fantasy seems to have played a bigger part than in literature. For example, and as we noted earlier, in 1803 a pantomime by Cuvelier was performed in Orléans. Joan and Dunois declare their love for one another early on, the God of Love appears and offers Joan a rose, which she burns. In the last tableau set in Rouen, the funeral pyre disappears to be replaced by a triumphal arch with a model of the statue of Joan to be erected in the town square. Ten years later this pantomime would be modified; all these features have been removed and at the end Joan is born away in triumph to heaven by a choir of angels.

From what evidence we have it seems that most of the pieces from the early years of the nineteenth century were minor and enjoyed only very limited success. On 15th February 1845, La Scala in Milan housed the first production of Guiseppi Verdi's opera *Giovanna d'Arco* with words by the popular resident librettist, Temistocle Solero. It would be the first major treatment of Joan in music.

Before this there had been an opéra-comique *Jeanne d'Arc* by Michel Carafa, produced in Paris, and two grander Italian operas by Nicolo Vaccai and Giovanni Pacini a decade later. Carafa's work is light and pastoral. There is nothing tragic about it and the religious dimension is played down in a complete reworking of the traditional story. At the end Joan is reunited with her peasant fiancé, Robert, who returns from the war and the pair sing a rich, joyous duet, but in general the music is simple with little ornamentation. In contrast the two Italian works are full of grand scenes and appropriate music with Joan in a role that is both heroic and visionary.

Verdi's opera, which has never enjoyed the status of such masterpieces as *La Traviata* or *Rigoletto*, for example, is somewhere between the two styles. It was well received in Italy where, with Erminia Frezzolini in the title role, it enjoyed twenty-five performances between 1845 and 1848. But the French were less sympathetic and critics with more than a little justification – though

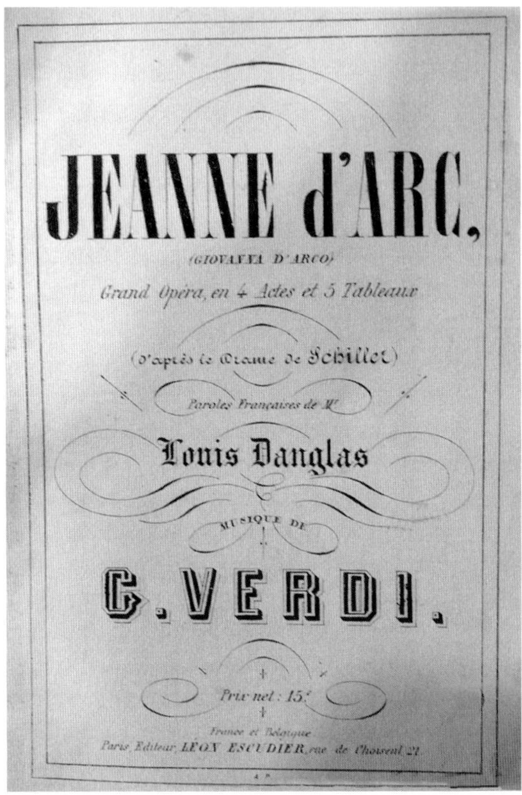

126. Cover of the French score for Verdi's opera with an acknowledgement to Schiller.

with seemingly no memory of the liberties taken by some of their compatriots – considered that it was not sufficiently faithful to the accepted story. As she sleeps Joan is tempted by devils who promise her endless earthly pleasures: 'You are beautiful... If you relinquish the flower of love now, it will quickly die, never to return....' However, angels persuade her instead to liberate her country, offering her a helmet and a sword; even so when she leaves on her mission her father, Giacomo, remains convinced that she is in league with devils. Moreover so ashamed is he of Carlo's lack of resistance to the English that he is willing to join and hand Joan over to them! Joan is successful, but at the coronation Giacomo again accuses her of having accepted the devils' aid, a view with which the crowd now agrees. When Joan remains silent her father takes this as confirmation and offers her the chance to redeem herself if she will accept to be burned. In addition to this reworking of the religious or supernatural elements in Joan's story Solero also has Carlo declare his love for Joan – a love she is willing to return. Joan is imprisoned and from her cell hears a battle and in her mind's eye sees Carlo surrounded by the English and about to be defeated. She prays to God and unbeknown to her is watched by her father who promptly forgives her. Joan joins the battle and the English are defeated but she is fatally wounded. The people kneel before her and she dies in the arms of her father and Carlo. When, in June 1996, Verdi's opera received its first performance at the Royal Opera House in London, French critics were no less dismissive than they had been a century before, calling it 'absurd' and 'historical romantic rubbish.'

However fanciful much of this opera may have been, an undertaking on this scale marked the beginning of others that stood out from the continuing production of very ordinary pieces. One such piece was the four-act opera *Jeanne d'Arc* with words and music by A. Mermet that ran for fifteen performances in April 1876.

127. The cover of a song and piano reduction of Mermet's score.

Despite this relatively modest success a year later an article in the *Moniteur universel* was scathing in its criticism. Any hopes for something new in an opera devoted to Joan were dashed, it was claimed. 'We are sorry to have to say that the work is a complete failure. And having already been murdered by so many operas, Joan can now add another palm to her martyr's crown.' But Joan

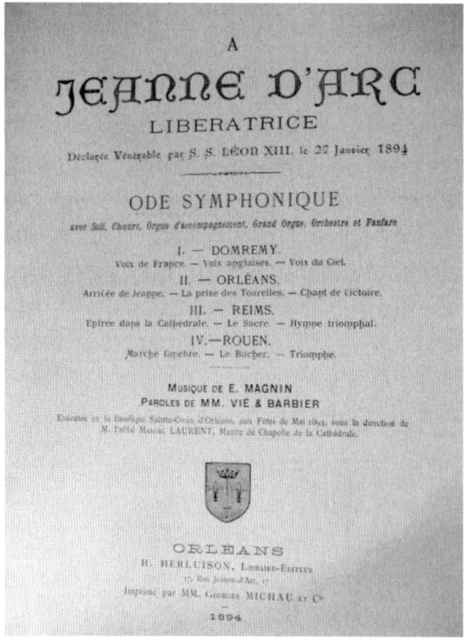

128. Gounod's Vision de Jeanne d'Arc, *and the cover of the score by Magnin and Barbier.*

continued to inspire. Magnin and Jules Barbier wrote their *Ode symphonique*, and Charles Gounod provided music for Barbier's 1873 play (in which as we have seen, Warwick falls in love with Joan and offers to save her), and wrote a

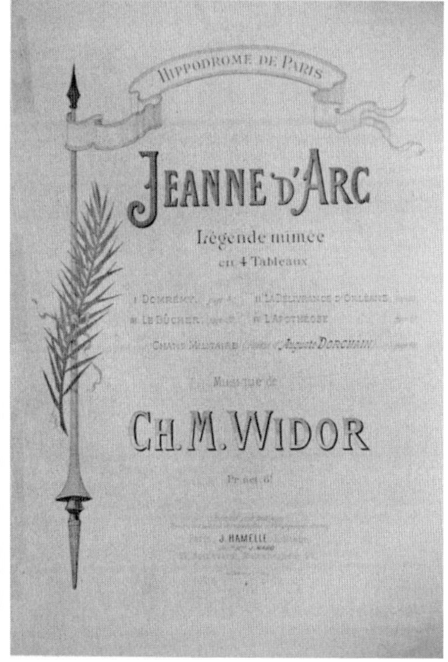

129. The opening bars of Liszt's Jeanne d'Arc au bûcher *and the cover of the programme for Widor's production.*

mass and a piece for solo violin with organ or two pianos in 1887. Even Franz Liszt was stirred to write a now nearly forgotten piece for voice and piano.

And if Gounod was motivated by the divine dimension of Joan's story, in 1890 Charles Widor wrote the music for a mime, *Jeanne d'Arc, légende mimée en 4 tableaux*, taking his inspiration from Joan's peasant origins and exploits as a soldier.

Both produced music that is rhythmically and harmonically more complex than most of what had been composed before and Widor's instrumentation would arguably not be matched until Honneger's nearly fifty years later. Meanwhile Joan had again attracted the attention of major composers abroad. In 1881, in Russia, Tchaikovsky's opera (with a libretto by Joukovski) was performed in St Petersburg to popular acclaim.

130. Cover of the original Russian score of Tchaikovsky's opera.

To a great extent the opera follows Schiller's play, not only in content but so closely that sections of the German text can be turned into vocal lines without its being necessary to adjust them to the music. The vocal highlight of the opera comes with the introduction of Lionel in Act Four. Joan fails to resist her passion for him and they celebrate their love in a glorious duet. But angels tell Joan that she has failed and that even though a place awaits her in heaven she will have to suffer. The English enter and attack the lovers, killing Lionel and taking Joan prisoner. No doubt because of the musical potential of the traditional ending to Joan's story Tchaikovsky now abandons Schiller's plot and has Joan die at the stake in Rouen. As the fire is lit a chorus of angels invite her 'to come to the heaven of God'. Elsewhere too Joan was a source of inspiration. In Germany Max Bruch had already composed accompanying music for Schiller's play in 1859 and in 1886 one of the few symphonic treatments, the *Symphonic Variations* by Thadewalt, was performed.

While such works as these suggest a more serious approach, Joan continued to be treated rather more light heartedly especially by the English. By the late nineteenth century a number of 'burlesques' and music-hall pieces were performed that were often farcical and even disrespectful. A good example of this is *Joan of Arc* by J. L. Shrine and Adrian Ross with music by F. O. Carr, performed in London in 1892, in which, as they appear, characters are accompanied by discordant, lively or ponderous music and so on, according to how they have been caricatured.

With the twentieth century Joan continued to be treated in music in much the same way. Imitations of medieval ballads (*Complainte sur la Pucelle d'Orléans*) with reproductions of period woodcuts in 1909; a cantata celebrating her entry into Orléans in the year of her canonisation; a mass which Hubert Parry who died in 1918 was rumoured to have been preparing for the five-hundredth anniversary of her death; a symphonic poem by Manuel Rosenthal, with words by Delteil in 1936, and a score for chamber orchestra *Paysage pour une Jeanne d'Arc à Domremy* ('Landscape for Joan of Arc at Domremy') a year later; collections of popular and patriotoc songs and countless small

One of the typical collecions of songs celebrating Joan

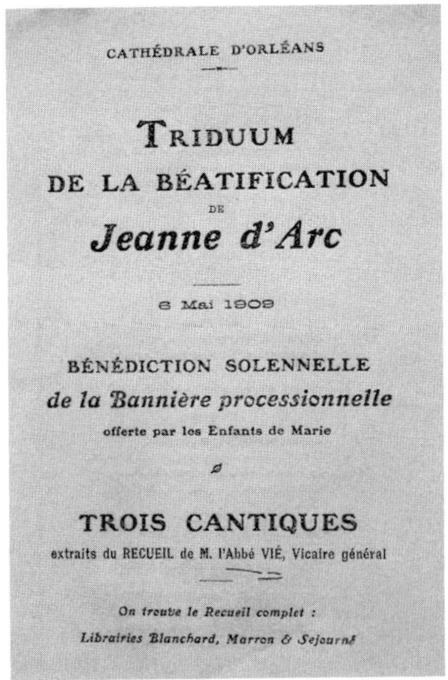

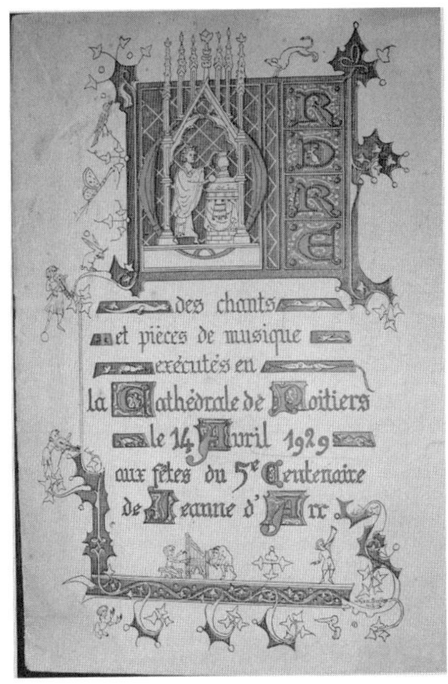

131. *Some examples of songs: a celebration of Joan's beatification; popular songs for workers; a patriotic pamphlet; an imitation medieval illumination manuscript celebrating the five hundredth anniversary of Joan's arrival in Orléans.*

pieces, mainly vocal.

Nor was Joan forgotten in school music. A popular collection of songs for children, edited by the librettist Marc Legrand and including his own *Jeanne la Bonne Lorraine* to music by Ernest Reyer, enjoyed frequent reprintings.

132. Opening bars of Reyer's simple score.

During the First World War Joan became the subject of a marching song for Canadian troops and when America entered the war, she attracted in turn

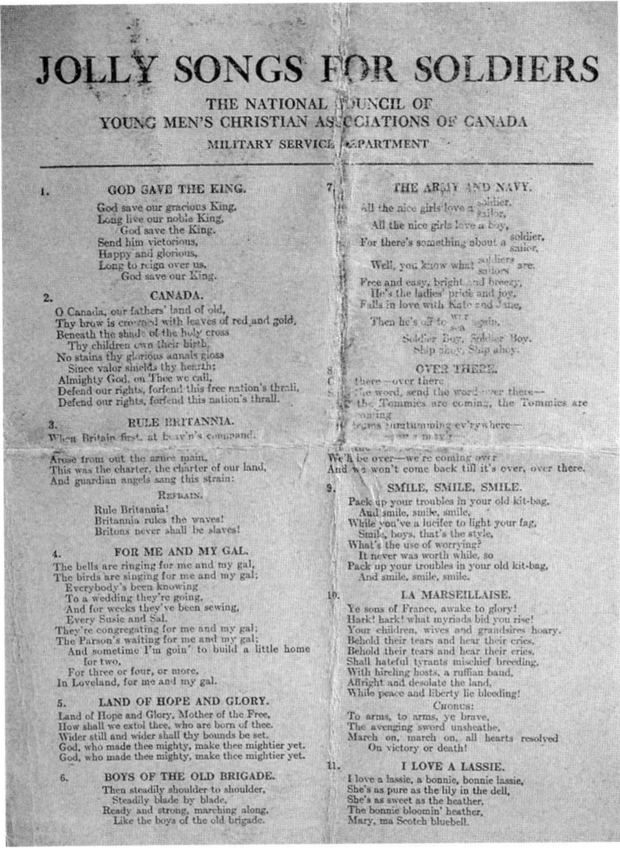

JOLLY SONGS FOR SOLDIERS

THE NATIONAL COUNCIL OF
YOUNG MEN'S CHRISTIAN ASSOCIATIONS OF CANADA

MILITARY SERVICE DEPARTMENT

1. GOD SAVE THE KING.

God save our gracious King,
Long live our noble King,
God save the King.
Send him victorious,
Happy and glorious,
Long to reign over us,
God save our King.

2. CANADA.

O Canada, our fathers' land of old,
Thy brow is crowned with leaves of red and gold,
Beneath the shade of the holy cross
Thy children own their birth,
No stains thy glorious annals gloss
Since valor shields thy hearth;
Almighty God, on Thee we call,
Defend our rights, forfend this free nation's thrall,
Defend our rights, forfend this nation's thrall.

3. RULE BRITANNIA.

When Britain first, at heav'n's command,
Arose from out the azure main,
This was the charter, the charter of our land,
And guardian angels sang this strain:

REFRAIN.

Rule Britannia!
Britannia rules the waves!
Britons never shall be slaves!

4. FOR ME AND MY GAL.

The bells are ringing for me and my gal,
The birds are singing for me and my gal;
Everybody's been knowing
To a wedding they're going,
And for weeks they've been sewing,
Every Susie and Sal.
They're congregating for me and my gal;
The Parson's waiting for me and my gal;
And sometime I'm goin' to build a little home for two,
For three or four, or more,
In Loveland, for me and my gal.

5. LAND OF HOPE AND GLORY.

Land of Hope and Glory, Mother of the Free,
How shall we extol thee, who are born of thee.
Wider still and wider shall thy bounds be set.
God, who made thee mighty, make thee mightier yet.
God, who made thee mighty, make thee mightier yet.

6. BOYS OF THE OLD BRIGADE.

Then steadily shoulder to shoulder,
Steadily blade by blade,
Ready and strong, marching along,
Like the boys of the old brigade.

7. THE ARMY AND NAVY.

All the nice girls love a soldier, / sailor,
All the nice girls love a boy,
For there's something about a soldier, / sailor,
Well, you know what soldiers / sailors are.
Free and easy, bright and breezy,
He's the ladies' pride and joy,
Falls in love with Kate and Jane,
Then he's off to war / sea again.
Soldier Boy, Soldier Boy,
Ship ahoy, Ship ahoy.

8. OVER THERE.

[illegible] there—over there
[illegible] the word, send the word over there—
[illegible] the Tommies are coming, the Tommies are coming
[illegible] drums rumtumming ev'rywhere—
[illegible]
We'll be over—we're coming over
And we won't come back till it's over, over there.

9. SMILE, SMILE, SMILE.

Pack up your troubles in your old kit-bag,
And smile, smile, smile,
While you've a lucifer to light your fag,
Smile, boys, that's the style,
What's the use of worrying?
It never was worth while, so
Pack up your troubles in your old kit-bag,
And smile, smile, smile.

10. LA MARSEILLAISE.

Ye sons of France, awake to glory!
Hark! hark! what myriads bid you rise!
Your children, wives and grandsires hoary,
Behold their tears and hear their cries,
Behold their tears and hear their cries,
Shall hateful tyrants mischief breeding,
With hireling hosts, a ruffian band,
Affright and desolate the land,
While peace and liberty lie bleeding!

CHORUS:

To arms, to arms, ye brave,
The avenging sword unsheathe,
March on, march on, all hearts resolved
On victory or death!

11. I LOVE A LASSIE.

I love a lassie, a bonnie, bonnie lassie,
She's as pure as the lily in the dell,
She's as sweet as the heather,
The bonnie bloomin' heather,
Mary, ma Scotch bluebell.

18. JOAN OF ARC.

Joan of Arc, Joan of Arc,
Do your eyes, from the skies, see the foe?
Don't you see the drooping Fleur-de-lis?
Can't you hear the tears of Normandy?
Joan of Arc, Joan of Arc,
Let your spirit guide us through,
Come lead your France to Victory,
Joan of Arc, they are calling you.

133. Marching songs for Canadian troops in the First World War.

the attention of songwriters there, perhaps for the first time. At least three pieces appear to have been written between 1915 and 1918. The first and best known is *Joan of Arc, they're calling you* from a 'Novelty Musical Production' *This Way Out*. (The show also contained such stirring numbers such as *King of the Ring*, *Auntie Skinner's Chicken Dinner* and *Ragtime Wagner's Ghost*.)

134. Score of 'Joan of Arc They Are Calling You',
a song written during the First World War.

There's a tear in my eye for the soldier,
As he lays *[sic]* among the slain.
There's a throb in my heart for this old world,
That sighs for peace in vain.
There's a hope in my prayer that some one above,
Will gaze down on earth through the blue,
And pitying all our sorrow and woe,
Will tell us what to do.

There's a sigh in the trench for the hedgerows,
For the tender last embrace,
And the babe held up high to hide from him
A woman's anguished face.
Oh, it's so hard to breathe when I think of the hearth,
And old folks in silent despair,
While dreaming of him in pale fire-light glow,
The boy they cannot spare.

Refrain (in slow march time):

Joan of Arc they're calling you,
From each trench they're calling you.
For through the haze comes the sweet Marseillaise,
Can't you hear it calling too?
They really say from your last breath
That a dove flew to the skies.
And if that was the Dove of Peace, Joan of Arc,
Send it down and dry a mother's eyes.

The second, *Joan of Arc* (1916) with music by James Kendis and lyrics by Robert Roden, accompanied the publicity produced for DeMille's film *Joan the Woman* by the Cadillac Moving Picture Series and the score has a large portrait of Geraldine Farrar on the front cover. The third, *Joan of Arc's answer* (1918) with music and lyrics by J. L. Lavoy, was 'Dedicated to the Fatherless Children of France.' The reverse cover of the score bears the notice:

> There are about 250,000 fatherless children in France that America is helping to support. This fund is being raised in various ways. The author of this composition will contribute 20 per cent of the net proceeds to their support. Every copy sold will help this charitable work.

The two verses of the song have Joan exalting the allied forces to continue their 'fight for their right to liberty', but the refrain closes with the promise of American aid:

Dear old France with listening ear and aching heart I hear you calling,
With great valor I can see your heroic stand,
My word to you in this great hour of need is 'Do not falter',
For America with millions strong is near at hand.

135. Joan leads the American troops and below soldiers from France, Britain, Australia and North Africa charge forward, bayonets at the ready.

Despite such attention from the world of popular music a major question remained, however. With the operas by Verdi and Tchaikovsky largely forgotten, was Joan ever going to inspire a musical work that would outlive the immediate circumstances of its composition – for example the celebration of her canonisation – and enjoy the reputation of, say, a play like Shaw's? Interestingly enough one of France's greatest twentieth-century composers, Maurice Ravel, could not bring himself to realise such a project, even though he thought about it. While he appears to have planned the individual scenes and had ideas about a 'sarcastic music' for the trial he seems not to have written a single note. 'I'll never write my Jeanne d'Arc', he said to Valentine Hugo in 1933. 'The opera is in my head, I can hear it, but I'll never write it. It's finished, I can't write my music any more.' But not all was lost. In the same year the dancer and writer Ida Rubenstein approached the Protestant Swiss composer Arthur Honneger. She had seen a production of some medieval mystery plays and conceived a project involving the story of Joan for a travelling theatre group, but Honneger rejected the proposal on the grounds that his music would not be suitable. But the idea was there and through Darius Milhaud Rubenstein contacted the Catholic poet and playwright Paul Claudel. At first he also refused to become involved but, on a train journey to Brussels, had a vision of Joan's hands: 'Suddenly I felt a shock, the idea came to me. I saw two hands tied together making the sign of the Cross. The play was ready. I only had to write it, a matter of a few days.' Claudel finished his text within two weeks. When he received Claudel's manuscript, Honneger needed no convincing and composed the music the following year.

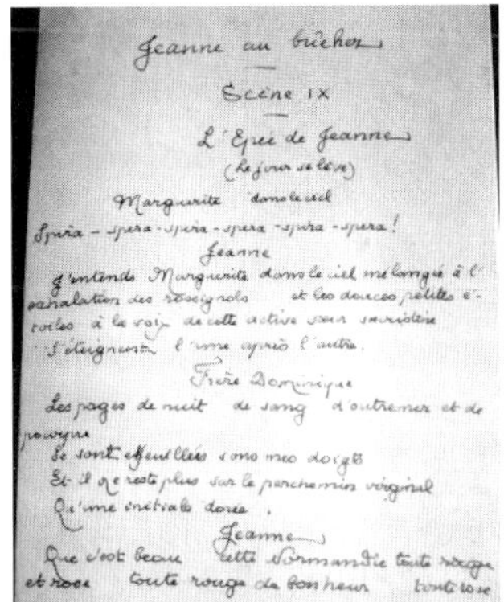

Jeanne au bûcher

Scène IX

L'Epée de Jeanne

Marguerite dans le ciel

Spera - spera - spera - spera - spera - spera!

Jeanne

J'entends Marguerite dans le ciel mélangée à l'exhalation des rossignols et les douces petites étoiles à la voix de cette active
s'éteignent l'une après l'autre.

Frère Dominique

Les pages de nuit de sang d'outrance et de pourpre
Se sont effeuillées sous mes doigts
Et il ne reste plus sur le parchemin virginal
Qu'une initiale dorée.

Jeanne

Que c'est beau cette Normandie toute rouge et rose toute rouge de bonheur toute rose

136. Claudel's and Honneger's manuscript pages of Jeanne d'Arc au bûcher, *1938.*

On account of administrative complications and delays in Paris the 'stage oratorio', *Jeanne d'Arc au bûcher*, had its first performance in Basel on 12th May 1938 with Rubenstein as Joan. A year later on 6th May a concert version was performed in Orléans, where anti-Semitic supporters of the extreme Right viciously attacked it, and a month later it opened in Paris. Given the circumstances the oratorio quickly assumed political significance. Claudel had first written somewhat conventionally in his preface: 'It is the eternal Joan we witness, the one on the threshold of our modern times and who is the patron of our national unity.' Now in 1940 he would ask: 'Is France going to be torn in two for ever?' Neither the Vichy government nor the Nazi censors in Paris seemed concerned by the oratorio, however, any more than they were, as we have seen, by various literary works. It was performed in Paris in June 1941 and went on to enjoy a prolonged provincial tour in the southern 'free' zone of the country. Three years later in November 1944, three months after the Liberation of Paris, the work was given a new prologue. In it Claudel likens France before Joan comes to save her to the chaos before the creation; the opening words are sung quietly by the chorus: 'Darkness! Darkness! Ah!! And France was without form and void, and darkness covered the face of the kingdom, and the spirit of God, not knowing where to rest, hovered over the chaos of souls and hearts.'

Whatever political significance the piece might have had, however, it is the unusual combination of spoken word and music – the former often over and against the music – as well as Claudel's imaginative text, that marks it out from anything that had been produced before. One small illustration of this is the way in which Honneger has a musical echo of Claudel's use of the pun Cauchon-cochon to portray the bishop as a pig and name him Porcus, by having the part sung by a high tenor, the voice traditionally given in French opera to figures of fun. Joan's spoken conversation with Brother Dominic as she attempts to understand episodes from her past life as it is described in the book prepared by her accusers and which he reads to her, is reflected in the singing and orchestral passages. Honneger introduces snatches of folk songs (Scene 8), for example, and has echoes of Bach's *Passions* in the bass passages and of Orthodox ritual hinted at by the tolling of bells in Scene 7. As the end approaches Heaven and Hell battle stridently before calm is restored – Honneger uses saxophones and heavy percussion – and Joan is joyfully received into heaven by the Virgin Mary and by Saints Margaret and Catherine. The closing words – 'Greater love hath no man more than this, that he lay down his life for those he loves' – echo those of Christ in the Gospel according to Saint John.

137. Illustrations from an HMV boxed set of 9 records of Jeanne d'Arc au bûcher.

138. *Posters advertising performances of* Jeanne d'Arc au Bûcher *in Paris and Orléans.*

On a smaller scale altogether but in some respects equally subversive is another oratorio *Jeanne d'Arc triomphante* by René Herval, performed in Rouen cathedral on 30th May 1943, the beginning of what was to be the bleakest period of the Nazi occupation. Unlike the work by Claudel and Honneger, Herval's is utterly conventional in its treatment of the Joan story, but his final chorus was surely a call to French people to resist:

Sweet France, the day has come
When you will emerge from your suffering, to be born again.
Thanks to the spirit that exalts you and brandished steel
The enemy flees. Joan guides you,
Joan whose intrepid heart
Shines in battle with a divine fire.
The God of the armies will lead you on as before,
Invisible and strong, across the blazing plains.
There will be fighting in the shadow of His sword,
And you will see Victory surrounded by a golden halo
In the rising dawn.

And as an example of a blatant post-Liberation use of Joan for political purposes we need look no further than Louis Ganne's traditional *Marche lorraine*. This was originally published in1892, but with De Gaulle now firmly (if temporarily) in control, a new title page neatly illustrates how it could be adapted to the contemporary situation.

139. Politics or music? Louis Ganne's Marche Lorraine.

Whether or not it was *Jeanne d'Arc au bûcher* that prompted a re-exploration of musical adaptations of Joan's story, not unlike the surge of interest in the world of film, is impossible to say, but from the mid twentieth century attention to it throughout the world has not been lacking. In New York the feminist choreographer Martha Graham produced a dance for solo performer, *The Triumph of Saint Joan*, in which Joan is Maid, Warrior and Martyr and in which, as in the Claudel-Honneger oratorio, she embraces the fire that consumes her. A few years later this piece was reworked for group performance, with music by Dellio Joio, with the title of *Seraphic Dialogue*. Ballets were staged in Paris in 1955 and in Moscow two years later Nikolaï Peïko's *Saint Joan* enjoyed considerable success. This was a vigorous, elaborate production with, for example, projections of black smoke and red flames during the battle scenes and in the court episodes the use of well over fifty performers

140. Violetta Bovt as Joan in Peïko's ballet, Moscow, 1958.

whose dances are a mix of classical steps and traditional folk pieces, the latter used to point to and undermine the decadent nature of Charles' court. In the last tableau that depicts the burning of Joan there is no dancing, only a row of soldiers in the market square. Above them through smoke and flames, Joan is silhouetted and finally bathed in white light.

In 1971, in America, Leonard Cohen recorded his song 'Joan of Arc' as part of his mainly lugubrious anti-war album *Songs of Love and Hate*: 'I'm tired of the war/ I want the kind of work I had before/ A wedding dress or something white.' He too has Joan willingly embrace the flames, presented as a seductive male:

> "Then fire, make your body cold,
> I'm going to give you mine to hold."
> Saying this she climbed inside
> To be his one, to be his only bride.

In 1984 the young British composer Luke Stoneham wrote a chamber opera, *La Pucelle* (originally entitled *Arms for the Maid*), evocative of eastern music and Japanese Noh theatre. And probably from around the same time there is an American oratorio, *Saint Joan*, by Al Carmines, the Pulitzer Prize winner and gay minister who was then pastor at the Judson Memorial Church in New York. In this work Joan is a drug addict, possibly bi-sexual and a revolutionary drop-out who has to be eliminated. The ecumenical council comprising a rabbi, a cardinal and a bishop, does not take long to find a way of compromising its position and of not opposing her execution by the electric chair. Carmines' work is at times comic but it is also typically and relentlessly satirical.

Act Two

CARDINAL: I call this meeting of the President's Ecumenical Religious Council to order. Item one: the case of this girl Joan. She blew up a building, claims to hear voices, is incarcerated awaiting trial. The President wants a recommendation from us regarding her sentence.

BISHOP: Well, it seems pretty straightforward. She's obviously insane; she should be sent to a hospital.

RABBI: Well . . . it's a little more complicated than that. There are certain political implications the President would like to see squelched.

BISHOP: Hm – I see. What's her religion?

CARDINAL: Jewish background, raised Presbyterian, and now she claims to have conversations with the Virgin Mary.

RABBI: The newspapers have been quoting Pope John about leniency and mercy.

CARDINAL: John, John, John – I'm sick of hearing that name. He's become a mouthpiece for every bleeding heart in the country. Oh God, how long, how long?

BISHOP: I just came out against capital punishment. I can't very well recommend what the President seems to want.

RABBI: Is there some way we could sound liberal but . . .

CARDINAL: But really have her executed? I don't know.

BISHOP: Wait a minute – did she shoot a policeman? That's an exception to the capital punishment statement.

CARDINAL: No, but I think a bathroom attendant was slightly wounded.

BISHOP: That's close enough – if he was uniformed – let's simply say that the President's wisdom in this case makes interference by the clergy unwise. Make a big case for religion-state separation. You're so good at that, Cardinal.

Equally subversive in tone is a rock opera, *The White Raven,* written in 1978 by the Ukranian poet Youry Rybtchinsky. Like Carmines, Rybtchinsky set out to attack what he saw as the oppressive political regime in the Soviet Union – an accusation that was quickly justified when his opera was banned!

Quite different in mood and intention, and once again from America, is the oratorio by Richard Einhorn, *Voices of Light*, (1995) inspired by Dreyer's film and sung by the female quartet Anonymous 4. In it Einhorn aims to underline the mystical quality of Joan's story. For his libretto he uses passages from the Bible, and from thirteenth- and fourteenth-century texts notably by female mystics in Latin and medieval French. The orchestral accompaniment is marked by heavy rhythmic string playing that creates a hypnotic effect and resolves in a rich and powerful ending in 'The Burning' and 'The Fire of the Dove'. For the recording the four singers were placed facing the orchestra and when interviewed claimed that this confrontation put them in exactly the same position as Joan at her trial and had thereby created in them the required emotional response.

Joan has also continued to inspire popular songs. In 2002 Elton John (with words by Bernie Taupin) produced his provocative 'Did anyone sleep with Joan of Arc?':

She swung a sword
She rode a horse
She wore her armour for the Lord
But did she cry by candlelight
Was she lonely after dark
Did she pray for something more
Did anybody sleep with Joan of Arc.

From all these activities, however, perhaps the one outstanding omission for many a year was a large-scale musical in the tradition of *Evita, Jesus Christ, superstar, Les Misérables* or *Cats.* In February 1997 this was made good with the staging in Montreal of *Jeanne la Pucelle, The Joan of Musical Drama,* in both French and English versions, with lyrics by Vincent de Tourdonnet and music by Peter Sipos. The production costs amounted to no less than 4.5 million dollars, but before opening over thirty thousand tickets had been sold. Reception was mixed. Kate Taylor, writing in *The Globe and Mail* deemed it 'at least bland and occasionally ridiculous'; Sylvain Cormier described it as 'a clumsy imitation of an Andrew Lloyd Webber musical [...] a kind of medieval *Evita* for American-loving Canadians.' But elsewhere praise was high –

141. Bilingual flyer for Jeanne la Pucelle.

'spectacular, flawless, dazzling, aesthetically impeccable' were just some of the tributes.

In large measure the plot follows that of Shaw's play, but it fails to sustain the tension and has none of the gravitas of the earlier work. We have yet another attempt to turn Joan and Charles into a romantic pair, and the failure to convey Joan's terror when faced with the prospect of being burned are just two examples of the way in which popular taste could exert an influence.

As with film the question that remains for music in the future is whether Joan will continue to inspire composers and librettists or whether she has run her course. No doubt anniversaries such as those of her death or canonisation will be reason enough for occasional pieces to be written and performed. It is also true that to date we still await a major 'Saint Joan' symphony or concerto. What does seem unlikely, however, is that a new, different *form* of musical interpretation is possible. There is no doubt that Einhorn went some way to achieving this, but it seems likely that for the foreseeable future Tchaikovsky's opera and above all the Claudel-Honneger oratorio will be difficult to surpass.

Afterword

Why, after more than five centuries, should we remain interested in a teenage girl whose achievements, while undoubtedly remarkable, could easily have become little more than a footnote in the history of France and of Anglo-French relations in particular? Why does she continue to inspire biographers and creative artists across the world? Why does she appeal so strongly to the popular imagination? In all these respects Joan is no different from any other similar iconic figure. As in most of such cases, details of her short life – at least those that can be historically accounted for – are well known and provide a simple but fixed framework for any imaginative treatment of her. But like Robin Hood, Cleopatra, Faust or Christ, Joan has become more than a simple historical figure. It is not what she was or what she said or achieved in early fifteenth-century France that matters, but what she has come to represent or symbolize. Like all such figures Joan has acquired a metonymic quality; her name evokes not simply a person but a range of values and issues that have varied and evolved according to time and circumstances. Canonisation, it is true, has ensured that Joan's image is linked in particular with the Catholic Church, not only in France but worldwide. At the same time, however, and as we have seen, it has been appropriated and used as an emblem by and for a variety of other institutions, factions and purposes, not a few of which barely relate, indeed if at all, to the values traditionally associated with Joan.

But what of Joan's future? Her story will undoubtedly be retold in schoolbooks and be subject to scholarly examination. It will just as surely continue to invite controversy and be challenged. In France, the anniversaries of the raising of the siege of Orléans, of her martyrdom and of her canonisation will be celebrated in various ways. It also appears likely that she will remain for the foreseeable future the figurehead for the proclamations and demonstrations of ultra-conservative Catholics and the politicians and supporters of the nationalistic extreme Right. Her name and image will no doubt promote goods and services of all kinds. She will also undoubtedly be evoked at moments of crisis or even of good-natured controversy between France and England. But the real test of her status as one of the outstanding iconic figures of European and indeed worldwide culture is surely her capacity to inspire writers and artists of all kinds. Already regular performances of the works by Péguy, Shaw, Anouilh and Claudel, exhibitions, and the release on DVD of major feature films ensure an ongoing interest, but it is in the way that her image can be imaginatively recast in new works that is particularly significant. As we have seen, while these may not be numerous, they are not lacking and are tellingly varied – proof alone that Joan's place in the panoply of major iconic figures is ensured.

142. A group of modern statuettes of Joan from a collection in Boston. Some reflect traditional images, some different cultures and others are simple and beautiful works of art.

Appendix
The American Maid

CLAUDE GRIMAL

At the end of Maxwell Anderson's play, *Joan of Lorraine* (1946), Mary, the actress who is to play Joan of Arc, declares with emotion that she has finally seized on how to interpret her character: 'I know now – and it's as if I knew it from Joan herself. It does not matter what we try to say about her. Nobody can use her for an alien purpose. Her own meaning will always come through, and all the rest will be forgotten'.[1] However, nothing could be less true: few historical personages have been used for other than their 'own, meaning' as much as Joan of Arc, as can be seen in the literature, art, films, and images of which she has been the subject over the centuries, serving purposes and causes quite foreign not only to France and the Middle Ages, but to herself. The ease with which her figure can be moulded and modulated – owing to its unusual and paradoxical association of femininity and warrior virtues, of naive ignorance and intelligence, of the spirit of revolt or loyalty to an ideal – has made her adaptable to innumerable purposes and in innumerable countries, including the United States.

A priori it seemed hardly likely that America would be a country to remodel Joan of Arc into a nationally suitable heroine. Neither its history nor its culture seemed predisposed to transforming her into a useful and productive myth. Nonetheless, American Joans soon appeared in answer to the needs of the times: with the birth of the new Republic, she was a symbol of Independence, and in the nineteenth and twentieth centuries, a rallying cry for soldiers as well as an inspiration for philosophical thought on the subjects of exceptional destiny and the individual's role in history. Chaste women warriors cropped up in American paintings, writings, speeches, especially between 1870 and 1920 when, echoing the French controversy over Joan of Arc which arose after the loss of Alsace and Lorraine and the subsequent debate over canonization, America took over the personage and adapted it to its own needs. Thus a study of the various metamorphoses of the American Joan of Arc, what they were and how they were engendered, leads us to re-examine certain moments of American cultural history. Yet while Joan may have a role to play in historical and intellectual matters, she is essentially an image that crosses national borders, an extraordinarily powerful and seductive fantasy of the human psyche: virgin warrior, sorceress-saint, super-lucid eternal child, and still more. It is these aspects which will be emphasized in the present study, leaving aside the Joan of Arc of the cinema, already well covered in a number of reference works, this one included.

At times, the American Joan of Arc was independent of the French Jeanne, at others their lives ran parallel. As we shall see, the American Maid was fashioned from existing European literature and scholarship, and became an important figure in the United States when she was also the centre of attention in her own country, in particular between 1850 and 1920. Before and after these years Jeanne's metamorphoses were perhaps more innocently coloured by her new context, but at the end of the nineteenth and the beginning of the twentieth century, America, well aware of adopting a subject that preoccupied France, was carefully reshaping it and ridding it of its national or political element, while at the same time allowing French thought and iconography to guide the American imagination. In the nineteenth century, it was the work of the French scholar Jules Quicherat that provided direct or indirect source material about Joan, while after the 1920s both European and American literature and cinema lead in shaping a vision of her, probably the most important single influence on a particular version of Jeanne in the Anglo-Saxon world being George Bernard Shaw's *Saint Joan*, which premiered in New York in 1923.[2] Thus from the outset, the French heroine arrived for her American career already clothed in diverse national, religious, and ideological attire – French, Protestant, warmongering and others – and in a variety of incarnations with which the Americans identified according to their own particular needs, whether or not they coincided with the intentions of Joan's many previous European impresarios. It is the result of this constant process of hybridization, the American Joan, of the arts, of literature, and of propaganda, who interests us here.

An Enlightened Joan

Joan of Arc's first appearance on the American continent was quite an oddity. In 1793, shortly after the birth of the Republic, John Daly Burk, a little known playwright, wrote and directed a play called *Female Patriotism or the Death of Joan of Arc*. The action took place during the French Middle Ages, and more or less followed historical events and Joan's life. The play was not very successful for various reasons, one of which was the strong anti-French sentiment of the time, the result of the serious disagreement between President John Adams and the Directoire.

Burk, an Irish revolutionary who had been forced to flee his country (and is said to have arrived in the New World disguised as a woman),[3] used Joan in a curious reversal of historical reality. The situation in fifteenth-century France was made into a replica of the problems facing the Americans struggling against England, and Joan herself was transformed not only into a heroine of independence but a spokeswoman for Republican ideas. The gap between Joan's reality and Burk's use of it made *Female Patriotism* a rather incongruous play, in which Joan and her story were pretexts for a heavy messianic drama promising happiness for all once humanity was delivered from the tyranny of its sovereigns. Obviously, a vision such as this one necessitated extensive changes in the 'real' person, even if Burk was already heir to a tradition that had given fantasy a measure of liberty with the facts concerning the Maid of Orleans. Reading Burk, though we may not he surprised to find a Joan in love already invented by others, we are indeed intrigued on encountering an anti-monarchist and deistic Joan who has never heard voices, two unusual metamorphoses of the French country girl, though they had in fact appeared slightly earlier in the Englishman Robert Southey's *Joan of Arc* (1795), probably one of the sources of Burk's play.[4]

Nonetheless – and from a literary point of view this is her central function in the play – Joan retains her heroic characteristics (courage, determination, solitude, and so on). She retains, however antithetical, the sentimental aspects of the ideal feminine figure as seen by the eighteenth century, with its modesty and gentleness. Thus at the end of the play she expresses a desire to go back to the place she has always felt was hers, far from the public eye and from the battlefield.

Yet in religious and political matters, Joan is an enlightened man of the eighteenth century, a Burk in skirts, a 'Tom Paine in petticoats'.[5] She believes in 'the Power Supreme', the 'universal Soul of the Universe',[6] to which she addresses long monologues. She confides that she has never heard voices nor received a divine mission to save France; 'my story was a pious fraud' (III. iii. 36), she says, before adding:

> No visions had I more than one of you.
> I saw no sights but all of you did see:
> France torn by feuds and foul dissentions;
> France desolate beneath a stranger sword [...]
> And these my country and my countrymen,
> Groan in the bondage of a meaner state.
> This only was my inspiration. (III. iii. 15–18, 21–3)

She has been sent by no one, certainly not by Heaven, and insists that she is simply human:

I am no more of heaven than yourselves;
No inspiration do I feel, beyond
The stretch and compass of the human mind. (III. iii. 11–13)

Burk's Joan denies any vision of herself and her commitment that might go beyond the limits of the 'human mind'. She squares accounts with the divine, and explains that it not the Heavens but her own patriotism that is to be thanked for the aid she brought to France. She presents her political, Republican stand and states that the crowning of the Dauphin is pure and simple strategy. Thus the 'pious fraud', thanks to which she passed herself off as having been sent by God, serves a cause of human society; yet this is only a stage before the 'golden age', before the Republic, the ineffable moment when all men shall be equals:

'Tis not to crown the Dauphin prince, alone
That hath impell'd my spirit to the wars,
For that were petty circumstances indeed,
But on the head of every man in France
To place a crown, and thus at once create
A new and mighty order of nobility
To make all free and equal, all men kings
Subjects to justice and the laws alone.
For this great propose have I come amongst you. (IV. i. 6–14)

In the name of 'Liberty and Equality', she proclaims:

The race of kings shall be but simple men
The human race becomes a race of kings
This may be called the golden age indeed. (IV. i. 23–5)

This picturesque Maid, improbable as she was, but armed with the strength of her convictions, was meant to represent very 'advanced' ideas. However, because her deism, rationalism and egalitarianism were too radical, and her nationality was (as we have already said) against her, she did not overly appeal to that public whose sympathies she might have aroused.

One wonders why Burk chose to clothe his ideas in the personage of Joan of Arc. Moral virtues and the heroic warrior ideal could have been incarnated in numerous other figures, any one of whom, given his casual attitude towards historical fact, could have served the playwright's ideological principles. We can only guess that Burk wanted a feminine warrior and also a 'real' historical personage, a domain in which historiography is in fact sorely lacking. Joan gave a feeling of reality to his play, and at the same time enabled him to develop both the heroic and the sentimental, normally difficult to reconcile. Joan's death, both a 'real' event and a summum of emotion, gives the audience not only the pain and pleasure of high pathos but a reassurance of the conventions befitting the feminine realm: feminine heroism is paid for by death because it is fundamentally a transgression, because it crosses the confines of the intimate and ventures into masculine territory – politics, war, thought. Joan of Arc allowed Burk to develop virile and feminine qualities in a single character and to punish what in the end will appear as a usurping of the masculine by the feminine. With Joan's death we find the feminine back in its sacrificial role, a realm of predilection used once again to re-establish the conventional view of women.[7] Joan's femininity makes up the sentimental counterpart of a play about protest and rationalism. However shocking for twentieth-century readers – though it was certainly less so for those of the eighteenth – social equality and the reign of reason are dreams borne by a woman who defies her own century only to defend implicitly, for herself and her sisters, a reactionary ideal of timidity and modesty that is better off at home than in the great wide world of politics and war.

The Warrior Maid

The theme of grace and modesty beneath courage and conviction was not the one that most interested another curious political protester who enlisted Joan under the Confederate flag during the Civil War. John Fentonhill's hundred-page essay, preceded by a committed introduction, gives us another interesting distortion of the personage of Joan. *Joan of Arc, an opinion of her life and character as derived from the ancient chronicles,* was published in Richmond, Virginia in 1864, when the Southern cause was just about lost after the battles of Gettysburg and Atlanta. The image that interested Fentonhill was that of Joan of Arc the fighter, the head of an army that would launch itself into a hopeless battle and win. The medieval conflict was an unhoped-for parallel in the midst of military collapse and humiliation. In Joan's story he found the only possible answer to disaster: the fantasy of a providential saviour. This imaginary character invented for the needs of the cause also made a mockery of Joan's reality.[8] To urge his Southern comrades to continue the fight, Fentonhill transformed Jeanne into a ruthless warrior with no qualms about massacring the enemy, perceived in both cases (the English and their allies or the Northerners) as a horde of killers and plunderers rather than a legitimate army. On the religious side, he makes the heroine into a precursor of Protestantism, a notion which had already appeared in English metamorphoses, and in a chapter entitled 'Joan's Protestantism Shown', explains that she is an example of how matters of belief are ruled by personal judgement and not ecclesiastical bodies.

At the same time as Joan became a source of inspiration for Fentonhill, the Unionists found a real Joan in flesh and blood: the young Anna Dickinson, held up by the Northerners as 'The Joan of Arc of the Unionist Cause', 'The American Joan of Arc', 'The Joan of Arc of the Civil War'. This young Quaker girl from Philadelphia gained fame during the war years thanks to oratorical gifts which she put to the service of the Northern cause, making speeches at political meetings, rousing troops before their departure to the front, speaking before Congress, and before Abraham Lincoln himself. When the press compared her to Joan of Arc, she identified with the image of the heroine and stepped into the personage – the parallel was there: she was young, from a modest family, made her ideas heard to great men, defended her country, and so on.[9] In no time, with or without ironic intention, almost every militant, political-minded woman would be dubbed 'Joan of Arc': at the beginning of the twentieth century, for example, suffragettes were ridiculed in cartoons as self-deluded Joans of Arc,[10] and the Labour union militant Elizabeth Gurley Flynn was nicknamed by workers, this time admiringly, 'Joan of Arc of the Wobblies'.[11]

But if the name of Joan of Arc appeared now and then in connection with women who engaged in public and political activities, it was World War I that aroused the desire for an imaginary or real virgin warrior, fighting on the field or speaking before the crowds. The First World War further intensified the heroic and sentimental theme, although by World War II Joan was completely forgotten: modern war no longer needed a woman for a talisman to serve the multiple purposes of yardstick for the justice of a cause, source of inspiration, and guarantee of success on the battlefield. But before going on to see how World War I prolonged the magic of Joan's image and carried it to the greatest heights, let us return to the second third of the nineteenth century, when a vision of Joan began to develop that was both close to historical fact and interested in a new definition of her personality.

The Morals and Politics of Joan

In the 1840s, quite another picture of Joan of Arc came into being both in the United States and in France thanks to new studies about her – the research of Jules Quicherat in particular, published between 1841 and 1849 – which triggered interest by providing access to historical documents. For instance, it is as an introduction to an English translation of the minutes of her trial that Mark Twain wrote one of his two texts on Joan, 'Saint Joan of Arc' (1899).[12] Thanks to the erudite work of Quicherat, Joan's own voice came directly across to nineteenth-century readers, and many authors described the emotion that had inspired them to transcribe her testimony word by word in their own works.

Thus it was on the basis of new historical facts that biographies – by Jules

Michelet (1841), Alphonse de Lamartine (1842), and Anatole France (1908) – and other works would soon be written. Atheists like Quicherat and Michelet as well as Catholic writers were fascinated by Joan, and as their works became known in English-speaking countries, the latter began producing their own.[13] Mark Twain, far example, for his *Personal Recollections of Joan of Arc by the Sieur Louis de Conte* (1906), read a series of studies both English and French, a bibliography of which can be found at the beginning of the book with an indication of eleven titles the humourist claims to have used as a basis for his own text, the works of Quicherat and Michelet, along with Janet Ticker's very popular English biography.

In the United States again as in France, a great number of historical, hagiographic, or simply moralizing studies appeared in the last third of the nineteenth century. Two aspects of Joan seemed to fascinate her creators – her inner strength and her fight against the powers that be, the second one being diversely interpreted and seen in line with each individual writer's ideology. The religious or psychological vision accentuated her character traits (their intensity, origin, and exemplary nature), and the other more political vision laid emphasis on the conflict between the personage and political authority.

But it was the vision of a pious Joan to the exclusion of any other facet of her character and reality that made its appearance where least expected. Sarah Grimké, for example, militant abolitionist and feminist like her sister Angelina, translated and adapted Lamartine's biography in 1867, preceding it with a brief introduction extolling Joan's exemplary nature for its piousness and moral qualities, a conventional and hardly pugnacious discourse in which Joan's virtues are those of 'a woman in all gentleness, tender yearnings, and fortitude sublime; a man in intellect, heroic daring and loftiest aspiration'. Making no allusion to the causes she and her sister ardently defended, Grimké saw Joan as having been sent by God:

> Next to Jesus, she seems to have been the grandest medium of divine communication; a being sent from a higher sphere to allure and busy us upward. Her inspiration was a summons from God, reverberating though a whole people, and concentrating its power in the exaltation and agony of a single soul.[14]

Be that as it may, in Grimké's insistence on the fact that woman is the subject of God (and of no one else) it is also possible to recognize the same spirit of protest as in her 1837 *Letters on the Equality of the Sexes.*

During the nineteenth and twentieth centuries, the image of a pious Joan often took the form of a soothing Christian model of piety, the embodiment of obedience to the divine word. It was during this period that she became a reminder to humanity of its religious duty, inspiring a host of mediocre literary works varying in accent and tone according to those to whom they catered –

women, children, Americans, Catholics ... thus, to take one American example among many, the author of *The Wonderful Story of Joan of Arc and the Meaning of Her Life for Americans* (1918), C. M. Stevens, repeats over and over the simple lesson with its confessional aim, that she is an example of Faith: 'The Domremy shepherd girl [...] reveals how the world's work is achieved through faith', 'She was faith', 'Joan of Are was the long, straight aim of Faith', 'Christ was a revelation of life [...] Joan of Arc is the revelation of Christian life. She was a vision and a message of the unconquerable Christian soul', 'Her faith is available to all'.[15] The putting forth of Joan as a model was aided and abetted by the French debate of the times, although its circumstances remained foreign to the United States.

Indeed, in France, the warning signs of what was to come and the defeat of 1870 revived interest in Joan of Arc. Campaigns to canonize her – she was proclaimed Venerable in 1894, Blessed in 1909 and Saint in 1920 – kept her in the public, eye, but although the United States was willing to accept a patriot, it did not feel the same way about a Saint, except for a Catholic minority. Some groups aligned themselves along the liberal and anticlerical lines formulated by Michelet, and other anti-Catholic groups chose to see Joan as a radical Protestant who found in herself the truth that it was not the business of the Church to preach. Again, the division between historians, biographers, rationalist or 'progressive' writers, and partisans of a conservative, religious Joan, could be found in the United States. For some, even if it meant exaggerating one side of her character at the expense of the rest, Joan was a religious personage with an exemplary faith, for others she was a revolted soul ready to challenge authority, firm in her convictions unto death.

Parallel to the conservative vision of Joan, a vague and impassioned feeling towards women was conveyed in texts and particularly in pictures. Her beauty, virtue, attire and allure were subjects of query. Some of the innumerable paintings of her crossed the Ocean and raised the question of how she should be represented. When the paintings by Jules Bastien-Lepage and Gustave Jacquet, two French artists, were shown in New York in 1881, a newspaper commented:

> There are in New York, at the time of writing these sentences two pictures of Joan of Arc [...] One is by Bastien-Lepage, an American [*sic*] painter [...] The other is by the French artist Jacquet[16] [...;] Jacquet's idealism is worthless, but so is Bastien-Lepage's pretended realism. Who wants to look at a repulsive peasant girl as an ideal of the Maid of Orleans? The artist, in his determination to discard all the glamour and false notion of the legendary and sentimental idealism, [...] has forgotten that Joan was only 18 [...] he refused to heed her gentle dignity, her pure and modest manners, and has thought fit to portray the maiden as a rustic of the rustics.[17]

In defence of the American journalist, it can be added that neither Emile

Zola nor J. K. Huysmans in France, nor Mark Twain, who all commented upon the painting, had much to say in favour of *Jeanne d'Arc écoutant les voix*, which was nonetheless immediately purchased by an American collector after its showing in Paris at the 1880 Salon (the painting is now one of the most popular works in the Metropolitan Museum of Art in New York). America left the pictorial depiction of Joan to France, though often using it to illustrate works about her. Sarah Grimké chose a reproduction of Marie d'Orléans' statue for her translation, and Mark Twain, disappointed with the illustrations he had commissioned froth the American artist F. V. Du Mont, replaced them with engravings from Jules Lenepveu's mural paintings for the Panthéon in Paris in a later edition of *Personal Recollections of Joan of* Arc. The statues dedicated to Joan of Arc erected in the United States were almost all casts or copies of French works.[18] The only American artist to venture on the terrain was Anna V. Hyatt, whose equestrian statue was inaugurated in New York in 1915.[19] Although American enthusiasm for pictorial and sculptural representations of Joan never reached the same level as in France,[20] to this day it has remained lively, as demonstrated by the fact that a U.S. Internet site sells seven different versions of *Jeanne à Domrémy by* Henri Chapu (1871), including one life-sized bronze, along with many other pictorial representations of Joan which are either affectionate portraits of the Maid, or the manifestation of 'Kitsch' taste in the representation of feminine figures.

Thus Joan's development in the United States at the end of the nineteenth and the beginning of the twentieth century often ran parallel to that in France, differing from the latter most often in matters relating to Catholic and Republican points of view. Interest for her as a symbol was a result of her popularity in France, at the time, as the object of a struggle between fundamentally opposed political and ideological camps indigenous to France. In the United States, as has been said before, she could be put to the service of a variety of causes, but these were not central to the evolution of American history or at the heart of issues concerning it. Her recruitment by the French Catholics in particular was met with reticence by a majority of English and Americans, whose scepticism as to the merits of her canonization has recently been summed up by a twentieth-century commentator:

> Although the canonization process made her story better known to Americans, the religious aspect of her character was not the primary source of her popularity here. The American view of Joan is perhaps best expressed by these words written in the *Saturday Review* in 1894: 'The Maid of Orleans has nothing to gain in honours from being canonized. She is canonized already in the hearts of all who love courage, truth, purity, gentleness and beauty [...][21]

'The Marvelous Child'

It was Joan's 'courage, truth, purity gentleness and beauty' that interested Mark Twain when he published *Personal Recollections of Joan of Arc by The Sieur Louis de Conte (Her page and secretary)* in 1895.[22] He so wanted this book, which he had written 'for love',[23] to be taken seriously that he had it published anonymously. 'I like *Joan of Arc* best of all my books, it *is* the best; I know it perfectly well',[24] he kept insisting. Few of his commentators were to agree with him on the qualities of this historical romance, that nonetheless sheds light on both Twain's own tendencies and those of the whole nineteenth century in matters of history, childhood, and women.

In *Personal Recollections,* Twain chose a fictional mode to talk about Joan. Her story, told by her page and by then aged secretary, Louis de Conte, combines the charmed vision of a young boy and the bitterness of an old man. One wonders what the violently francophobic, misanthropic and anticlerical Twain saw in the deeply believing young French patriot left to burn at the stake. Certainly it was not Joan's 'saintliness' that interested him. Nor was it her politically providential character, considering Twain's profoundly pessimistic view of the series of uninterrupted catastrophes called History. Nor was it the magnificence of her defence of her country. For Twain, disgusted by 'the damn human race', Joan was an extraordinary human exception that embodied all virtues, or rather the one virtue which for him summed up all the others, and which was innocence.

To begin with, Joan was a young girl, and Twain, who later surrounded himself with his famous pre-adolescent 'Angelfish', had a fascination for pre-puberty femininity that he shared with a number of other writers such as Edgar Allan Poe, Charles Dickens, and Lewis Carroll. Joan, 'the marvelous child', corresponded to his ideal. Louis de Conte/Mark Twain was moved by the young virgin both as an adult man with a curious passion for purity and as a young boy upholding the heroic ideal of rescuing a 'damsel in distress'. The idealization of Joan was of course both physical and moral, 'a dainty little figure [...] gentle and innocent [...] winning and beautiful in the fresh bloom of her seventeen years' (*PR*, I, 23) and 'the most noble life that was ever born into this world save only One' (*PR*, I, 18). Joan was one of the little girls who moved him in the same way as the sweet young things he wrote about – Becky Thatcher, the 'wonder child', Marjorie Fleming, the 'sweetheart' of his fifteen years, and others. She also bears a resemblance to mistreated young women like Harriet Shelley, for whom he wrote a posthumous 'defense' at about the same time, in 1894.

Yet Joan also posed a historical question for Twain, a man enamoured with logic. She caused him to ask how, given her social origin, her sex, and the context of the times, she had been able to accomplish such extraordinary feats.

But oddly enough, finding no rational answer to the question, he simply dismissed it. In the 'Translator's Preface' to *Personal Recollections,* Twain states that the Middle Ages was the most appalling age of humanity, but makes no effort to understand how such barbarous centuries were able to produce a creature so perfect. He accepts and enjoys the wonder of it, and strange though it may seem for a rationalist, takes it for a miracle:

> When we reflect that her century was the brutalest, wickedest, the rottenest in history since the dark ages, we are lost in wonder at the miracle of such a product from such a soil. The contrast between her and her century is day and night (*PR*, I, xi).

No, he writes later in 'Saint Joan', 'there is no blemish in that rounded and beautiful character!' and taking up once again the mysterious question of the origin of such perfection, he repeats:

> Taking into account [...] all the circumstances – her origins, youth, sex, illiteracy, early environment, and the obstructing conditions under which she exploited her high, gifts and made her conquests in the field and before the courts that tried her for her Life – she is easily and by far the most extraordinary person the human race has ever produced (SJ, 595-6).

Thus Joan is a mixture of innocence, goodness, abnegation, et cetera, as in the stereotypes of sentimental fiction ... and is also Twain's ahistorical answer to history. For Twain, extraordinary human beings appeared on earth from time to time, their influence was negligible (in Joan's case anyway), they had no use even as models, but they could be considered quasi perfect. Twain's judgement remained confined to hyperbole, refusing to enter a world of relativity and rational analysis. Joan's character 'can be measured by the standards of all times without misgivings or apprehension as to the result. Judged by any of them, judged by all of them, it is still flawless, it is still ideally perfect' (*PR*, I, xi). For Twain the great sceptic, Joan was a mystery, a miracle that served no other purpose than to illustrate the imperfection and abomination of the rest of the world.

In his 1910 article, 'The Turning Point of My Life', Twain went so far as to reproach God, declaring that a human being with Joan's character would have better served humanity than his first creatures, Adam and Eve. With his usual humour and brio, he chose the two personages who, in a light and optimistic scenario, could have prevented the Fall: 'What I cannot help wishing is that Adam and Eve had been postponed, and Martin Luther and Joan of Arc put in their place – that splendid pair equipped with temperaments not made of butter, but of asbestos. By neither sugary persuasions nor by hellfire could Satan have beguiled *them* to eat the apple'. To which he adds, concluding in a comical vein: 'There would have been results! Indeed, yes. The apple would be intact today; there would be no human race; there would be no *you*; there would be no *me*' (485).

'Joan of Arc, they are watching you'

The First World War, the years following and the period surrounding her canonization in 1920 were in France the apogee of the version of Joan as a national heroine, whereas in the United States at that time she was mainly enlisted for war propaganda. She inspired no major literary or iconographic work, but flourished as the subject of sentimental fiction and war novels, articles, songs, posters and diverse objects.

Haskell Coffin's poster for Savings Stamps, intended for American women, shows the traditional image of an armoured Joan with raised sword, a comparison suggesting that frugality in the household is tantamount to bravery on the battlefield. American men adopted Joan along with soft drinks, and stories are told of how the troops embarked singing 'Joan of Arc, they are watching you', the best known though not the only war song in her name.[25]

The statue of Joan on Riverside Drive in New York was inaugurated on December 6th, 1915, before America's entry into the war.[26] The work of Anna Vaughan Hyatt, who had received an Honourable Mention for a first version of the statue at the 1910 Paris Salon, it had been intended as a celebration of the five-hundredth anniversary of Joan's birth. Erected in the midst of war, it gave rise to patriotic declarations on the part of French officials, while the American government, still neutral at the time, was appreciative, but more reserved. President Woodrow Wilson sent a letter which was placed in the pedestal and which read: 'Joan of Arc is one of those ideal historic figures to whom the thought of patriotic people turns back for inspiration. In her seems to have been embodied the pure enthusiasm which makes for all that is heroic and poetic'.[27] In his speech, the French Ambassador stated: 'this statue, the noble work of an American maiden, appropriately recalls the similitude of what both our countries cherish most in this world'.[28]

Finally, in 1917, when the United States landed in France to defend in person what they 'cherish[ed] most in this world', American troops happened to be stationed near Domremy (General Pershing's headquarters were in Chaumont), and the press was soon full of the love of the 'doughboys' for the young woman warrior.[29] Christian and patriotic fires made occasional appearances in American propaganda literature, whose sentimentality all but equalled that of the French:

> The little cottage [at Domremy] for two years opened its door to hundreds of thousands of Americans. These new Americans came, like Joan of Arc, to fulfill a mission. Doughboys from ranches and from colleges, from coal-mines and from

> offices gazed about them earnestly at the low-walled dwelling as humble as that in which Lincoln first saw the light. To some Joan was a Saint, to others a strange wonderful girl; for all of them she had a vivid interest. Most of them never had heard of her before they went to their training camp, but not one of them reached France without knowing the words of the song that taught them that the maid's spirit was as thrilling in France in the twentieth century as it had been when she led her men in many a sally almost 500 years ago. Every day they sang 'Joan of Arc, they are calling you'. In token of their willingness they hung on one of the altars the unconquered flag under which they fought.[30]

Joan's New Causes

The image of Joan as the defender of a nation faded after the First World War, particularly after the 1920s. During World War II, patriotic spirit was little apt to be kindled by the mise en scène of a feminine warrior; the image of Joan doubtless seemed unusable also because the nature of war had changed: in France, only a few members of the Resistance, among them Claude Vermorel in his *Jeanne avec Nous*, published in 1942, and René Char in *Jeanne qu'on brûla verte*, published after the war, saw her in their own image, as a fighter in the shadows.

Nevertheless, the enthusiasm and emotion aroused by the personage of Joan of Arc was used to uphold other causes, some rather vague and others more precise. It was the theatre that changed the image of Joan for the Western world, America included: Bernard Shaw's *Saint Joan* (1923), which premiered in the United States, Bertolt Brecht's *Saint Joan of the Stockyards* (1932),[31] Jean Anouilh's *L'Alouette* (1953), adapted by Lillian Hellman. But it was of course the cinema that recreated Joan's image with the greatest force and intensity.

The plays of Shaw, Brecht, and Anouilh shaped and modulated Joan's character each in its own way. Certain features already exploited were brought to the fore in a more striking manner: Shaw reinforced the Protestant, individualistic, nationalistic and political version of Joan. In his introduction, he criticized the tone of 'idolatrous romance' or 'belittling scepticism' with which she had been treated; in his eyes she was that celebrated personage who showed, as his Joan herself says, that the earth is not ready to receive its saints, or to put it differently that all evolution in thought and in conduct must first appear as heresy and misconduct.[32]

Jean Anouilh's approach was more 'existentialist'; his Joan is a young girl who 'says no', who is guided by her personal conscience to the point of refusing Cauchon's suggestions for a solution of compromise, comfort, and happiness. This adamant version of Joan left her open to the unexpected political interpretations in Hellman's adaptation.

Bertolt Brecht took advantage of the twentieth century to exploit Joan for the singularity of her character and situation. His play is set in the United

States where Joan Dark is a lieutenant in the Chicago Salvation Army. Engaged in promoting the cause of charitable reformism, she becomes awakened to the combat against capitalism and dies. Chosen by Brecht for her moral and militant qualities, Joan enabled the playwright to suggest an interesting contrast between the historical context of the Middle Ages, more or less familiar to the audience, and a new political context hardly related to the former but which needed morally committed heroes as much as did the fifteenth century, this time for a combat not against the Church or the English but against capitalist exploiters. Misled at first, Joan rallies and ends up espousing the Marxist cause with the same tenacity and courage as the original Jeanne.

Among the American creations, the best known of those that came after the war is Maxwell Anderson's *Joan of Lorraine* (1946), a rather facile version of Shaw's *Saint Joan.* The momentary popularity of the play was due more to its modern composition of a play within a play and to Ingrid Bergman in the role of Joan than to any new treatment of Joan's character or situation. Joan is the protagonist who proves her inner strength, who doubts and then returns to beliefs that Anderson deliberately leaves undefined. Before going to her death, she says to Cauchon:

> Each must believe for himself. Each soul chooses for itself. No other can choose for it; in all the world there is no authority for anyone save his own soul. [...] Yes, you did choose [your faith]. You choose to keep it. As I choose to keep mine. And, if I give my life for that choice, I know this too now. Every man gives his life for what he believes. Every woman gives her life for what she believes. Sometimes people believe in little or nothing. One life is all we have, and we live it as we believe in living it, and then it's gone. But to surrender what you are, and live without belief – that's more terrible than dying – more terrible than dying young. (III)

The play sets out to illustrate the drama surrounding personal conviction and moral doubt. But for lack of analysis of the underlying ethical aspects of these questions, it leaves us with the assertion that only the individual, ahistoric conscience guides one's choice of values. It was probably this meagre intellectual substance and the fact that it came just after the War that accounted for its success, and it was thus on Anderson's Joan that Victor Fleming based his 1948 film, with Ingrid Bergman once more in the central role.

The work of Jean Anouilh interests us here because of Lillian Hellman's adaptation.[33] For Hellman, a victim of McCarthyism – she was summoned in 1952 before the House Committee on Un-American Activities, like her friend Dashiell Hammett, who was sentenced to prison – Anouilh's play was about courage and refusal. She herself, Hammett and their friends opposed the authorities and refused to cooperate in any denunciations. Her version of *The*

Lark was therefore one of defiance and protest, and was perceived as such by the audiences who attended its 229 performances, between 1955 and 1956, and whose aim in so doing was to see a play about American reactionary despotism – superbly played by a celebrated trio of actors (Julie Harris, Boris Karloff and Christopher Plummer) – and about how one could rise up against it. Hellman, however, was well aware of having made use of a play that had little political intent, which only the McCarthy era had allowed her to transform into a fiery tract. She later admitted, in 1968: 'I don't like Anouilh's *The Lark* very much. But I didn't discover I didn't like it until I was halfway through [the translation]'.[34] Nonetheless, Anouilh's play had served her purposes at a time when, except for Arthur Miller's *The Crucible* (1953), few works had given form to the problem of personal conscience tyrannized by the pressures of suspicion and terror.

In the second half of the twentieth century, Jeanne continued to lend herself to specific, causes unrelated to her own times – feminism, pacifism and others – that used her more and less interestingly, mostly as an epitome of moral grandeur. However, it also became fashionable to perceive her with a certain irony and derision: Jules Feiffer's Broadway play *Knock Knock* (1976) gave the audience a blond-wigged Joan in a farce midway between 'Shaw and Disney [...], a wild spree', at the same time 'fairytale and [...] free-wheeling vaudeville'.[35]

One modern theatre group made serious use of Joan however, though again in a rather curious manner. In 1977 at the World Theatre Festival in Nancy, then elsewhere in the world, the Bread and Puppet Theater, equally disinterested in the conventional notion of heroism, premiered their *Joan of Arc*,[36] a sort of poetic and counter-cultural cavalcade that combined, in the words of director Peter Schumann, 'the mythic, the spiritual and the political'. The idea was to say once more that 'war and hunger have to be abolished; water, air, soil have to be brought back to life [...] Our mind is hungry and Jesus says: man does not live by bread alone, but from puppet shows as well'.[37] The programme was decorated with naive drawings and divided into four parts featuring short texts on the subjects of 'Why', 'For Whom', 'Who', 'What' is Joan of Arc:

> Why Joan of Arc: Because our civilisation is a dead-end, because it's dark, because we die, because we suffer – and in order to break the logic of the story, and in order to light a light, and in order to raise a flag.
>
> For whom Joan of Arc: For all who die, for all who suffer, for all who fight against unsurmountable obstacles, for all women-warriors. If we can make an angel who conquers the impossible, then you can make an angel who conquers the impossible too.
>
> Who is Joan of Arc: A peasant-child, a woman-warrior, born in 1412, listened to the voices of heaven, defeated the invaders, crowned the dauphin, burnt at the stake when she was 19, canonized in 1919.

> What is Joan of Arc: A legend in 2 parts. Part 1: a book unfolded, a series of pictures and demonstrations of her life and death, accompanied by a Chinese jazz-band. Part 2: the story of her horse, our society on a train pursuing the white horse, getting it, killing it. Cruelty succeeds. Mourners mount. It takes an angel to resurrect the dead.

The play, performed by Schumann's neo-primitive marionettes, was both a lament over the state of modern society and the ills of mankind, and a vision of hope in which the young girl, the white horse and the angel of Heaven all played their role in the disjointed, falsely naive manner of Bread and Puppet productions. Their modern symbolism turned back the clock to take up the subject of wars and flying banners for a combat in the name of 'light', spiritual flame, and moral force against contemporary brutality. A drama not far from some religious visions of the nineteenth century, but with the humour, fantasy and political drive of counter-culture.

One of the recent dramas at the opposite end of Joan's historical reality is Carolyn Gage's The *Second Coming of Joan of Arc* (1988). In her introduction, she makes Joan into a spokeswoman for the feminist and lesbian cause:

> a character conspicuous in her absence from heteropatriarchal theatre: the angry young woman. This Joan of Arc is a far cry from the eroticized and idealized Joan of Anouilh or Shaw. This Joan, like the historical one, is a teenager, a runaway from an alcoholic home with an incestuous father, a girl with severe eating disorders, and a lesbian. No longer a martyr and a victim, this Joan redeems her experience through unmasking her betrayers and rallying contemporary women with a rousing call to arms.[38]

The play, a thirty-page soliloquy, reveals that in fact, behind 'the sterile patriarchal stereotypes' exists 'the angry teenage lesbian'.[39] Gage was not the first to create a homosexual Joan, the ground having already been laid by works such as Vita Sackville-West's *Saint Joan of Arc* (1937), in which Joan's travesty plays an important role and where her indifference to men is emphasized at length.[40] (Sackville-West herself, disguised as 'Julian', had in fact escorted her lover Violet Trefusis to Paris.) In Gage's play, Joan speaks to women in the language of today and warns them that they are still victims of oppression: 'Today you women are allowed to go out and work in the men's world but when I did back in 1430, I was a real freak. But the men haven't changed, the rules haven't changed, and the institutions haven't changed. The fact that there are more of us doing it, just means they're ready to build a bigger fire'.[41] In a tone of eloquent militancy, Joan denounces sexual, social, arid political violence against women, and advocates the combat against men, their institutions and beliefs, in view of a feminine cause left unexplicit:

> God the Father was a lie then and is a lie now, and all the hierarchies modeled after him – the governments, the armies, the churches, the corporations, *the*

> *families!* – are illegitimate. We will not convert them. They will martyr us. *We will not convert them.* We must fight for our own causes, women's causes. We must clothe ourselves with our finely-tempered rage, and obey only those voices that we women alone can hear. (32)

In 1950, John Steinbeck wrote in the *Saturday Review of Literature* that Joan of Arc had constantly been used by writers and artists to find 'some corroborations of [their] convictions, no matter what they may be'.[42] And in the examples we have seen, rather than as a historical character in her own right, Joan clearly appears in the form of a 'solution' to the problems haunting the writers and artists when they chose her as a subject. Very few of these writers and artists attempted to understand the fifteenth century and the mentality of a woman – let alone an exceptional woman – of the Middle Ages. Each had his own agenda: Burk's was a promotion of the ideals of the French Revolution, and in however different ways, Fentonhill's and Twain's were a groping for the miraculous in the face of massive defeat or disappointment. Yet whatever the role played by the artist's 'convictions', as Steinbeck put it, Joan's metamorphoses can perhaps best be accounted for by transformations in religious, political, and moral concepts, by changes in broad ideological phenomena rather than by differences in individual commitments and beliefs. This is evidenced by the extent to which in recent years, for example, Joan has been less and less used to confirm mythologies of a collective order (religious or political) and more and more to secure today's very fertile myth of individual authenticity and uniqueness.

In her American incarnations, we find a Joan who is solidly anchored to common human projects (the universal Republic and deism in Burk, Marxism in Brecht, separatist femininism in Gage, world peace for the Bread and Puppet, etc.), yet she also embodies individual belief, which, though often religious, is without obedience to an institutional or general credo. This latter incarnation in particular has led her to become the support of modern individuality, an 'individualized' individuality, so to speak, as in Anderson and Anouilh, one that seeks a moral sense instinctively, and within the self. Joan's drama is that of the self looking for 'answers [...] in her heart', in Maxwell Anderson's words, and that of the refusal of authority, metaphorically represented by the Catholic Church. Joan sets herself against the law and against general beliefs because for her 'there is no other authority' than that of 'the church from [her] heart' (III). This is the Joan who embodies the contemporary ideal of authenticity, because truth – constantly perceived in modern works as being difficult to hear or in danger of being lost, owing to the conformity of the outer world – is dictated to her by her inner voice. 'To surrender what you are [is] more terrible than dying', says Anderson's Joan with a typically modern, egocentric bravura, implicitly adhering to the mythical project of a self-created subject impervious to historical and sociological forces and asserting that moral sensitivity and judgement are strictly individual.

Finally, apart from being a heroine at the service of the truths found in her heart and soul, Joan is also a strange fantasy, one that suggests a fascination with a being that is feminine, yet devoid of sex. For some authors, the images of child and virgin serve to vindicate a personal dreamworld, for others they inspire reveries more influenced by the ideas and ideologies of the times. Invested equally by male and female authors, a human but sexless Jeanne seems to arouse a devotional passion oblivious of its own death-loving and narcissistic components. Of the American authors, only one, Carolyn Gage, chooses to see her as clearly sexual, but by taking the risk of giving Joan a sex life and making her into an anti-male militant, she superimposes yet another crude fantasy, that of superimposing the distinction between good and evil on that of woman and man.

But rather than Joan the woman, it is the chaste, angelical, and androgynous Joan that generally kindles the flame of all desire. 'Fire, make your body cold', she sings in Leonard Cohen's melancholy song, 'I'm going to give you mine to hold'.

It may be this evasive image of the bride of fire, sufficiently suggestive to inspire any and all fantasies, that best suits the Joan of the arts and letters.

Notes

This article was first published in Dominique Guy-Blanquet, (ed), *Joan of Arc. A Saint for All Reasons*. Aldersthot: Ashgate, 2003, 123–141.

1. *Joan of Lorraine* (Washington, D.C.: Anderson House, 1947), III. interlude 3.
2. Otto Preminger's 1957 film, for instance, is an adaptation of the play's scenario.
3. See Nadia Margolis, *Joan of Arc in History, Literature, and Film. A Select Annotated Biblography* (New York: Garland, 1999), 25.
4. On the politics of Southey and Coleridge's *Joan*, see D. Goy-Blanquet's essay in Dominique Goy-Blanquet, *Joan of Arc: A Saint for All Reasons* (London: Ashgate, 1999).
5. Coleridge's phrase. The poet, who had worked with Southey on the first version of *Joan of Arc*, later annotated his copy of the poem in the following way: 'How grossly unnatural an anachronism, thus to transmogrify the fanatic votary of the Virgin into a Tom Paine in petticoats, a novel-palming proselyte of the Age of Reason', quoted in John Taylor Brown, 'Bibliomania', *The North British Review* 40 (Feb. 1864), 83.
6. II. i. 15–16 See the play on the Internet site, Chadwyck Literature on Line.
7. On these issues, and the evolution of the character in American film, see Robin Blaetz's essay in Dominique Goy-Blanquet, *Joan of Arc: A Saint for All Reasons* (London: Ashgate, 1999).
8. See Marcelline Brun, 'Jeanne d'Arc des Pays de la Loire à ceux du Potomac', *Annales de Bretagne*, II (1986), 281–97.
9. After the war she became a speaker in favour of Black rights and Women's rights. More information about her can be found in Elizabeth C. Stanton *et al.*, eds., *History of Woman Suffrage* (New York: Fowler and Wells, 1881–7), II, 40–50.

10. See the cartoon in *Life*, 27 March 1913, reproduced in Robin Blaetz, *Visions of the Maid: Joan of Arc in American Film and Culture* (Charlottesville and London: University Press of Virginia, 2001), 32.

11. It is for her that Joe Hill, the famous Wobbly organizer and song writer, composed 'The Rebel Girl' in 1915.

12. The text was only published in 1904, in *Harper's Weekly*.

13. See Marcelline Brun's bibliography in her unpublished thesis 'Jeanne d'Arc aux U.S.A. De l'Histoire au Mythe' (Université de Tours, 1981), and that of Nadia Margolis, *Bibliography*.

14. Sarah M. Grimké, *Joan of Arc, A Biography* (Boston: Adams, 1876), 4.

15. *The Wonderful Story* ... (New York: Cupples and Leon, 1918), 8, 12, 344, 338.

16. Jules Bastien-Lepage (1848–1884), a painter from Lorraine, often represented scenes from country life. Jean-Gustave Jacquet (1846–1909) was a minor artist who had studied with Bouguereau; his *Jeanne d'Arc Arc priant pour la France* (1878) won a Third Medal at the Exposition Universelle of Paris.

17. Anonymous review, *Appleton's Journal* (June 1881), 570–71.

18. They are often casts of Emmanuel Frémiet's statue (1875), which stands on the place des Pyramides in Paris, or of Paul Dubois's statue (1895) on the place Saint Augustin in Paris, and in Rheims.

19. She also did a high relief of the Saint for the Cathedral Saint John the Divine in New York in 1920. There are few American iconographic representations of Joan of Arc, and the replicas of French ones were often given by France after the First World War.

20. One will find interesting statistics of the representations of Joan of Arc at Paris Salons in *Images de Jeanne d'Arc* (Paris: Hotel de la Monnaie, June–Sep. 1979), 192–3. The 'Boulangiste' crisis, the decree in venerability (1894), the post-war period and the canonization are the high points of this representation.

21. Anne B. Powers, 'The Joan of Are Vogue in America, 1894–1929', *American Society of the Legion of Honor Magazine* 49, 177–92 (1978), 183.

22. The complete title is *Personal Recollections of Joan of Arc by The Sieur Louis de Conte (Her page and secretary), freely translated out of the ancient French into modern English from the original unpublished manuscript in the National Archives of France by Jean François Alden*. The references to Twain's *Personal Recollections* come from the Harper & Row edition of 1924. The references will be preceded by *PR* and the number of the volume. The references to Twain's article 'Saint Joan of Arc', which will be preceded by *SJ*, come from Louis J. Budd's edition, *Mark Twain: Collected Tales, Sketches, Speeches and Essays* (New York: Literary Classics of the United States, Library of America, 1992). On *Personal Recollections*, see Albert E. Stone Jr., *The Innocent Eye: Childhood in Twain's Imagination* (New Haven: Yale University Press, 1961), and William Searle, *The Saint and The Skeptics: Joan of Arc in the Works of Mark Twain, Anatole France and Bernard Shaw* (Detroit: Wayne State University Press, 1976).

23. 'Possibly the book may not sell, but that is nothing – it was written for love', 29th Jan. 1895, in A. K Paine, *Mark Twain's Letters* (New York: Harper and Bros, 1917), 624.

24. In 1900, quoted in A. B. Paine, *Mark Twain: A Biography* (New York: Harper and Bros, 1912), II, 1034.

25. See Ch. H. Lightbody, *The Judgements of Joan: A Study in Cultural History* (Cambridge: Cambridge University Press, 1961). There were war songs, but also up to the 1970s, half a dozen popular songs as well, among them the charming Leonard Cohen 'Joan of Arc' of 1971.

26. There exist other Hyatt statues of Joan in the United States, and one in Blois (France), donated by the American Legion.

27. A private group, the Joan of Arc Statue Committee, raised money for the statue. The committee was composed of twenty-one members, most of them Americans; among the French members were the writer Pierre Loti and Louis d'Arc, a supposed collateral

descendant of Jeanne d'Arc. The booklet about the unveiling was written by one the members of the Committee, George Frederic Kunz, *The Dedication of the Statue of Joan of Arc in the City of New York* (New York: s.n., 1916).

28. *The Dedication*, 44.

29. A website, www.scuttlebuttsmallchow.com/joan.arc.html, 15 June 2002, presents photographs of American and French soldiers at Domremy, and pageants staged by the YMCA in 1918 in honour of Joan.

30. M. S. C. Smith, *The Maid of Orleans: The Story of Joan of Arc for Girls* (Thomas Y. Cromwell Company, 1919), chap. XXIX.

31. Brecht actually wrote two other plays about Joan. The first one on which he worked between 1941 and 1946 is *The Visions of Simone Machard* [*Die Gesichte der Simone Machard*]; he wanted to call it 'Jeanne d'Arc 1940'. In 1952 he wrote *The Trial of Joan of Arc in Rouen 1431* [*Der Prozess der Jeanne d'Arc zu Rouen 1431*] for the Berliner Ensemble; it was an adaptation of a radio play by Anna Seghers.

32. George Bernard Shaw, Preface to *Saint Joan* (Harmondsworth: Penguin, 1966), 22. It is in the same preface that Shaw also famously described Mark Twain's Joan as 'an unimpeachable American school teacher in armour', 25.

33. *The Lark* (New York: Random House, 1956).

34. *Conversations with Lillian Hellman*, ed. Jackson R. Bryer (Jackson: University Press of Mississippi, 1964), 58–9.

35. Internet site, www.auroratheatre.org/knockknock.com 10 June 2002.

36. See the video cassette, *Bread and Puppet theater: Joan of Arc*, Prolefeed Studios, 1999.

37. Internet site, www.sp.uconn.edu/~wwwsfa/Mckenna.html, 10 June 2002.

38. Carolyn Gage, *The Second Coming of Joan of Arc and Other Plays* (Santa Cruz, Calif.: HerBooks, 1994), 1.

39 Quotation on the book jacket.

40. To Vita Sackville-West, *Saint Joan of Arc* (Leipzig, Paris, Bologna: The Albatross. 1937), 17: Joan 'clearly aroused neither the natural desire of men nor the competitive mistrust of women'.

41. *The Second Coming*, 11–12.

42. 'The Joan of Arc in All of Us', *Saturday Review of Literature*, (14 Jan. 1956), 17.

Selected Bibliography

Details of particular editions of the primary texts consulted are to be found in the notes as are suggestions for further reading. The amount of secondary literature relating to Joan is immense; what follows is a list of works that have proved particularly interesting and relevant.

Acocella, Joan, 'Burned Again', in *The New Yorker*, 15th November 1999.

Alain, *Jeanne d'Arc: Sept propos d'Alain.* Nîmes: Fabre, 1921.

Allen, C., 'The schizophrenia of Joan of Arc', *History of Medicine*, 6, 1975.

(Anon.) *Jeanne d'Arc par elle-même. Histoire de Jeanne d'Arc dictée par elle-même à Ernance Dufaux.* L'Etang-la-ville: Editions Philonam, 1999.

(Anon.) *The First Biography of Joan of Arc.* Translated and annotated by Daniel Rankin and Claire Quintal. Pittsburgh: University of Pittsburgh Press, 1964.

(Anon.) *Journal d'un bourgeois de Paris (1405–1449).* Translated by Janet Shirley as A *Parisian Journal, 1405–49.* Oxford: Clarendon Press, 1968.

Anouilh, Jean, *L'Alouette.* (1952) Translated Christopher Fry as *The Lark*, London: Methuen, 1955.

Ashley, Tim, 'The Sexuality of Sainthood', in *Giovanna d'Arco* Programme of first performance at the Royal Opera House, London, 24th June 1996.

Astell, W. Ann and Wheeler, Bonnie, *Joan of Arc and Spirituality.* New York and Basingstoke: Palgrave, 2003.

Balladur, Edouard, *Jeanne d'Arc et la France. Le Mythe du sauveur.* Paris: Fayard, 2003.

Bancquart, Marie-Claire, *Anatole France, un sceptique passioné.* Paris: Calmann-Lévy, 1984.

—*Anatole France polémiste.* Paris: Nizet, 1962.

—*Les Écrivains français et l'histoire d'après Maurice Barrès, Léon Bloy, Anatole France, Charles Péguy.* Paris: Nizet, 1966.

Barrès, Maurice (*et al.*), *For Joan of Arc.* London: Sheed and Ward, 1930.

Barstow, Anne Llewellyn, *Joan of Arc. Heretic, Mystic, Shaman.* Lewiston and New York: Edwin Mellen Press, 1986.

Beaune, Colette, *Jeanne d'Arc.* Paris: Perrin, 2004.

Belloc, Hilaire, *Joan of Arc.* Boston and London: Little Brown and Cassell, 1930.

Bermel, Albert, 'The Virgin as Heretic: *Saint Joan* by Bernard Shaw (1923)', in *Contradictory Characters: An Interpretation of the Modern Theatre.* New York: Dutton, 1973.

Blaetz, Robin, 'Cecil B. DeMille's *Joan the Woman*', in Katherine Verduin (ed.) *Medievalism in North America.* Cambridge: D .S. Brewer, 1994.

—'*La Femme vacante* or the Rendering of Joan of Arc in the Cinema' in *Postscript,* 12, No 2, Winter, 1993.

—'Joan of Arc and the Cinema' in *Joan of Arc. A Saint for all Reasons.* (ed.) Dominique Goy-Blanquet, Aldershot: Ashgate, 2003.

—'Retelling the Joan of Arc Story: Women, War, and Hollywood's *Joan of Paris*' in *Film Literature,* 22, No 4, 1994.

—*Visions of the Maid. Joan of Arc in American Film and Culture.* Charlottesville and London: University Press of Virginia, 2001.

Bloom, Harold (ed.), *Joan of Arc,* New York: Chelsea House, 1992.

Bloy, Léon, *Jeanne d'Arc et l'Allemagne,* Paris: Georges Crès et Cie Éditeurs, 1915.

Boas, Frederick S., 'Joan of Arc in Shakespeare, Schiller and Shaw', in *Shakespeare Quarterly,* 2, 1951.

Bonnaire, Sandrine, *Le Roman d'un tournage: Jeanne la pucelle.* Paris: Lattès, 1994.

Bordwell, David, *Filmguide to 'La Passion de Jeanne d'Arc'.* Bloomington: Indiana University Press, 1973.

Bostock, J. Knight, 'The Maid of Orleans in German literature', in *Modern Language Review,* 27, 1927.

Boutet de Monvel, Louis-Maurice, *Jeanne d'Arc.* Paris: Plon-Nourrit, 1896.

Bouzy, Olivier, *Jeanne d'Arc, mythes et réalités.* Paris: L'Atelier de l'Archer, 1999.

Brecht, Bertolt, *Die Heilige Johanna der Schlachthöfe.* Trans. Frank Jones *(Saint Joan of the Stockyards)* in *Bertolt Brecht. Plays,* Vol. 2, Methuen, London, 1962.

— *Die Gesichte der Simone Machard.* Trans. Ralph Manheim (*The Visions of Simone Machard)* in *Bertolt Brecht, Collected Plays,* Vol. VII, Vintage Books, New York, 1975.

— and Anna Seghers, *Der Prozess der Jeanne d'Arc zu Rouen, 1431.* 1959. Trans. Ralph Manheim and Wolfgang Sauerlander (*The Trial of Joan of Arc at Rouen, 1431*) in *Bertolt Brecht, Collected Plays,* Vol. IX, Vintage Books, New York, 1979.

Bresson, Robert, *Le Procès de Jeanne d'Arc.* Paris: Julliard, 1988.

Butterfield, John and Butterfield, Isobel-Ann, 'Joan of Arc: A Medical View', in *History Today*, September 1958.

Cabot Lowell, Francis, *Joan of Arc*. Boston: Miflin, 1896.

Cahiers du Cinéma, 476, February 1994.

Cahm, Eric, *Péguy et le nationalisme français*, Paris: Cahiers de l'Amitié Charles Péguy (no.25), 1972.

Calmette, Joseph, *Jeanne d'Arc*. Paris: PUF, 1946.

Cardoze, Michel, *Jeanne d'Arc. Dossier non classé*. Paris: Librairie Séguier, 1987.

Caze, Pierre, *La Vérité sur Jeanne d'Arc*. Paris: Rosa, 1819.

Caute, David, *Communism and the French Intellectuals*. London: André Deutsch, 1964.

Contamine, Pierre, 'Naissance d'une historiographie. Le souvenir de Jeanne d'Arc, en France et hors de France, depuis le "procès de son innocence" (1455-1456) jusqu'au début du XVIe siècle', in *Francia,Forschungen zur westeuropäischen Gesichte*, 15, 1987.

Darmesteter, James, *Jeanne d'Arc jugée par les Anglais*. Paris: La Nouvelle Revue, 1883.

Deary, Terry, *The Real Joan of Arc? A History mystery*. London: Franklin Watts, 1996.

Debout, Henri, *Sainte Jeanne d'Arc*. Paris: Maison de la Bonne Presse, 1907.

Deteil, Joseph, *Jeanne d'Arc*. (1925) translated Malcolm Cowley, London: Allen & Unwin, 1926.

Donot, A., 'Jeanne d'Arc dans la littérature du 18e siècle', in *Dictionnaire des lettres françaises. Le 18e siècle*. Paris: Fayard, 1960.

Dufaux Ermance, *Jeanne d'Arc par elle-même. Histoire de Jeanne d'Arc dictée par elle-même à Ermance Dufaux*. Vies dictées d'outre-tombe, LÉtang-la-ville, 1999.

Duff, Mildred and Hope, Noel, *Joan of Arc*. London: Salvationist Publishing and Supplies, 1929.

Dunn, Susan, 'The Myth of Jeanne d'Arc in Michelet and Lamartine', *Romanic Review*, 80, 1989.

Dufreigne, Jean-Pierre, 'Quelques Pucelle inoubliables' in *L'Express*, 28th October – 3 November 1999.

Edmée, Marie, *Histoire de notre petite sœur Jeanne d'Arc*. Paris: Plon et Cie, 1874.

Endore, Guy, *The Sword of God: Jeanne d'Arc*. New York: Farrar and Rinehart, 1931.

Études cinématographiques, 18–19, 1962.

Fabre, Joseph, *Jeanne d'Arc. Libératrice de la France*. Paris: Delagrave, 1882.

Fawcett, Mrs Henry, *Joan of Arc*. London: National Union of Women's suffrage societies, 1912.

Ffoulkes, Charles, 'The Armour of Joan of Arc', in *Burlington Magazine*, 16, December 1909.

Flower, John, *Literature and the Left in France*, London: Macmillan and

Methuen, 1983.

Fraioli, Deborah A., *Joan of Arc.The Early Debate*. Woodbridge: Boydell Press, 2000.

France, Anatole, *Vie de Jeanne d'Arc*. Paris: Calmann-Lévy, 1908.

Funck-Bretano, Frantz, *Jeanne d'Arc*. Paris: Boivin, 1912.

Garland, H. B., *Schiller the Dramatic Writer*. Oxford: Clarendon Press, 1969.

Goy-Blanquet, Dominique (ed.), *Joan of Arc. A Saint for All Reasons*. Aldershot: Ashgate, 2003. Translated from *Jeanne d'Arc en garde à vue* (Brussels: Le Cri Éditions, 1999) by D. Goy-Blanquet with revisions and an additional essay by Claude Grimal, 'The American Maid'.

—'Shakespeare and Voltaire set fire to History' in *Joan of Arc. A Saint for All Reasons, op.cit.*

Gordon, Mary, *Joan of Arc*. New York: Lipper Publications and Viking, 2000.

Grillot de Givry, Émile, *La Survivance et le mariage de Jeanne d'Arc*. Paris: Arché, 1914.

Grimal, Claude, 'The American Maid', from Dominique Guy-Blanquet, (ed), *Joan of Arc. A Saint for All Reasons*. Aldersthot: Ashgate, 2003, 123–141.

Grimod, Jean, *Jean d'Arc a-t-elle été brûlée?* Paris: Amiot-Dumont, 1952.

Guérin, Jeanyves, 'La figure de Jeanne d'Arc dans le théâtre contemporain' in M. Perrin (ed.), *Dire le Moyen Age, hier et aujourd'hui*. Paris: PUF, 1990.

Guillemin, Henri, *Jeanne dite Jeanne d'Arc*. Paris: Gallimard, 1970.

Guitton, Jean, *Problème et mystère de Jeanne d'Arc*. Paris: Fayard, 1961.

Hanna, Martha, 'Iconology and Ideology: Images of Joan of Arc in the idiom of the Action Française, 1908-1931', in *French Historical Studies*, 14, 1985.

Hanotaux, Gabriel, *Jeanne d'Arc*. Paris: Hachette, 1911.

— *Jeanne, la Pucelle d'Orléans*. Paris: Plon, 1938.

Harmand, Adrien, *Jeanne d'Arc, ses costumes, son armure*. Paris: Aulard, 1929.

Harty, Kevin J., 'The Nazis, Joan of Arc and Medievalism gone awry: Gustav Ucicky's 1935 film *Das Mädchen Johanna*', in *Rationality and the Liberal Spirit*, Louisiana: A Centenary Publication, 1997

—'Jeanne au cinéma', in Wheeler, Bonnie and Wood, Charles T., (eds), *Fresh Verdicts on Joan of Arc*. New York: Garland, 1996.

Headly, L.C., *The Passion of Joan of Arc*. London: Purnell and Sons, 1930.

Heppenstall, Rayner, *The Fourfold Tradition*. London: Barrie and Rockliff, 1961.

Heimann, N. M., *What Honour for the feminine sex?* New York: City University, 1994.

— *Joan of Arc in French Art and Culture (1700–1855)*. Aldershot: Ashgate, 2005.

Hill, Holly, *Playing Joan: Actresses on the Challenge of Shaw's Joan of Arc*. New York: Theatre Communications Group, 1987.

Hirschfeld, Gerhard and Marsh, Patrick (eds), *Collaboration in France: Politics and Culture during the Nazi Occupation, 1940-1944*. Oxford, Munich and New York: Berg, 1989.

Hisiao, Karen, 'Joan of Arc may have had epilepsy', *Boston Herald*, 25th May 1990.

Huet, Émile, *Jeanne d'Arc et la musique*. Orléans: Librairies Jeanne d'Arc – Marcel Marron, 1909.

Ireland, W. H., *The Maid of Orléans or La Pucelle of Voltaire*, trans. into English verse with notes. 2 vols, London: Miller and Wright, 1822.

Jackson, Gabriele B., 'Topical Ideology: Witches, Amazons, and Shaw's *Joan of Arc*', in *English Literary Renaissance*, 18, 1988.

Jacobs, Gabriel, 'The Role of Joan of Arc on the Stage of Occupied France', in Kedward, Roderick and Austin, Roger (eds), *Vichy France and the Resistance. Culture and Ideology*. London and Sydney: Croom Helm, 1985.

Jacoby, Jean, *Le Secret de Jeanne d'Arc, pucelle d'Orléans*. Paris: Mercure de France, 1932.

John, Benyon S., *Anouilh: L'Alouette and Pauvre Bitos*. London: Grant and Cutler, 1984.

Jussem-Wilson, Nelly, *Charles Péguy*, London: Bowes and Bowes, 1965.

Kedward, Roderick and Austin, Roger (eds), *Vichy France and the Resistance. Culture and Ideology*. London and Sydney: Croom Helm, 1985.

Keneally, Thomas, *Blood Red, Sister Rose*: London: Collins, 1974.

Ker, David, *Cross and Sword. A Tale of Joan of Arc*. London and Edinburgh: Chambers, 1930.

Krumeich, Gerd, 'Jeanne d'Arc vue de l'Allemagne', in *Jeanne d'Arc entre les nations*. Amsterdam: Rodopi, 1998.

— 'The Cult of Joan of Arc under Vichy' in G.Hirschfeld and P. Marsh (eds), *Collaboration in France, op. cit.*

Krushelnycky, Askold and Burrell, Ian, 'At stake: the reputation of a French heroine, after expert dismisses Joan of Arc's story as a royal fable', *The Independent*, 23rd December 2003.

Lanéry d'Arc, Pierre, *Jeanne d'Arc et la Guerre de 1914*, Paris and Nancy: Berger-Levrault, 1916.

Lang, Andrew, *La 'Jeanne d'Arc' de M. Anatole France*. Paris: Perrin, 1909.

—*The Maid of France*. London, New York, Boston and Calcutta: Longmans Green and Co., 1908.

Lanhers, Yvonne, 'Jeanne d'Arc vue par ses contemporains', in *Bulletin de la société des amis du Vieux Chinon*, 8, No 3, 1977.

Le Bouvier, Gilles dit le Héraut Berry, *Les Chroniques du roi Charles VII*. Published for the Société de l'histoire de France by Henri Courteault and Léonce Celier with the collaboration of Marie-Henriette Jullien de Pommerol. Paris: Klincksieck, 1979.

Leibovici, Solange, 'Ceci n'est pas une femme. La Jeanne de l'extrême droite', in *Jeanne d'Arc entre les nations*. Paris: CRIN, 1998.

Le Nordez, Albert, Léon, Marie, *Jeanne d'Arc*, Paris: Hachette, 1898.

Le Pen, Jean-Marie, *La France est de retour*. Paris: Michel Laffon, 1985.

Lewis, Wyndham, 'Joan of Arc', in *The Atlantic Monthly*, January 1954.

Lightbody, Charles H., *The Judgements of Joan. A Study in cultural history*. Cambridge: Cambridge University Press, 1961.

Lucie-Smith, Edward, *Jeanne d'Arc*. Paris: Perrin, 1977.

—*Joan of Arc*. London: Allen Lane, 1976.

Malraux, André, 'Commémoration de la mort de Jeanne d'Arc (au nom du Gouvernement français) Orléans, daté Rouen, 31 mai 1964', *Oraisons-funèbres*. Paris: Gallimard, 1971.

Maquet, Florence, *Jehanne la Pucelle, l'histoire, les documents*. Millau: Imprimerie Maury, 1982.

Margolis, Nadia, *Joan of Arc in History, Literature and Film*. New York: Garland, 1990.

— 'La Chevauchée solitaire du Professeur Thalamas: rationalisme et réactionnaires dans l'historiographie johannique (1904-1945)', in *Bulletin de l'Association des Amis du Centre Jeanne d'Arc*, 15, 1991.

— 'Rewriting the Right: High Priests, Heroes and Hooligans in the portrayal of Joan of Arc (1824–1945)', in D. Goy-Blanquet (ed.), *Joan of Arc. A Saint for all Reasons, op., cit.*

Marnant, Marcel, *Maurice Ravel*. Paris: Fayard, 1986.

Marot, Pierre, 'La Genèse d'un roman: Pierre Caze, l'inventeur de la bâtardise de Jeanne d'Arc', in *Jeanne d'Arc, une époque, un rayonnement*. Paris: CNRS, 1982.

Marsh, Patrick, 'Le Théâtre à Paris sous l'occupation allemande', in *Revue d'Histoire du Théâtre*, III, 1981.

Meltzer, Françoise, *For Fear of the Fire: Joan of Arc and the Limits of Subjectivity*. Chicago: University of Chicago Press, 2001.

Michelet, Jules, *Joan of Arc*, translated with an Introduction by Albert Guérard, Ann Arbor, 1959

Michener, Wendy, '*Jeanne d'Arc* in Moscow' in *Dance and Dancers*, September, 1958.

Milet, Jacques, *Mistère du siège d'Orléans*. (1450). Ed. V. L. Hamblin, Geneva: Droz, 2002.

Money-Kyrle, Roger, 'A psychoanalytic study of the voices of Joan of Arc', in *British Journal of Medical Psychology*, 13, 1933.

Nichols, Roger, *Ravel Remembered*. London and Boston: Faber and Faber, 1987.

Oakes, Philip, 'Family says Joan of Arc escaped burning', in *Boston Sunday Globe*, 10th December 1967.

Oliphant, Mrs (Margaret O. Wilson), *Jeanne d'Arc. Her Life and death*. New York and London: Putnam's Sons, 1896.

Paine, A. B. *Joan of Arc. Maid of France*. London: Macmillan, 1925.

Péguy, Charles, *Œuvres Poétiques complète*. Paris: Pléiade, Gallimard, 1941.

Pernoud, Régine, *J'ai nom Jeanne la Pucelle*. Paris: Gallimard, 1994.
— *Jeanne d'Arc*. Paris: Seuil, 1981.
— *Jeanne d'Arc par elle-même et par ses témoins*. Paris: Seuil, 1975.
— and Marie-Véronique Clin, *Jeanne d'Arc*. Paris: Fayard, 1986.
Pisan, Christine de, *Ditié de Jehanne d'Arc*. Ed. Angus J. Kennedy and Kenneth Varty. Oxford: Society for the Study of Medieval Languages and Literatures, (Medium Aevum Monographs, n.s. IX), 1977, reprinted 2003.
Prolo, Maria, Adriana, *Storia del cinema muto italiano*. Milan: Poligono, 1951.
Quicherat, Jules, *Procès de condamnation et de réhabilitation de Jeanne d'Arc dite la Pucelle*. Paris: Jules Renouard, 1841-49.
Quincy, Thomas De, 'Joan of Arc', in Purcell, Alfred A., S.J. (ed.), *The English Mail Coach*. New York, Boston, Chicago and Toronto: Longmans, Green and Co., 1938.
Rabbe, Félix, *Jeanne d'Arc en Angleterre*. Paris: Savine, 1891.
Raknem, Ingvald, *Joan of Arc in History, Legend, and Literature*. Oslo: Universitetsforlaget, 1971.
Reyniers, Marcelline-Brun, *Jeanne d'Arc aux USA. De l'histoire au mythe*. Unpublished thesis, University of Tours, 1981.
Rigolet, Yann, *Jeanne d'Arc ou l'étonnante pérennité d'un mythe, à Orléans, de 1945 à nos jours*, unpublished Masters thesis, Univesity of Orléans, 2003.
Roberts, Yvonne, 'Joan of Arc's skeleton in the closet', *The Independent*, 28th December 2003.
Robo, Etienne, *Saint Joan. The Woman and the Saint*. New York: Spiritual Books Associates, 1948.
Sackville-West, Vita, *Saint Joan of Arc*. New York: Doubleday, 1936.
Salomé, Laurent *et al.*, *Jeanne d'Arc: Les Tableaux de l'Histoire 1820–1920*. Paris: Réunion des musées nationaux, 2003.
Schneider, Edouard, *Jeanne d'Arc et ses lys, la légende et l'histoire*. Paris: Grasset, 1932.
Scott, W. S., *Joan of Arc*. London: Harrap, 1974.
Searle, William, *The Saint and the Skeptics: Joan of Arc in the Work of Mark Twain, Anatole France, and Bernard Shaw*. Detroit: Wayne State University Press, 1976.
Sémolué, Jean, ' 'Douleur, noblesse unique' ou la passion chez Carl Dreyer', in *Études cinématographiques*, 10–11, 1961.
Shakespeare, William, *Henry VI, Part I*. Ed. Edward Burns, The Arden Shakespeare, London, 2000.
Sharpe, Lesley, *Friedrich Schiller. Drama, Thought and Politics*. Cambridge: Cambridge University Press, 1991.
Shaw, G. B., *Collected Plays with their Prefaces*. London: Bodley Head, 1973.
Soons, J. J., *Jeanne d'Arc au théâtre. Étude sur la plus ancienne tragédie, suivie d'une liste chronologique des œuvres dramatiques dont Jeanne d'Arc a fourni le*

sujet en France de 1890 à 1926. Purmerend: Musses, 1929.

Stanton, Mary, *The Everlasting Ego. Lives of Joan of Arc exemplifying reincarnation in History*. London: The Free Society, 1970.

Stolpe, Sven, *The Maid of Orleans*. New York: Pantheon, 1975.

Swanwick, Anna, *The Works of Frederick Schiller*, London: Henry G. Bohn, 1847.

Tame, Peter D., *La Mystique du fascisme dans l'œuvre de Robert Brasillach*. Paris: Nouvelles Éditions latines, 1986.

Thalamas, François-Amadée, *Jeanne d'Arc, l'histoire et la légende*. Paris: Paclot, 1904.

Thomas, Édith, *Jeanne d'Arc*. Paris: Hier et aujourd'hui, 1947.

Thomas, Nicholas, *The International Dictionary of Films and Filmmakers*. Chicago, 1990.

Tournier, Michel, *Gilles et Jeanne*. Paris: Gallimard, 1983.

Trask, Willard R., *Joan of Arc: In Her Own Words*. New York: Turtle Point Press, 1996.

Twain, Mark, *Personal Recollections of Joan of Arc*. Introduced by Justin Kaplan, New York and Oxford: Oxford University Press, 1996.

Vercruysse, Jeroom, 'Jeanne d'Arc au siècle des lumières', *Studies on Voltaire and the Eighteenth Century*, 90, 1972.

— Ed. *La Pucelle d'Orléans* in *The Complete Works of Voltaire*, Vol. 7, Geneva, 1970.

Vidal, Philippe, *Jehanne d'Arc... laquelle? L'énigme enfin résolu*. Nantes: Opéra éditions, 1994.

Waldmann, Milton, *Joan of Arc*. London, New York and Toronto: Longmans, Green and Co., 1935.

Warner, Marina, *Joan of Arc: The Image of Female Heroism*. Berkeley and Los Angeles: University of California Press, 1981.

Wheeler, Bonnie and Wood, Charles T., (eds), *Fresh Verdicts on Joan of Arc*. London and New York: Garland, 1996.

White, Hayden, *Metahistory: The historical Imagination in nineteenth-century Europe*. Baltimore: John Hopkins Univesity Press, 1973.

Wohl, Louis de, *Saint Joan. The Girl Soldier*. London and New York: Vintage Books, 1957.

Winock, Michel, 'Jeanne d'Arc et les Juifs', in *H-Histoire*, 3, 1979.

Winwar, Frances, *The Saint and the Devil: a biographical study in Good and Evil*. New York and London: Harper and Hamish Hamilton, 1948.

Wood, Charles T., *Joan of Arc and Richard III: Sex, saints and government in the Middle Ages*. New York and Oxford: Oxford University Press, 1988.

Wooster, Nora, *The Real Joan of Arc*. Lewes: The Book Guild Ltd, 1992.

Index

Figures in **bold** type refer to pages containing illustrations